"The approach is fresh, the writing accessible and engaging. The authors have deep knowledge of the subject and convey it with clarity and enthusiasm [...] Han and Tomori are far and away the best scholars for the job."

—Carole H. Browner, Co-editor of *Reproduction, Globalization, and the State (Duke 2012), UCLA*

"Care is taken to situate human reproduction holistically; this is useful not only for students with a background in anthropology—it gives students in other disciplines a different and more complete picture of human reproduction."

—Keri Canada, *Colorado State University*

"Anthropology's holistic approach makes it an ideal discipline for studying reproduction. This text utilizes that comprehensive perspective, emphasizing the importance of understanding diverse contexts—political, economic, historical, and racial—to educate readers on social inequalities."

—Angela Castañeda, *DePauw University*

ANTHROPOLOGY OF REPRODUCTION

THE BASICS

Anthropology of Reproduction: The Basics is a clear and accessible guide to topics in reproduction from the perspective of anthropology, emphasizing the central importance of reproduction in human sociocultural and biological experience. It examines why reproduction matters so much to human beings and what anthropology offers to better understand their decisions about having or not having children, and their experiences with periods, infertility, contraception, abortion, pregnancy, pregnancy loss, birth, and care for children. The book shows that all of reproduction is shaped by our evolution, prehistory, and history, as well as the cultural, social, political, and economic contexts and conditions that impact our lives. It tells the story of how these conditions enable, support, constrain or coerce reproduction—and how people around the world survive or thrive within, comply with, or resist against these forces to create their reproductive futures. Its primary goals are:

- to promote an understanding of human reproduction as sociocultural and biological experience
- to spread awareness of and attention to the sociocultural, historical, political, and economic contexts and conditions influence the ideas and practices of human reproduction, particularly how social inequities shape reproduction and, in turn, how we can move toward more equal and just reproductive futures
- to introduce and reinforce an understanding of anthropology as a discipline taking a holistic approach to human experiences. This student-friendly text provides an overview of the

fundamental principles of reproduction and is an invaluable guide for anyone wanting to learn more about this fascinating subject.

It is an essential read for students approaching the subject for the first time, as well as researchers coming to the topic from another discipline in the sciences and humanities.

Sallie Han is Professor of Anthropology at SUNY Oneonta, USA. She is the author of *Pregnancy in Practice: Expectation and Experience in the Contemporary US* (2013) and co-editor of *The Anthropology of the Fetus: Biology, Culture, and Society* (2018) and *The Routledge Handbook of Anthropology and Reproduction* (2022).

Cecília Tomori is Associate Professor at the Johns Hopkins School of Nursing and the Johns Hopkins Bloomberg School of Public Health, Department of Population, Family and Reproductive Health, Johns Hopkins University, USA. She is the author of *Nighttime Breastfeeding: An American Cultural Dilemma* (2014) and co-editor of *Breastfeeding: New Anthropological Approaches* (2018) and *The Routledge Handbook of Anthropology and Reproduction* (2022), and numerous other publications.

The Basics Series

The Basics is a highly successful series of accessible guidebooks which provide an overview of the fundamental principles of a subject area in a jargon-free and undaunting format.

Intended for students approaching a subject for the first time, the books both introduce the essentials of a subject and provide an ideal springboard for further study. With over 50 titles spanning subjects from artificial intelligence (AI) to women's studies, The Basics are an ideal starting point for students seeking to understand a subject area.

Each text comes with recommendations for further study and gradually introduces the complexities and nuances within a subject.

For more information about this series, please visit: www.routledge.com/The-Basics/book-series/B

ANTHROPOLOGY OF REPRODUCTION

THE BASICS

Sallie Han and Cecília Tomori

Routledge
Taylor & Francis Group

NEW YORK AND LONDON

Designed cover image: Hiraman

First published 2025
by Routledge
605 Third Avenue, New York, NY 10158

and by Routledge
4 Park Square, Milton Park, Abingdon, Oxon OX14 4RN

Routledge is an imprint of the Taylor & Francis Group, an informa business

© 2025 Sallie Han and Cecília Tomori

Library of Congress Cataloging-in-Publication Data
A catalog record for this title has been requested

ISBN: 978-1-032-45955-4 (hbk)
ISBN: 978-1-032-45956-1 (pbk)
ISBN: 978-1-003-37941-6 (ebk)

DOI: 10.4324/9781003379416

Typeset in Bembo
by Taylor & Francis Books

To our families

CONTENTS

BOXES

WHY REPRODUCTION MATTERS AND WHAT THE ANTHROPOLOGY OF REPRODUCTION OFFERS

Pregnancy and birth are often considered as the beginning and end of the story of human reproduction. In this book, however, these topics are intertwined among many others that make little or no sense unless we tell these stories together. Menstruation, birth control, abortion, infertility and childlessness, reproductive technologies, pregnancy, pregnancy loss, birth, breastfeeding, and infant care are all discussed as part of a much more complex story in these pages.

Reproduction, as we define it here, includes every aspect of having and not having children. It is simultaneously biological, social, and cultural, and is both broader and deeper than the medical and legal practices and ideas that many readers will associate with it. The experiences of reproduction in the present take their form from manifold pasts that include the life courses of individual parents and the generations preceding them; the histories of communities and countries that came into consequential and often catastrophic encounters with each other; and indeed, the deep time of our biological evolution as a species with its distinct features of reproduction. We often use the word context to refer to this larger span of time, space, and people and the interactions among them. Context is, of course, everything for scholars and especially for anthropologists engaged in the study of reproduction. Our purpose is to unwind and unravel the long and various threads of context so that we can better understand each one and the patterns weaving them together in our experiences of reproduction.

DOI: 10.4324/9781003379416-1

People who do not wish to have children may be forced to do so while others who desire them are discouraged or even actively blocked from doing so and parents struggle for the resources they need and want to raise their children as well as they can. Anthropologists of reproduction undertake the project of documenting and describing what people do and explaining how and why. Our interest is in telling these stories so that each is revealed as distinct, but also not isolated. A *reproductive trajectory* that leads to having children takes shape in relation to a trajectory that does not. Grounded in studies of **kinship**—describing and explaining how relatedness and families are made in and through social and cultural practices, not simply given as "natural" biological facts—anthropologists also understand that all of us experience reproduction as not only individuals and selves, but also as people encumbered within relationships with various other people, such as partners and kin and family, and as members of our communities, societies, and cultures.

The approach we introduce in this chapter and take throughout this book may be new to readers who have learned and been taught to think about reproduction as more narrowly defined as simply producing children and to regard these human experiences as biological processes and medical concerns. In the anthropology of reproduction, we take the perspective that reproduction is all of this and more. In the following pages we invite you to join us on a journey to learn about what the anthropology of reproduction offers to better understand what is at stake in reproduction and why it plays such a crucial role in social life.

FOUR-FIELD ANTHROPOLOGY AND THE STUDY OF REPRODUCTION

Defined as the study of humanity, **anthropology** is well positioned to ask and answer questions about human reproduction. Established in the middle of the nineteenth century, the discipline is concerned with human society, culture, and language of the past and present as well as the evolution and biological diversity of our species. In the United States, the discipline is organized into the **four fields of anthropology** that have developed their own theories, methods, and historical trajectories apart from each other.

Archaeology enables us to know the histories of people even when no written records are available to us. We can look instead at the structures (buildings), artifacts, and other material remains across the broad timespan of the human past. Archaeological evidence also gives insight into practices of everyday life that were considered insignificant by, or were hidden from, men or other people keeping records, like women's birth control practices (see Chapter 2).

Biological anthropology investigates questions about human evolution by comparing modern humans and other living primates like chimpanzees, a specialization known as **primatology**, and by looking at fossil evidence of now extinct ancestral humans such as Neanderthals, an area of study called **paleoanthropology**. The evolution of human birth, with a focus on the female pelvis, has been an area of special interest (see Chapter 4). From studies of infancy and parental care, and nutrition, child survival, and growth, we gain understanding of the optimal behaviors for human survival, like breastfeeding and the close proximity of parents and infants in shared sleep (see Chapter 5).

Cultural or sociocultural anthropology is engaged in both the close and specific examination of people's ways of living as members of a given culture and a broad comparison across cultures. **Culture** refers to the totality of our learned and taught habits of acting, talking, thinking, and feeling that includes humans as members of a group. It describes the patterns of behavior and belief that are shared among people in the same group or a closely related one and it explains the differences between people from different groups. How cultural anthropologists come to know a culture is through their immersion into a group of people whose experiences they undertake to document and understand—a research process and strategy that is called **ethnography**. By giving careful, detailed, and sympathetic attention to people's lives, ethnographic accounts of reproduction allow us to understand the wide range of practices and ideas surrounding human experiences of menstruation and menopause, infertility and pregnancy, and birth and loss. In this book, the discussions of these topics draw heavily from ethnographies analyzing not only cultural differences, but also economic, political, and social inequalities (discussed below).

Linguistic anthropologists examine our engagements in language as significant forms of human action. Everyday practices of language reflect and reinforce people's social identities and unequal statuses within a community. One example is that pregnant and birthing women may be discouraged from speaking or have their expressions of complaint or concern discredited or dismissed in their spoken interactions with healthcare workers. We frequently overlook the fact that language, too, is a practice of reproduction. Children learn and are taught not only the languages of their families and communities, but also the habits that make them recognized members of their human societies and cultures. Expectant parents in the United States talk to their expected children even while in utero as part of the process of constructing their human status and identity (see Chapter 4).

All four fields have their own particular aims, approaches, and histories that may overlap more closely with research and scholarship outside of anthropology than within it. Yet, **holism** remains an ideal across the four fields so that being human is never reduced to a single dimension like genetic heritage. Humans are always simultaneously biological, social and cultural, and linguistic beings. Our capacities and activities across all aspects of human experience shape and influence each other. For example, how people give birth is defined by not only the requirements of biology, but also the lived context that includes cultural difference and economic, political, and social inequality. **Biocultural** perspective on human health and reproduction can make us rethink some of the advice on what we "should" do. For these reasons, the integration of insights across the four fields is especially important and necessary in the study of human reproduction (Han and Tomori 2022; see also Han et al. 2018 and Tomori et al. 2018). There are also important applications of anthropology, as with the recent revisions to policy recommendations concerning breastfeeding and infant sleep (see Chapter 5).

The words **society** and culture (or social and cultural) are often used interchangeably. In anthropology, however, the terms have distinct and also connected meanings. Society refers to groups of individuals co-existing in large, organized groups and shared arrangements within these groups, as people do in households and families. Culture, as we have defined here, refers to patterns of behavior and belief that are shared among people in the same group. Anthropologists also use the term **sociocultural** to call attention to the connectedness of society and culture.

In anthropology, the concept of culture can enable us to talk about the differences in behaviors and beliefs observed between groups of people without thinking about them as hierarchical, or ranked. Humans are members of the same human species with common capacities of body and mind, and cultures equally represent human efforts. There are no superior or inferior cultures. **Cultural relativism** is the principle that any given practice or idea cannot be fully understood, let alone appreciated or evaluated, in isolation from its larger cultural context. It is a stance against **ethnocentrism**, or the tendency of people to assume that the practices and ideas they learned and were taught in their own culture are or ought to be the normal or correct and even superior ones.

While it may help us to talk and think about human differences in terms of culture, it also limits or even prevents us from understanding the inequalities that also shape and influence people's everyday experiences. Ask yourself, for example, when a person with less money receives lesser quality services than a person with more money, is this situation one of different or of unequal circumstances? In the anthropological study of reproduction, it is important and necessary to recognize difference vs. inequality.

HOW DOES THE ANTHROPOLOGY OF REPRODUCTION HELP US UNDERSTAND REPRODUCTION?

Consider how laws shape people's reproductive lives. In the wake of the US Supreme Court's decision overturning Roe v. Wade, new bans and restrictions have made not only abortion, but also pregnancy and birth less safe for millions of women. In Texas, for example, emergency abortion care has been denied to women, imperiling their lives and future fertility. The right to abortion care is supported by majorities of people. In the United States, 67% of women say that abortion should be legal in all or most cases. Voters in Mexico, Argentina, Ireland, and elsewhere have successfully pushed for legal and safe abortion care in their countries. Around the world, new parents need a range of support to care for their new babies, including support for breastfeeding, but many lack paid leave or access to skilled lactation support while being awash with virtually unregulated misleading marketing even from their trusted healthcare providers. For anthropologists of reproduction, these policies are examples of **reproductive governance**, which refers to the ways that state and non-state actors influence people's experiences of reproduction. These actors can include various branches of the government that create and implement laws and regulations, as well as non-governmental organizations like Planned Parenthood, religious institutions, or even for-profit corporations like the pharmaceutical companies that lobby lawmakers to shape infant feeding policies (see Chapters 2, 5, and 6). From laws to direct appeals to people or lobbying state officials, these actors may engage in activities to promote and advance their own priorities that shape and constrain available options or consequences of reproductive behaviors.

Around the world, people contending with unwanted childlessness and infertility find hope in reproductive technologies, but access to treatment may be denied to individuals who are unmarried or LGBTQ+ or the costs may be prohibitively expensive. (LGBTQ+ stands for lesbian, gay, bisexual, transgender, queer, plus other identities not named, and it is a common acronym used throughout this book.) Before, during, and after pregnancy and birth, people in communities marginalized by poverty, racism, sexism, and homophobia suffer from poorer health originating in the poor health of their mothers or their own in utero exposures to adverse environmental conditions. Marginalized people may also suffer neglect and abuse at the hands of healthcare workers who are charged with providing their care. These inequities are core issues in the anthropology of reproduction. Anthropologists have used the term **stratified reproduction** to describe people's unequal access to the resources, power, and opportunities enabling them to have and raise children based on race, ethnicity, gender, sexuality, class, or other social categories of discrimination. Importantly, people's experiences of inequality may be compounded and amplified by overlapping systems of discrimination, such as the treatment of people who are both Black and identify as a woman or poor and disabled. Anthropologists use **inter-sectionality** to describe these combined forms of oppression. The reader will find discussion of stratified reproduction and intersectionality woven throughout this volume.

BOX 1.1   REPRODUCTION GOES BEYOND BIRTH

Global news media turned the spotlight onto maternity leave in 2018 when New Zealand's Prime Minister, Jacinda Ardern, became the world's first elected leader to take it. She had been in office for less than a year, prompting her critics to ask whether she or any woman preparing to have a child should be hired for a position. Ardern responded: "It is a woman's decision about when they choose to have children, and it should not predetermine whether or not they are given a job or have job opportunities" (Quackenbush 2018). During the six weeks of her leave, the country's Deputy Minister handled the responsibilities of her office. When Ardern returned to work, her partner, with whom she was not married at the time, became their child's primary caregiver. The Prime Minister also made headlines around the world for bringing her daughter, then three months old, into the UN General Assembly meeting because she was breastfeeding.

Ardern's story can be read as an exceptional one about a powerful person enjoying privilege that is not available to everyone, but this is exactly why we ought to pay attention. Ardern was only the second leader of government to give birth—in 1990, Pakistan's Prime Minister, Benazir Bhutto, gave birth to her second child while in office—which reminds us of the continuing gender gaps in political representation globally. New Zealand is noted for having been the first country in the world where women gained the right to vote in 1893 and for having one of the lowest gender gaps in pay. Notable health inequities exist, however, between Indigenous and non-Indigenous people. Maori women suffer poorer health and higher rates of pregnancy and birth-related deaths than non-Maori women of white European descent like Ardern. Even with the country's system of socialized universal healthcare and **midwifery** model of care intended to offer more holistic and humane treatment of people during pregnancy and birth (see Chapter 4), other social determinants of health, like access to housing and food, rooted in a history of **colonialism**, shape the inequities of Maori women's reproductive experiences (Dawson et al. 2022; also see Chapter 6). In this case, we see that context is on the one hand global and broad—for example, the financing of healthcare systems and housing and food security may not be obvious as concerns of reproduction. Simultaneously, context is also local and specific, which anthropologists and especially ethnographers enable us to better appreciate in their attention to social and cultural practices and ideas.

At the time of Ardern's leave, New Zealand's legislature had been in the process of extending paid parental leave from 22 weeks to 26 weeks. The United States is one of six countries in the world where there is no guaranteed paid leave. The Family Medical Leave Act allows up to 12 weeks of unpaid leave for parental or other caregiving. In many countries, the duration of leave differs for women and men, so that an average paid maternity leave is 29 weeks and an average paid paternity leave is 16 weeks (Miller 2021). Even when paternity leave is available, however, men are less likely to take it, worsening already existing inequities between men and women (gender gaps) in the pay received for the same work and in their employment and opportunities to advance in their jobs. Sweden has assigned a minimum number of leave days for each parent in a couple so that fathers and mothers take their time away from work more equitably (Savage 2024). Economists describe a "motherhood penalty" for women with children, who may be perceived as less capable or reliable than people without children. In the United States, the gaps and penalties are felt most acutely and keenly by Black and Latine mothers who are raising children on their own, unlike Ardern and her partner, who later married in 2024. The impacts on solo mothers and mothers of color point to **intersectionality**, or the overlaps, or intersections, of multiple systems of discrimination, which in this case include sexism and racism that already filter their experiences in the other arenas of their lives. Consequently, over their life courses, these women and mothers contend with poorer physical and mental health and financial disadvantages with accumulating and compounding effects for themselves and their families.

What might our lives look like if and when we think about reproduction as more than birth and intentionally center reproduction in our economic, political, and social structures? One step in this direction is being taken in Sierra Leone, in West Africa, a generation after a decade-long civil war (1991–2002) entirely ruptured people's lives there. In 2023, resulting from the efforts of women's rights activists there, the legislature passed the Gender Equality and Women's Empowerment Act with requirements to increase the numbers of women in paid employment and government, mandates on equal pay and access to employment and educational opportunities, and 14 weeks of maternity leave. Each of these elements may itself be modest, but the approach is one recognizing the interconnectedness of work, pay, and reproduction.

What we see in all these areas of struggle is that reproduction is not simply about the production of children. Instead, the anthropology of reproduction is concerned with how the entire scope of reproductive trajectories is tied up with *reproducing existing systems of power and inequities*. Who gets to exercise their human rights to decide if, when, and how they have children and how to raise them depends on these systems. As these systems assert powerful control over every aspect of reproduction, they also reproduce these inequities. As previous generations of anthropologists have argued, *reproduction is at the center of social life* because it plays such a crucial role in making families and also in reproducing communities, nations, and entire ways of being. When a group of people is provided with support to achieve their reproductive desires while others are systematically hindered from realizing them, the stakes are extremely high. These decisions are, in the end, matters of life and death, and the survival and continuity of entire people. At an even broader scale, decisions that create enabling or harmful environments for reproduction may threaten the collective reproductive capacity and survival of the human species.

Importantly, anthropologists have also shown that even in times and places of war and armed conflict, mothers teach their daughters what to do when they get their periods, people celebrate their pregnancies and births, and parents do what they can to raise their children safe and healthy. People around the world find ways to create new opportunities for making families, resist forms of oppression, and move toward a better future as we show later in this chapter.

KEY AXES OF OPPRESSION: COLONIALISM AND RACE, SEX, AND GENDER INEQUALITIES

Anthropology offers crucial insight into contemporary inequities in reproduction and beyond. A major insight is that these inequities are continuing legacies of **colonialism**, or the historical projects of territorial expansion and resource extraction undertaken by wealthy nations located in Europe, North America, and Australia. Together, these wealthy nations constitute the **Global North** and continue to assert considerable control over the **Global South**, referring collectively to countries previously under colonial rule. Commonly used in the recent past were terms like First World and Third World, originating in the Cold War between the United States and the Soviet Union (the Second World), and not adequately describing the interconnected global structures of economic and political power and influence. What has been called "the West" is also not a geographical location, but an ideological construct that historically had been used to distinguish and elevate European Christian societies from their Arab and Muslim neighbors in the Middle East and people still further in the Far East. Today, the continuing use of West sets the Global North apart from the Global South, usually accompanied by incorrect beliefs about the superiority of Western cultures and religions.

The main object of colonialism was to exploit land, natural resources, and labor—that is, people—in the colonies and transfer the wealth they generated to the colonizers. In 1950, Britain controlled about half of the world's territories through its colonies. It is estimated that Britain extracted the equivalent of $45 trillion in today's US dollars from India alone between 1765 through 1938 (Patnaik 2017). The enrichment of the Global North is rooted in colonialism. **Settler colonialism** refers to colonialism that establishes permanent occupation of the territory by forcibly displacing or removing people already living on the lands, historically causing untold numbers of deaths, as witnessed in the dispossession of Indigenous people in North America.

Reproduction is profoundly implicated in colonialism. First, reproduction was the source of people. For colonial powers, people were valued primarily as the source of human labor required to cultivate or mine the earth for other wanted resources. The natural resource of people was exploited through enslavement and forced labor. Colonial economies produced not only sugar, tea, and rubber, but also made people into commodities through the slave trade. The entirety of the colonial enterprise was built on various unfounded justifications of its practice based on false racial hierarchies and religious beliefs painting people in the colonies as "primitive," "heathen," and "backward." The systematic exploitation of colonial populations and the accumulation of wealth and capital based on these racial concepts is called **racial capitalism**.

These strong financial interests were coupled with the cultural and religious beliefs of the colonizing powers. Colonial projects were also concerned with "civilizing" people and "saving" their souls by introducing or, in fact, imposing European customs and Christian teachings. What resulted is that colonial administrations were intimately involved with managing and regulating the reproductive practices of local populations to ensure that they had more labor—and therefore wealth—available to them. They directed their efforts at reshaping how local people bore and raised children to their own liking.

Colonial administrators employed medical officers to implement what they perceived to be more "modern" and "civilized" ways of birthing, feeding, and caring for babies. In turn, many populations were forced to abandon their cherished traditions of reproductive knowledge and practice that had ensured safe birth and healthy infant care for generations. Being forced to assimilate meant abandoning the cultural inheritance passed down among women. Many faced extremely high rates of death due to violence, heavy labor loads, and inability to adequately care for birthing people and children under these circumstances. The close relationship of Western biomedicine with these administrations and the legacies of these medical interventions is of sustained interest to the anthropology of reproduction. While other disciplines often depict biomedicine solely as a vehicle of progress and improved health, anthropologists take a critical view and examine how **biomedicalization** can have both beneficial and harmful effects (see Chapter 2). Without acknowledging this history, we will continue to struggle with what many researchers call racial disparities in risks to health and life that we can better address when we understand them as continuing historical inequalities.

The **biomedicalization** of reproduction refers to the historical shift from seeing reproduction as experiences in the broader context of people's lives to more narrowly reducing them to biological events, processes, and functions that may require specialized intervention (see Chapter 2). A more widely used term is medicalization, but in this chapter, and throughout this book, we use the terms biomedicalization and biomedicine, following the lead of scholars who note that medicine, or a system of practices and ideas concerning health and sickness, can be observed in every community. **Biomedicine** refers more precisely to a medical system that is grounded in biological sciences and technologies and accessed through institutions like hospitals. It is now the globally dominant form.

Colonial cultural and religious beliefs also played an important role in shaping local norms of sexuality and gender. Colonial administrations imposed their own social and moral order on local populations whose behaviors included some that were judged and condemned as "immoral" and "unnatural." In India and in large parts of Africa, the British imposed prohibitions against non-binary sexualities and gender identities and criminalized homosexuality. Their cultural norms became institutionalized as laws that were later also reproduced in postcolonial policies (see Chapter 6). Human rights observers today note the continuing restrictiveness on sexualities in African countries where some locally have claimed that recent movements for LGBTQ+ inclusiveness represent the continuing efforts of former colonizing Western nations to impose their own ideas on African people. The claims are challenged by the gender diversity, flexibility, and array of sexual practices extensively documented in the work of ethnographers and historians here and elsewhere around the world. Undoubtedly, people in local cultures did not uniformly accept these behaviors and indeed may have expressed and enacted their own disapproval, but the framing of diverse practices of sexuality and gender as novel Western inventions is incorrect.

While gender-based oppression and violence is troublingly common across cultures, it is also true that in many cases women had more power in the precolonial era and were more protected by kin networks. The balance of authority between women and men in their marriages and their families and households was unsettled by other, larger disruptions. For instance, we know that forced labor practices displaced large numbers of men to mines in Tanzania, where they lived impoverished and away from their families for lengthy periods of time. At the same time, women were left on their own to care for children while also undertaking all of the responsibility for farming and food production. The systematic exploitation of the population left families and communities destitute. In turn, people were unable to participate in locally significant traditions of gift exchange that forged connections between families, cutting out individuals from the marriage process and undermining men's abilities to meaningfully fulfill cultural expectations of manhood and masculinity as well. This larger context, alongside religious prohibitions preventing women from seeking recourse against their spouses, explains what led to men's alcoholism and engagement in risky sexual behavior and how and why women were made vulnerable to HIV through the activities of their partner, as well as their own to secure an income and feed their children.

The violence inflicted and the systems of exploitation imposed on populations in the context of colonial projects have had far-reaching consequences that stretch into the present, with significant implications for people's everyday experiences of reproduction. This book explores some of these legacies as they are manifested today in the inequities that shape whether individuals can live freely regardless of their sexuality or gender identity and make families on their own terms and can access and receive respectful, high-quality care as well as other resources needed to address their reproductive challenges and disruptions like infertility or pregnancy and birth complications.

The key struggles in reproduction are the efforts that people themselves have been making to restore and reclaim important and meaningful cultural traditions that have been attacked under colonialism, such as midwifery and birth practices (Chapter 4) and postpartum traditions of rest and recovery for new parents and breastfeeding as well as other aspects of infant care (Chapter 5; for a more comprehensive discussion of these topics, see Chapter 6).

In the United States, the concept of **race** is and has been used to highlight differences between groups of people. It is a social label associated with skin color and other observed features of physical appearance and has been a historically powerful cultural idea based on false claims about differences in human biology that were used to justify social hierarchies. Like money, race is a social construction, or a fiction with the force of society behind it. This means that while claims about human difference based on race have no scientific basis, racism has very real and devastating consequences.

Racism is the system of economic, political, and social discrimination, or unequal treatment, based on race. While racism is and has been a consequential form of inequality and source of historical trauma for untold numbers of people, it remains underacknowledged, even denied.

There have been recent and continuing concerns in the United States about the disparities in maternal mortality rates across different racial and ethnic groups (Hill et al. 2022). The number of Black women who die from pregnancy-related causes is three times as high as for white women. The rate of maternal deaths is twice as high among Native American mothers than among white mothers. Black and Native American women's babies also die in greater numbers.

Why? We can begin with what is not a valid explanation for these disparities. There is no evidence of unique "Black biology" and there are no exclusively "Black genes" that explain the higher rates of maternal and infant mortality than for white mothers and babies. The idea of separate races with superior or inferior capacities was used to justify settler colonialism and the violence and exploitation associated with it, including enslavement in the case of African people, or genocide in the case of Indigenous people as discussed above. In fact, the history of biological, or physical, anthropology itself can be traced to nineteenth century efforts to identify the distinctive racial biologies of Black, Indigenous, and other non-white people, an undertaking that we now call **scientific racism**.

Today, anthropologists confirm for us the evolution of one species of humans exhibiting variations in their appearance, including skin color—not multiple separate races. We understand that differences in skin color and other physical features associated with race, like hair texture, are just part of a wide array of small variations within populations of our human species, but these traits do not delineate "races" as there is more variation among than between groups. Moreover, traits are demonstrated to have no concordance, or correlation, with other more significant human characteristics, such as cognitive abilities, resistance to disease, or reproductive health.

The fact that pregnancy and birth pose much higher risks of death for Black and Indigenous women than for white women is a consequence of the unequal systemic treatment, or racism, directed at them—and built into the very biomedical systems that are ostensibly there to provide care. Yet, policy makers frequently look to specific factors that they can isolate, like promoting health education in Black and Indigenous communities that, on their own, create little or no benefit. Even well-educated and wealthy Black women, however, suffer worse outcomes than their white counterparts. In fact, maternal mortality rates were as high among high-income Black women as among low-income white women (Miller et al. 2023).

The disparities in maternal mortality rates for Black, Indigenous, and white women reflect and represent inequalities. The numbers of Black and Indigenous mothers and babies who die are the consequences of racism accumulating and compounding within individual life courses and across generations.

REPRODUCTIVE JUSTICE

The importance of our study of reproduction is not only to satisfy our curiosities, which is still a meaningful goal. What we see, however, is the possibility of even more. By sharing what we have learned, and continue to learn, about reproduction, our goal here is to serve the aims of **reproductive justice**.

Reproductive justice gives name to a set of principles and to the movements for social change that people have organized around the world around these ideas. Scholar-activists Loretta Ross and Rickie Solinger outlined three basic principles of reproductive justice: "(1) the right not to have a child; (2) the right to have a child; and (3) the right to parent children in safe and healthy environments" (Ross and Solinger 2017, 9). These rights are claimed as fundamental to human beings. As anthropologists, we take inspiration from the acknowledgement in these principles that reproduction is a centrally defining experience of being human. Reproduction both influences and is influenced by everything a human does and does not do. It is not only an individual, private, and personal matter, but also an institutional, public, and political one. How people live their lives, with whom, and whether they can do what matters most to them are questions of reproduction. These points are the foundational observations of the anthropology of reproduction, an area of study that is especially relevant now, in the context of scientific and technological developments and, especially, continuing struggles for reproductive rights, freedom, and justice.

The principles and movements of reproductive justice originate in the thought and action of Black feminists recognizing the direct connections between historical injustices of racism and present-day inequities that continue to be felt in communities of color. During the 1990s, they founded organizations like SisterSong, based in Atlanta, and built a coalition of activists and scholars to address the unmet needs and wants as they are experienced in the everyday lives of women, mothers, and people who are parents. These words are purposefully chosen here and throughout this book. The terms women and mothers refer to meaningful identities, but their use does not assume biologically determined status. Not every person who identifies as a woman has the capacity to become pregnant and birth a child, not every person who does identifies as a woman, and not every woman becomes a mother. Men and fathers, like women and mothers, are social and cultural identities that are distinguishable from biologies. They, too, feel the impacts of reproductive injustices as people who wish to not have or have children and as partners and parents. People may have a partner or spouse of different or same gender or sex, as in male-female (heterosexual), same-sex, or gender diverse unions or marriages. These uses of language point to the intersections, or interconnections, between gender, sex, and sexuality and particularly the unequal values associated with them. Reproductive justice provides us with the words, knowledge, and courses of action to confront this fact: our experiences of reproduction are not only different, but they are also made unequal by the economic, social, political, and historical systems that form the context in which we live.

REPRODUCTION AS RECKONING

When we take the discussion above seriously, the study of reproduction is no longer an academic exercise. It is an opportunity to recognize, resist, and challenge the racist, colonial legacies built into the contemporary systems in which people do not have or have children and raise them. It is a reckoning. Additionally, the study of reproduction offers a critique of the colonial structures within anthropology. Scholars who claim to have perspective on what it means to be human also need to turn this lens onto themselves. Anthropology was founded as part of the larger colonial enterprise. Historically, the work of this discipline was used to justify the subjugation and oppression of human beings whose differences in appearance and habit became a basis of their unequal treatment. Anthropologists have challenged these legacies, including their explicit demonstration of how the constructs of race, gender, and sexuality have been used to make false claims and empirically untrue arguments about people based on cultural ideas developed in Europe and North America and sustained around the world. Anthropologists today have more awareness also of the shortcomings of our disciplinary practices shaping who becomes trained as an anthropologist and whose research and scholarship become elevated. Anthropology today remains a community of predominantly white scholars from and in the Global North, many of whom come from privileged backgrounds enabling them to pursue advanced degrees. Accounting for and addressing these inequities is critical and necessary alongside the many ongoing struggles for reproductive justice.

OVERVIEW OF THIS BOOK

In the chapters that follow this one, we consider a broad range of topics in reproduction. They are arranged in clusters addressing the themes of not having children, having children, and raising children in safe and healthy environments, which are the basic principles of environmental justice. After reading Chapter 1, the following chapters need not be read in the order they are presented here. Each chapter is written so it can be read on its own. Every chapter includes specialized terms in bolded type with a short definition or explanation; the terms are compiled in the Glossary at the back of the book. Some chapters also include boxes highlighting a focal point or example. All the chapters end with a bulleted list of takeaway points in the Summary and suggestions for additional or other resources, like films or videos, podcasts, and websites, in a section titled Further Exploring.

Chapter 2 discusses menstruation, contraception, and abortion. Not having children is a reproductive experience that is important and meaningful to consider as a matter of reproductive justice. Menstruation, as a sign of fertility, carries a range of meanings. How we perceive it gives insight into the social status of girls, women, and people who menstruate. Deciding whether to have children, when, and how many is a longstanding human concern. Historically and cross-culturally, people have used various means of contraception to avoid pregnancy and methods of induced abortion to end an unwanted one. Control over people's access to contraception and abortion is control over people. Curtailing access denies human rights and creates unnecessary risks to their health.

Chapter 3 considers the topics of infertility, assisted reproductive technologies, and reproductive losses. Infertility represents the challenges of not having children when they are desired and the disruptions of cultural norms and gendered expectations for parenthood. Over the last 40 years, people have turned to assisted reproductive technologies for hope. Cultural and religious norms influence their use of technologies such as in vitro fertilization and gamete provision; structural inequities shape people's access to them. The chapter ends with an examination of reproductive losses. Reproduction is always uncertain and how people make sense of losses depends on their lived circumstances and the larger sociocultural context.

Chapter 4 is focused on pregnancy and birth as biocultural processes central to human experience. These processes are shaped by human society, history, and culture as well as by human biology and evolution. Across historical and sociocultural contexts, pregnancy and birth have been experienced as life events affirming connections among kin and women supporting each other. The perception that they require biomedical supervision is a relatively recent development. Knowing this history, particularly the broad and deep interconnections between biomedicine, racism, and colonialism, is an important and necessary step toward addressing the inequities and injustices of pregnancy and birth, such as the higher health risks for communities marginalized by racism.

Chapter 5 examines postpartum, infant, and other care, topics that demonstrate how reproduction is a process that continues beyond birth. Across settings, cultural practices and ideas have guided the physical recovery and social reintegration of parents after birth. The biomedicalization of reproduction, shaped by historical colonialism and racial capitalism, have had profound impacts on the models of postpartum and infant care and the policies today enabling or undermining care for children around the world. An urgent example is the aggressive pushing of infant formula by multinational corporations that reflects and reinforces a range of inequities. The final section of this chapter explores the significance, and significant challenges, of collective and cooperative care. Throughout our evolutionary and more recent history, it has been not only parents who look after infants and children.

Chapter 6 addresses continuing struggles and movements for reproductive justice. It begins with fertility crises as a site of struggle between the reproductive desires of individuals and the interests of a state (country) and its ability to assert control over people with the implementation of pronatalist or anti-natalist policies. Next, what we witness in Gaza and Ukraine is that wars are also sites of reproductive struggle. By threatening the survival and continuity of entire communities—including targeted violence especially impacting women and children in possible violations of international human rights law—states assert the most extreme forms of control over reproduction. The third section highlights the movements for access to birth control and abortion, demands for LGBTQ+ recognition, and fights against racism and colonial legacies in sexuality, birth, and infant care as ongoing struggles for reproductive rights, freedom, and justice. The final section of the chapter calls attention to environmental and climate crises, planetary health, and pandemics as urgent concerns for our collective reproductive futures. In this chapter, and throughout the book, the focus is on how people resist, overcome, and reinvent the possibilities and opportunities of reproduction toward a more just future.

SUMMARY

- As a human experience, reproduction is simultaneously biological, cultural, historical, social, political, and economic. Anthropology, as a discipline organized around the study of human complexity, provides important and necessary perspectives.
- Reproduction includes experiences of not having and having children, extending well beyond pregnancy and birth.
- All the various dimensions of human reproduction, from biology to history and culture, interconnect with each other in every experience. Acknowledging this context leads us to recognizing that ideas and practices of human reproduction are

shaped by cultural differences and historical inequalities of racism and colonialism.
- Righting the wrongs of reproductive injustices that we see daily impacting people's lives requires understanding and addressing the inequities.

FURTHER EXPLORING

READINGS IN THE ANTHROPOLOGY OF REPRODUCTION

Much of the significant research in the anthropology of reproduction has been published in edited volumes bringing together the works of various scholars who are in collaboration or conversation with each other. One recent example is *The Routledge Handbook of Anthropology and Reproduction*, edited by Sallie Han and Cecília Tomori (2022). A classic in the field is *Conceiving the New World: The Global Politics of Reproduction*, edited by Faye D. Ginsburg and Rayna Rapp (1995).

Over the years, a number of these collections have been recognized for their enduring influence by the Council on Anthropology and Reproduction (CAR). Founded in 1979, CAR is an organization of graduate students, emerging scholars, and senior researchers working in and out of academic institutions around the world. These books include:

- *Reproduction and Biopolitics: Ethnographies of Governance, "Irrationality" and Resistance*, edited by Silvia De Zordo and Milena Marchesi (2015).
- *Assisting Reproduction, Testing Genes: Global Encounters with the New Biotechnologies*, edited by Daphna Birenbaum-Carmeli and Marcia C. Inhorn (2009).
- *Reproduction, Globalization, and the State: New Theoretical and Ethnographic Perspectives*, edited by Carole H. Browner and Carolyn F. Sargent (2011).
- *Reconceiving the Second Sex: Men, Masculinity, and Reproduction*, edited by Marcia Inhorn, Tine Tjornhoj-Thomsen, Helene Goldberg, and Maruska La Cour Mosegaard (2009).
- *Beyond the Body Proper: Reading the Anthropology of Material Life*, edited by Judith Farquhar and Margaret Locke (2007).

- *Barren States: The Population Implosion in Europe*, edited by Carrie B. Douglass (2005).
- *Consuming Motherhood*, edited by Janelle S. Taylor, Linda L. Layne and Danielle F. Wozniak (2004).
- *Birthing the Pacific: Beyond Tradition and Modernity?*, edited by Vicki Lukere and Margaret Jolly (2002).
- *Childbirth and Authoritative Knowledge: Cross Cultural Perspectives*, edited by Robbie Davis-Floyd and Carolyn Sargent (1997).
- *Pragmatic Women and Body Politics*, edited by Margaret Lock and Patricia Alice Kaufert (1998).

For more information about CAR and the CAR book prizes, see the organization's website: www.anthrorepro.org.

RESOURCES ON REPRODUCTIVE JUSTICE

The civil rights organization Color of Change produced three short videos about reproductive justice, its history, and its continuing relevance. View part 1 here, then follow the links to parts 2 and 3: www.youtube.com/watch?v=mWyJ2Gz52fw.

Dorothy Roberts, a renowned scholar on issues of race and reproduction, delivered the annual Pembroke Publics Lecture at Brown University in April 2023 on the topic, "All of Reproductive Justice": https://youtu.be/iQVdojLf41M?si=1ISkWRBWHKgoBCMN.

REFERENCES

Dawson, Pauline, Benoit Auvray, Crystal Jaye, Robin Gauld, and Jean Hay-Smith. 2022. "Social Determinants and Inequitable Maternal and Perinatal Outcomes in Aotearoa New Zealand." *Women's Health* 18: 17455065221075913. doi:10.1177/17455065221075913.

Han, Sallie, Tracy K.Betsinger, and Amy B.Scott, eds. 2018. *The Anthropology of the Fetus Biology, Culture, and Society*. New York and Oxford: Berghahn Books.

Han, Sallie and Cecília Tomori, eds. 2022. *The Routledge Handbook of Anthropology and Reproduction*. Abingdon and New York: Routledge.

Hill, Latoya, Samantha Artiga, and Usha Ranji. 2022. "Racial Disparities in Maternal and Infant Health: Current Status and Efforts to Address Them." *KFF*, Nov. 1. www.kff.org/racial-equity-and-health-policy/issue-brief/racial-disparities-in-maternal-and-infant-health-current-status-and-efforts-to-address-them/.

Kapp, Caroline. 2023. "Women This Week: Women's Rights Victory in Sierra Leone." *Council on Foreign Relations Blog*, Jan. 27. www.cfr.org/blog/women-week-womens-rights-victory-sierra-leone.

Miller, Claire Cain. 2021. "'The World 'Has Found a Way to Do This': The US Lags on Paid Leave." *The New York Times*, Oct. 25, updated June 22, 2023. www.nytimes.com/2021/10/25/upshot/paid-leave-democrats.html.

Miller, Claire Cain, Sarah Kliff, and Larry Buchanan. 2023. "Childbirth Is Deadlier for Black Families Even When They're Rich, Expansive Study Finds." *The New York Times*, Feb. 12. www.nytimes.com/interactive/2023/02/12/upshot/child-maternal-mortality-rich-poor.html.

Patnaik, Utsa. 2017. "Revisiting the 'Drain,' or Transfer from India to Britain in the Context of Global Diffusion of Capitalism." In *Agrarian and Other Histories: Essays for Binay Bhushan Chaudhuri*, edited by Shubhra Chakrabarti and Utsa Patnaik, 277–317. New Delhi: Tulika.

Quackenbush, Casey. 2018. "New Zealand's Jacinda Ardern Is About to Take Maternity Leave: Why That's a Good Thing for Both Women and Men." *Time*, June 14. https://time.com/5310676/jacinda-ardern-maternity-leave-new-zealand/.

Ross, Loretta J. and Rickie Solinger. 2017. *Reproductive Justice: An Introduction*. Berkeley, CA: University of California Press.

Savage, Maddy. 2024. "Sweden: Where It's Taboo for Dads to Skip Parental Leave." *BBC*, Feb. 1. www.bbc.com/worklife/article/20240130-sweden-where-its-taboo-for-dads-to-skip-parental-leave.

Tomori, Cecília, Aunchalee E.L. Palmquist, and E.A. Quinn, eds. 2018. *Breastfeeding: New Anthropological Approaches*. Abingdon and New York: Routledge.

MENSTRUATION, CONTRACEPTION, AND ABORTION

Whether or not one's period comes when expected is commonly taken as a sign of not being or being pregnant, which in turn may be cause for relief or grief. To avoid pregnancies, people have employed various methods and materials, including medications. Yet, while we want and need contraception to be effective without harm to our bodies, the "control" we seek may be elusive and we may turn to other means of ending an unwanted or unviable pregnancy.

In this chapter, menstruation, contraception, and abortion are considered together. While each topic is important and necessary to examine on its own terms, they also represent human experiences of not being pregnant, which is as meaningful to consider as topics like being pregnant and giving birth. Not being pregnant and avoiding and ending a pregnancy are, and long have been, human concerns. To not have a child is a basic tenet of **reproductive justice**, a framework of principles organizing scholarly and activist efforts that asserts reproductive rights as human rights. Drawing on studies in sociocultural anthropology, biological anthropology, and archaeology, this chapter demonstrates the range of insights that can be applied to our understanding of human reproductive experiences. Practices and policies that shape how individuals can or cannot take care of themselves while menstruating—such as those creating the conditions for clean water or safe and private spaces—as well as what access they have to contraception and abortion are significant assertions of power

DOI: 10.4324/9781003379416-2

over not only reproduction, but people themselves. Deciding whether and when to have a child, including the choice to continue or end a pregnancy, is a profoundly important and meaningful exercise of an individual's agency. However, these reproductive decisions and choices are made within the contexts of not only relationships with other individuals including partners, but also of the priorities of governing bodies, which become asserted through policies and practices that empower or disempower individuals.

The first part of the chapter will discuss menstruation in sociocultural and evolutionary perspectives. In many present and past societies, menstruation is a symbol of fecundity and femininity. Its association with both the power to conceive and carry offspring and the pollution of menstrual effluvia have shaped the shared attitudes as well as individual experiences of periods as positive or negative ones. Cultural and societal biases about girls and women have shaped even the scientific ideas about why human females menstruate in the first place. Even as recently as the 1990s, one prominent theory suggested that periods had an immunologically cleansing function. Only in the last decade have more coherent explanations emerged so that we now have a better understanding of the biology and evolution of menstruation. How people who menstruate (including non-binary and masculine or male-identifying individuals) are enabled or not to manage their periods continues to be as much about the value that a culture or society ascribes to girls and women as it is about hygiene and health. Closing this section is a consideration of **menopause**, or the permanent cessation of menstruation. When menopause is discussed at all, we often talk about it as the end of women's reproductive experiences. Yet, as we expand our vision of what reproduction is—beyond pregnancy and birth—the significance of grandmothers comes more clearly into view.

The second part of the chapter is focused on contraception. An anthropological consideration of contraception begins with the understanding that whether and when to have children are basic human concerns of individuals and groups. People have long devised various methods and means to avoid pregnancy, sometimes less reliably and sometimes more. (Note: The focus here is on birth control, not with protection against HIV and sexually transmitted infections.) Presumptions about what people want and need—including gendered assumptions about sexuality—also become built into the development and promotion of modern contraceptive technologies. In fact, the distinctions we tend to make between want and need—alongside other terms and concepts like choice and right—deserve to be considered carefully. The quest for birth control and the uses of contraception raise important and meaningful questions about the conflicting interests and priorities of individuals in their everyday lives and of governing bodies which assert, even impose, their priorities for growing or slowing population.

The final section of this chapter will discuss abortion. Evidence from archaeology and history illustrates the longstanding human concerns with managing fertility. The development of methods of **surgical abortion** and medical or **medication abortion** have introduced safer means to end pregnancies which individuals may be unable or unwilling to continue. Yet, at this moment, there have been attempts around the world to restrict access to abortion care, which makes reproduction less safe for everyone. These exercises of power over reproduction and over people have necessitated abortion travel. People themselves also have been forming movements to assert their agency and demand reproductive justice.

MENSTRUATION

A period can be experienced as regular or "late." It might be dreaded when it arrives—or when it does not come at all. It can be a cause for pride or shame as well as abdominal pain. Menstrual cycles are interpreted as signs of our bodily condition, not only as indications of conception, but also of health, both reproductive and more general. Historically and cross-culturally, menstruation has been significant as a symbol of femininity, so that **menarche**, or the onset of menses, may be treated as a passage from girlhood to womanhood. It can be hard to square the idea that menstruation is a healthy and normal process, however, when it is often accompanied by pain, other physical discomforts like abdominal bloating, and emotional upset that can feel overwhelming. This is not to mention the attitudes and assumptions prevailing in many communities that periods are shameful, menstrual blood is disgusting, and by extension, so are the bodies that menstruate. In recent years, there has been activism to resist the stigmatization of periods and assert girls' and women's own human worth. At the same time, it is not surprising that menstruating people—including those who identify as girls and women and those who do not—may turn to the biomedical management of their periods to relieve their symptoms or suppress their cycles.

Menstruation is overwrought with meaning (Renne 2022). The elaboration of beliefs and behaviors surrounding it across cultures and societies has long fascinated anthropologists interested in religion and ritual. In the 1930s, British anthropologist Audrey Richards documented the puberty rites of the Bemba, an ethnic group in Zambia (central Africa), publicly marking the transformation of girls into women who were now eligible to become wives and mothers. **Puberty** is a time of not only observable physical and biological changes signifying reproductive maturation, but also the occasion for cultural and social shifts in the identity, status, and responsibility of individuals. Like the Bemba, many communities have marked these occasions with **rites of passage**, which may be performed as a ceremony or series of ceremonies initiating children and youths as adults. An important insight of Richards' work is that the "natural" fact of menstruation alone does not make a woman—or a wife or mother. After all, these are cultural and social roles. Thus, they require cultural and social acknowledgement and action. This insight also applies to an understanding of male initiation rites and the making of boys into men.

THE MEANINGS OF MENSTRUATION

The passage from girlhood to womanhood may be welcomed as entering into the common experience and knowledge of women and coming into one's own power as a woman. In the past, many North American Indigenous communities regarded this occasion as a sacred one and celebrated it according to their own religious teaching and practices. In recent years, there have been movements to revive and revitalize these rituals, which had been banned and abandoned under white settler colonialism and Christian missionization. Karuk (Native California) community members, including girls and women themselves, describe these practices as even more relevant today for young adults seeking guidance and sense of self while navigating the uncertainties of their everyday lives (see Further Exploring below).

Yet, also, menarche and menstruation may be greeted with dismay because it can represent the loss of the relative freedom of childhood to the responsibility of adulthood. Historically, in patrilineal and patrilocal societies like the Bemba, a young woman was expected to leave her father's home for her husband's father's home where it was hoped she would bear and raise her own children, especially sons. It is impossible to understand the meaning of menstruation without examining it within its larger historical, cultural, and social contexts.

The symbolic power of menstrual blood, or menses, itself has been intriguing to anthropologists, as Thomas Buckley and Alma Gottlieb (1988) noted in *Blood Magic: The Anthropology of Menstruation*. In various cultures and societies, there may be **taboos**, or symbolically meaningful avoidances. For example, girls and women on their periods may be restricted from participating in a range of activities, including cooking or even touching food with their own hands. Other taboos prevent their contact with other members of the community, particularly boys and men, and specifically prohibit sexual intercourse during menstruation. Taboos like these have been explained as practices to avoid what British anthropologist Mary Douglas (1966) called **pollution**, or symbolic contamination, which carries the threat of unwanted and even harsh consequences for individuals and communities. In addition to menstrual blood, other bodily substances—notably, semen—may be considered polluting in some cultural and social contexts. To prevent others from coming into contact with menstrual blood, girls and women may be expected to conceal all traces of their periods. In the western part of Nepal, actively menstruating people are forced to leave their homes and isolate themselves, sometimes in poorly maintained huts constructed for this purpose and sometimes in sheds built for animals. This practice of menstrual exile, called chhaupadii, exposes girls and women to risks to their health and personal safety, yet remains in force despite attempts to abolish it, such as a 2017 national law criminalizing it (Joshi and Acharya 2022).

Although menstrual taboos may reflect a given culture or society's belief that menstrual blood and, by extension, the menstruating bodies of girls and women are polluting, Gottlieb (1988) cautioned that such explanations must account for the larger context of the community's ideas and practices. Living and working among the Beng, an ethnic minority in Cote d'Ivoire, Gottlieb observed that men were prohibited from eating food cooked by their wives while they were menstruating. The reason was not that the food was considered polluted, but, as Gottlieb learned, that the Beng made important and meaningful distinctions between human fertility, represented by menstrual blood and human children, and Earth fertility, represented by forests and fields and the food crops they produce. In Beng cosmology, or worldview, these two forms of fertility must remain separate because both were regarded as powerful.

How anthropologists have portrayed menstruation has reflected their own unexamined presumptions. Much of the scholarship in the past emphasized the negative meanings of menstruation and menstrual blood. While people in different cultures and societies no doubt made these associations, it was anthropologists who chose to emphasize taboos and pollution in their studies. So, it is important and necessary both to take seriously what people themselves do, say, and think and to check how anthropologists talk and think about people.

THE ENDOMETRIAL CYCLE

Speakers of English and other languages frequently use the word period as well as euphemisms like time of the month to refer to menstruation, which itself is rooted in the Latin word for month. In actuality, some of us may not have such predictable cycles, but the regularity of blood loss in healthy, normal women has caused consternation for a number of (male) thinkers, as Emily Martin (1987) noted in her influential book, *The Woman in the Body*. In humoral theory, a European medical tradition dating to ancient Greece, the human body encapsulated the environment, with bodies themselves composed of human analogues of the elements of earth, water, fire, and air. Similarly, male and female reproductive anatomies were analogues of each other. Their bodies equally required cleansing, but men released their impurities through sweat because they were generally more active, and women experienced a "flush" through their monthly periods. Interestingly, Martin observed that through the eighteenth century, European medical texts discussed sex differences, but did not necessarily assign hierarchical value to them. A significant shift is evidenced in nineteenth century texts now claiming a "natural" causal link between women's lesser social status and their purportedly lesser and even dangerously flawed biology, which also justified the need for the interventions of gynecology and obstetrics, then emerging as new specialties of biomedicine.

Notions of the cleansing purposes of menstruation persisted through the end of the twentieth century, as biological anthropologists Mary P. Rogers-LaVanne and Kathryn B.H. Clancy (2022) discuss, with scientists publishing on the hazards of female "menotoxins" said to cause a range of ailments, including infants' colic, when not expelled or handled sanitarily. While these claims finally became discredited by the 1970s, other hypotheses about the immunological protections of menstruation—for example, against pathogen-bearing sperm—were proposed, without evidence, in the 1990s.

For Rogers-LaVanne and Clancy and other scientists currently investigating menstruation, the key to understanding it is the menses itself. Far from being merely a bloody excretion ridding the body of toxins and pathogens, it is in fact a build-up of rich tissue lining the uterus that is necessary for a fertilized egg to implant and develop into an embryo, which the endometrial lining continues to nourish until the placenta is formed to support it. This tissue is expensive for a body in terms of the energy required to make and maintain it. So, what is puzzling about periods is why the bodies of humans (and a few other mammals) have evolved to regularly use-or-lose this tissue; in fact, some of it is resorbed, not shed. By undertaking studies of both humans and select non-humans that menstruate, researchers now think it may be less costly to renew than retain the lining (see Kramer, Veile, and Ivey Henry 2022). They suggest that the continual repair and regrowth of the endometrial lining set up the optimal and necessary conditions for forming the placenta and sustaining a pregnancy.

People with smartphones may use period-tracking apps to know where they are in their ovulatory cycles so they can identify their fertile days to have or avoid sex and even plan vacations or other major events around their periods. Many of us have been accustomed to thinking about our periods in terms of ovulation and the ups and downs of the hormones associated with it. Yet, another way to understand menstruation is in terms of the endometrial cycle and its significance for the health of our reproductive capacity, which individuals may decide for themselves to exercise or not. Concerns about period-tracking apps have been raised in the aftermath of the US Supreme Court's 2022 decision in Dobbs v. Jackson undoing the right to access abortion care. There are fears that in US states now outlawing abortion, data from these apps can be used as evidence to prosecute people for obtaining them even when they travel to another state (see below). Additionally, the companies developing these apps may be interested in selling the private data they collect to corporations such as those with a stake in the market for period products.

PERIOD PRODUCTS

US readers who attended elementary or middle school from the late twentieth century onward may recall the talk or lesson they heard about puberty. Girls were taught to manage their periods with disposable sanitary pads, which were commercially manufactured starting in the 1920s and marketed as more hygienic, modern, and convenient to use than the cloths that women washed and reused or other materials they improvised. Tampons were developed in the 1930s and sold as a more reliable and discreet modern alternative to leaky, old-fashioned pads. Their use was denounced by Christian and other religious leaders who believed their use violated virginity—upheld as paramount for unmarried women. To this day, tampons may not be considered acceptable in religious and culturally conservative communities. The highest rates of tampon consumption are reported in the United States, Germany, and Austria, with none reported bought in Nigeria, the United Arab Emirates, Turkey, Kenya, Morocco, and Thailand (Chalabi 2015). Tampon usage was reported by 4.2% of women in South Korea (Choi et al. 2021) and only 1.9% of women in China (Ren et al. 2018). Additionally, questions about the safety of tampons continue to linger in the aftermath of hundreds of cases of toxic shock syndrome (TSS). Between 1970 and 1980, 73 women died and hundreds more were sickened by TSS, which is caused by a bacterial infection and associated with the use of tampons made with synthetic "superabsorbent" materials (Vostral 2017).

In the last decade, there have been movements around the world, led by girls and women, pushing back against the dictum that periods should not be seen or discussed. Their aims are to bring visibility to the consequences of menstrual **stigma** and voice to the girls and women burdened by the added expenses of period products that make them inaccessible in poor households and in low-income societies. Period poverty refers not only to the unaffordability of commercially produced pads and tampons, but also to the inaccessibility of other resources needed for menstruating people to take care of themselves, including toilets, clean water, and safe and private spaces. There are compounding effects of period poverty, as girls may be forced to skip school or give it up entirely. Menstruating people not only bear the costs of purchasing disposable pads and tampons, but they may also pay a so-called tampon tax. India introduced a 12% sales tax in 2017, then rescinded it from period products in 2018, under pressure from menstrual activists (BBC 2018). As of May 2023, 22 US states continued to charge sales tax on these items because they were legislatively classed as not necessities, as food and medicine are (Elsesser 2023). Activists call for what they call menstrual equity, pointing to the example of Scotland, where schools, universities, and local authorities are required to make period products available for free.

Stigma is a concept used widely in social and behavioral sciences to describe how the devaluing of a particular attribute of a person or group of people results in the devaluing of the person or people themselves. Stigmatization is always a social process and is built into and reinforced by systemic, structural inequities. In the case of menstrual stigma, because periods may be perceived negatively—for instance, seen as unclean—people who have periods are themselves also viewed and treated with negativity. Medical anthropologists observe that social stigma has consequences for the quality of healthcare that people receive and even whether they seek it at all.

Some scholars are, however, skeptical about what these efforts accomplish. Chris Bobel and Breanne Fahs (2020, 1009) are especially critical of a turn toward "a neoliberal engagement with menstrual management" in menstrual activism which is more focused on having "something to bleed on" than confronting the misogyny at the root of menstrual stigma. Malissa Kay Shaw (2024) outlines how the FemCare (feminine hygiene) industry exploits the perception of menstruation as a problem that its products can solve, perpetuating the idea of female uncleanliness. The globalizing market for period products is also prompting concerns about the environmental impacts of the waste that is generated by disposable pads and tampons. There has been growing interest in menstrual cups, typically made of soft silicone and inserted into the vagina to collect menstrual blood, but their use assumes some knowledge and willingness to engage intimately with the body. New products like reusable period underwear are designed to withstand washing and wearing. Others suggest turning to reusable cloth pads, with instructions online to teach people to make their own (like this one from the UK Women's Environmental Network: www.wen.org.uk/wp-content/uploads/Menstrual-pad-template-NEW-2020.docx.pdf).

Menstrual activists also question the negative value placed on menstrual blood itself as waste. In 2015, feminist poet Rupi Kaur, then a university student in Canada, posted on social media a series of photographs of herself with menstrual blood visibly staining her clothes and bedsheets. Instagram, the platform where Kaur posted the pictures, removed them without her permission, restoring them only after her written protest went viral. (One of the photographs, and Kaur's comment, can be viewed here: www.instagram.com/p/0ovWwJHA6f/?hl=en.) Instagram's actions—as well as the responses of internet trolls who called the images disgusting and hurled racist and misogynist vitriol against Kaur—demonstrated the very points that the project itself made.

REGULATING MENSTRUATION

Managing menstruation includes more than wanting materials to absorb the effluent. It may also involve other means and methods to regulate, stimulate, or suppress menstrual flow, as Elisha P. Renne (2022) observes. In southwestern Nigeria, where Renne conducted ethnographic fieldwork in rural Yoruba communities, women paid attention to the regularity of their periods as well as the color, consistency, and quantity of their menstrual blood as indications of their bodily health. When needed, they might treat their perceived ailments with herbal teas. In other settings, like rural Guatemala, where fecundity is highly valued culturally and socially, **amenorrhea**, or the absence of periods, and perceived menstrual delay might themselves be considered conditions of poor health, which might be treated with massages and plant-based **emmenagogues**, or remedies to stimulate menstruation. In such a context, the concern with bringing on a period may be an earnest one and not a euphemism for ending a pregnancy; however, the **abortifacient** properties of some menstrual remedies might also be well known and recognized in the community.

The pharmacological management of menstruation is an option for people in those parts of the world where access to hormone-based contraception is affordable and relatively convenient. In the US, 14% of girls and women ages 15 to 44 report taking hormonal contraceptive pills for non-contraceptive purposes that include the lessening of menstrual-related pain and making their periods more regular (Cooper and Patel 2024). The pill is also an option for trans or non-binary people seeking treatment that allows them to align their bodies and identities, or **gender affirming care** (Schwartz et al. 2023). On the pill, a "regular" period every 28 days is a product of the decisions of the drug manufacturers to package 21 active and 7 placebo pills. "Extended cycle" pills, however, reduce the number of periods to four times a year. The case for fewer periods also became popularized in a 1999 book, *Is Menstruation Obsolete?* written by a Brazilian doctor, Elsimar Courinho, who claimed not only did it free girls and women to put their time, effort, and energy into education, career, and other modern pursuits, but also that it falls in line with their evolved health based on the reasoning that women in the past had more pregnancies and longer durations of breastfeeding and thus fewer periods over their life courses. This popularized argument actually rests on the work of biological anthropologist Beverly Strassman (1997), who documented that women living in a contemporary Indigenous Dogon population in Mali experienced multiple-fold fewer periods than what was documented in wealthy Western settings primarily due to multiple pregnancies and longer periods of breastfeeding, which suppresses ovulation. Strassman and her colleagues have built on these argu-ments further to conceptualize evolutionary norms for human menstruation and their implications for reproductive cancers (Rogers-LaVanne and Clancy 2022; also see Chapter 5). Here, again, we see a contest among the meanings of menstruation. This time, the claims are about what it means to live in social conditions that vastly differ from those under which major evolutionary adaptations have taken place that shape our bodies.

MENOPAUSE

Menopause is not often or openly discussed in many social and cultural settings. This silence does not serve people who menstruate and eventually will experience this transition. Some women may dread menopause as the end of their fertility and a sign of their age, which shape the lack of respect and regard they may experience from other people, given the persistence of sexist assumptions that women's worth lies primarily in childbearing. Other women may look more positively on menopause as being released or freed from the pain and physical discomforts of menstruation and the efforts and costs of managing their periods as well as from the social and cultural expectations on women to have children. What all of us miss is that the cessation of menstruation is as significant a passage in a woman's life course as its onset and that menopause is an issue of reproductive justice.

The social and cultural biases equating women with childbearing appear to be reflected in the dearth of scientific research into the topic of menopause. Our lack of knowledge is disproportionate to our need for it. Lynnette Leidy Sievert and Subho Roy (2022) noted the unprecedented numbers of women currently going through the transition of menopause and starting their post-menopause lives. The world's population in 2020 included an estimated 978 million women between the ages of 50 and 99; this number is projected to reach more than one billion by 2030. Sievert and Roy (2022, 578) explain that in menopause, the ovaries "don't exactly dry up or 'shrivel,' but there is a process of degeneration (atresia) of the ovarian follicles across the lifespan." Menopause is not a singular event, then, but part of a larger, and longer, biological course. Human females, as with other mammals, are born with many more eggs than will become viable, much less become fertilized and result in pregnancies and births of living offspring. There are many questions about what predicts menopause and what may or may not be the connections with an individual's age at menarche, or the onset of menstruation, or other lived experiences and environments. We do not understand what causes hot flashes, a common complaint associated with menopause, so we do not know exactly how to address it or other bodily symptoms.

Significantly, menopause poses an evolutionary dilemma. The ovaries produce not only eggs, but also hormones supporting the health of organs, such as bone, so that the reduction of estrogen after menopause is associated with diseases like osteoporosis, or the loss of bone mass. Given this situation, menopause appears to be evolutionarily disadvantageous. In comparison with other mammals, including primates, human females live much longer past the time when they are able to have children, or offspring, from their own bodies. Interestingly, whales have become a focus of attention for scientists examining the evolution of menopause. A recent study of toothed whales suggests that menopause enabled the extended longevity of females (Ellis et al. 2024). It also supports what is called the **grandmother hypothesis**, proposing that the survival of offspring depends upon the efforts of not only mothers and parents, but also of grandmothers or older females (see Chapter 5). Notable in this research and others is the continuing use of wording like "post-reproductive" lives. We suggest that it is more accurate to approach grandmothering as another reproductive experience, and this framing may open us to new questions and answers with further study.

CONTRACEPTION

People have used a range of methods and means in their attempts to avoid or prevent pregnancy and manage whether and when they have children and how many of them. These include behaviors like withdrawal (*coitus interruptus*) as well as breastfeeding, or more specifically reliance on the effects of lactation in suppressing ovulation. Body-based devices, including condoms worn over the penis and other "barrier" forms inserted into the vagina, appear to have long histories. Middle Kingdom Egyptian texts advised women's use of honey or animal feces as a cervical cap or coating (Eichner and Wilkie 2015). In addition, historical archaeologists have recovered vaginal syringes from nineteenth century US sites associated with midwifery and sex work (Eichner 2013); the syringes would have been used for vaginal douching with water or various solutions, including acids, before or after intercourse. Not only have medicinal plant compounds been used in the past, but interest in them still persists in the present, such as the substances recognized as emmenagogues and abortifacients, as discussed in the sections on menstruation and abortion. Today, there is also a range of hormone-based contraception, including pills taken daily (containing either a combination of estrogen and progesterone) as well as the emergency contraceptive, or "morning after" pill (containing synthetic progesterone). Hormone-based injections and implants are designed to be long acting and reversible. While many methods and means of contraception block fertility only temporarily, there are also surgical forms of permanent birth control, or **sterilization**.

The decisions surrounding contraception are not necessarily made by individuals themselves, particularly not by women and especially not by poor and Black or Brown women. Importantly, family planning is a critical area of population policy, with national governments asserting and even imposing their priorities through laws and practices shaping which methods can be made available and to which people (Browner and Sargent 2022). People who wish to avoid pregnancies may be denied access to contraception, and people who wish to have children may have their ability to do so coercively or forcibly taken away. It is not only nations and states and their policies and laws, but also a range of other bodies from religious organizations to pharmaceutical companies and for-profit corporations that shape people's experiences of reproduction through a range of activities—a process that anthropologists call **reproductive governance** (Morgan and Roberts 2012).

According to a 2019 report of the United Nations, almost half (48%) of females of reproductive age (15–49 years old) in the world use some form of contraception. Another 10% reported wanting to avoid pregnancy, but using no birth control, indicating an unmet need. Worldwide, the most common means of avoiding pregnancy is female sterilization (24% of women currently using contraception). The next most common means were the male condom (21%); intrauterine device, or IUD (17%); and the female contraceptive pill (16%). Significant to understand are the patterns of birth control use, which vary widely by region. For example, reliance on female sterilization is highest in regions of the Global

South, notably Latin America and the Caribbean as well as central and southern Asia. The use of injections is highest in Latin America and the Caribbean and in sub-Saharan Africa; in contrast, this form of birth control is among the least used in Europe and North America.

Often, these patterns of birth control use are described as examples of cultural differences influencing individual preferences. Or they may be explained as evidence of social factors like lack of education for girls and women leading to lack of their awareness of contraceptive options. Significantly, however, these patterns reflect the exercises of power over people (Appleton 2024). For example, in the United States, the female contraceptive pill has become synonymous with birth control. Yet, a larger share of women aged 15–49 use female sterilization (18.1%) than the pill (14.0%)—and more than twice as many non-Hispanic white women (17.87%) used the pill as compared with Hispanic (7.9%) and non-Hispanic Black women (8.1%) (Daniels and Abma 2020). The pill became approved for use in 1960; however, distributing contraception or even information had been made illegal by the Comstock Act of 1873 and remained so in many states until the Supreme Court struck down these laws in two major decisions in 1965 and 1972. The pill became a symbol of sexual "freedom" and modernity for white women especially (Tone 2001). It did not, however, represent liberation for the Puerto Rican women who suffered ill effects on their bodies when it was tested on them during the 1950s. These women were particularly targeted because they were perceived as an "overpopulation" problem—a perception drawn from colonial and postcolonial efforts to control these communities' reproduction. Whereas producing more workers for colonial administrations was a key aim of earlier policies, in the postcolonial era "excess fertility" of the same populations came to be seen as problematic and was the basis of implementing racist "population control" policies (see also Chapter 6). The unequal value placed on people and the inequitable support or lack of it for people to have children are described as **stratified reproduction** (Colen 1995). Indeed, as Dorothy Roberts (1997) has recounted, the birth control movement of the early twentieth century—and the impetus to develop the pill specifically—has its origins in the American eugenics project to curtail births among Black people deemed "unfit" to reproduce. Yet, all of these women, white and Brown and Black, shared the want and need for some means of deciding for themselves when to have children and how many.

GENDERED DIVISION OF BIRTH CONTROL

Gendered assumptions about sex, sexuality, and reproduction have shaped and influenced cultural ideas and social practices as well as the scientific development of contraception and laws and policies enabling and disabling access to it. In keeping with various cultural presumptions about heterosexual marriage as a precondition for sexual activity, unmarried individuals, particularly women, may be prevented from access to contraception or even information and knowledge about it. Within the context of marriages, wives may feel pressure from their husbands to not use birth control. Alternately, wives and husbands may agree with each other, but still acquiesce to the demands of in-laws and extended families, as observed in couples in Pakistan (Sarfraz et al. 2023). Health workers also act as gatekeepers to birth control and information about it, refusing to provide it to a wife without assent from their husband, even when there is no legal requirement. Religious strictures on particular or even all forms of male and female birth control may prevent or at least discourage people from using them.

People with the capacity to get pregnant want and need the knowledge and means to avoid pregnancies. Indeed, many means of contraception are intended for female bodies, with information about them historically constituting what has come to be seen as traditional forms of "women's knowledge." Yet, in Europe and the US, sociologists have observed a gendered division of birth control and specifically a feminization of contraception that shifts the burden of preventing undesired pregnancies entirely to women (Fennell 2011; Kimport 2018). It is assumed that women feel more responsibility for birth control and that the responsibility should be solely theirs; however, this reasoning is based on reducing and naturalizing reproduction as female biology and feminine sentiment. When the responsibility is assigned to women in larger social, cultural, and political contexts that are not, in fact, empowering of them, it is experienced as an unfair burden or even blame when contraception fails. Moreover, women taking the pill also bear the risks and adverse effects associated with hormonal contraception, which range from unwanted spotting and "break-through" bleeding to nausea and headaches to rare but serious complications like increased risks for heart attack or stroke (Planned Parenthood n.d.).

Some men are, indeed, motivated by their awareness of the responsibilities and risks that women take, as Matthew Gutmann (2007) documents in his study of Mexican men choosing vasectomy. Yet, what men do, think, and feel about reproduction is much less studied in anthropology and in other disciplines (for discussion on recent anthropological studies of men and reproduction, see Wentzell et al. 2024 and for an overview of perspectives from biological anthropology, see Gray, Straftis, and Anderson 2022). The assumption that reproduction is primarily, if not solely, a female concern also has effects for thought and action on whether and how the responsibility for birth control can be shared. Notably, there are still fewer means of contraception for male bodies today than for female bodies. There has been a perception that masculine sexuality and male reproduction are more difficult to "control." In Japan, women's attempts to regulate their own fertility was perceived to require an extensive and lengthy process of governmental review, while men's exercise of sexuality was viewed as a much more acceptable right. The female contraceptive pill was not approved for use until 1999, after close to 40 years of study on its effects. In contrast, Viagra, the medication used to enhance male virility (not the same as fertility), became approved for use in the same year after only six months of deliberation.

In the now-classic article, "The Egg and the Sperm: How Science Has Constructed a Romance Based on Stereotypical Male-Female Roles," anthropologist Emily Martin described how gender stereotypes about women and men have been projected onto sex cells (e. g., passively waiting eggs, aggressively racing sperm), producing inaccurate understanding of human conception even among reproductive scientists. In addition, persistent stereotypes about male sexuality have affected the uptake of existing male body-based contraception, including condoms and vasectomies, as well as the further development of effective alternatives. In fact, the scientific know-how to create a "male pill" has existed since the 1970s, as Nelly Oudshoorn (2003) has documented, but pharmaceutical companies have been reluctant to invest in costly research for a male pill that they believed was unlikely to sell. Innovations in male birth control are blocked, then, not by the purportedly challenging nature of male biology or the limitations of science and technology to contend with it, but instead by social and cultural assumptions about masculine sexualities and male bodies.

STERILIZATION AND LONG-ACTING REVERSIBLE CONTRACEPTIVES

Most contraceptive methods block fertility only temporarily. However, surgical sterilization offers the possibilities of more permanent birth control, which individuals may want or need at some point in their reproductive lives. Female surgical sterilization, as noted above, is the most widely used form of contraception in the world; it includes **tubal ligation** (the blocking of the fallopian tubes by surgically cutting or "tying" them, thus preventing eggs from reaching the uterus) and **hysterectomy** (the removal of the uterus). Male surgical sterilization accounts for only 2% of birth control users (United Nations 2019) and includes **vasectomy** (the blocking of the vas deferens, preventing sperm from reaching the semen). While vasectomies can be surgically "reversed," these procedures cost several thousands of dollars, which patients in the US usually pay out-of-pocket because medical insurance typically does not cover them. There is, however, a growing interest in vasectomies that has been documented after the Dobbs decision with the rapid implementation of restrictions on abortion (Zhu et al. 2024), signaling that people are seeking out these procedures to avoid the often severe consequences of unintended pregnancies in abortion-restrictive states (see also Chapter 6).

The example of Puerto Rican women illustrates some of the concerns surrounding how and why female sterilization is the form of birth control most widely used in the world. Tubal ligation is so familiar to Puerto Rican women that it is known simply as la operación (operation). In a study spanning 25 years, Iris López (2008) details the concerns of women who want to have children while also limiting how many they have and spacing their births. Their options are constrained by the political and economic interests of the US, which holds the island as a territory, as well as the continuing influence of the Catholic Church, which forbids "artificial" birth control. There has also been a long-lasting negative perception of the pill directly resulting from the history of Puerto Rico as a site for US companies to test contraceptive technologies while they were still in development and the harm done to women who became involved in these experiments. When Puerto Rican women have "chosen" sterilization, they have not done so freely or with accurate or complete information about the irreversibility of "tying" the fallopian tubes.

While permanent birth control may be desirable for individuals in specific circumstances, there has been a history of sterilization abuse around the world. Enacted by governments claiming the necessities of population control, the abuses include the targeting of marginalized groups for involuntary sterilization, which has continued into the present day. In the US, individual states began enacting eugenicist policies in the name of improving population "quality" during the 1900s. Sterilization laws were aimed at people who were deemed unfit for society because they had developmental or intellectual disabilities, suffered from mental illness, or were poor. Black, Indigenous, and Latine people were the focus of especially aggressive sterilization campaigns throughout the twentieth century. In the 1960s, civil rights leader Fannie Lou Hamer, among others, brought to light the numbers of Black women whose uteruses were removed without their knowledge or consent—a practice grimly known as the "Mississippi appendectomy." In 1970, the Indian Health Service began paying for the sterilization of Medicaid recipients, with the result that an estimated 25% of Native American women were made infertile (Roberts 1997). In 2020, the involuntary sterilization of 16 Latin American women detained in a US Immigration and Customs Enforcement center was brought to light by a whistleblower complaint made by a nurse who had formerly worked at the facility (Mullings 2022). Incarcerated people have been vulnerable targets. More than 100 women held in California prisons underwent procedures without their voluntary consent between 2006 and 2012, and women and men in Tennessee prisons were offered a 30-day reduction in their sentences contingent on their agreement to be sterilized (Sufrin 2018).

Similar to sterilization, for individuals who want and need long-acting reversible contraceptives (LARCs), there are advantages to this form of birth control, but there is also a history of its abuse and the targeting of marginalized people, as documented in a systematic study (Boydell et al. 2023). LARCs are effective forms of birth control and their use may be more convenient and discreet. In contrast with the male condom which is put on immediately before intercourse or the pill which is taken daily, an injection is given every three months; an implant, once inserted, is effective for three years; and IUDs (intrauterine devices) last five years or more. Condoms and pills, however, remain within the immediate control of individuals themselves to use while LARCs require a healthcare worker to administer or insert and remove them. There also have been concerns about the safety of specific LARCs, such as Norplant. In a review of 92 papers reporting on programs promoting LARCs, Victoria Boydell and colleagues (2023, 11) came to what they called "one clear conclusion: all instances of coercive practices in LARC programs target marginalized, disadvantaged and excluded population(s)." The targeted people include Adivasi and Dalit women in India and Black and Native American women as well as incarcerated women in the United States, among others. Until 2021, the insertion of a LARC was required for women in the United Kingdom seeking access to substance use treatment.

As much as people have wanted and needed it for themselves, birth "control" has proved elusive. Conversations in the media often frame this challenge as one rooted in the complex, even difficult nature of human reproductive biology. Yet, it is equally if not more a result and reflection of the conditions of human culture and society, in particular the assertion of power over individuals by governing bodies to gain and maintain population control. This situation is made even more clearly visible when examining the wants, needs, and assertions of power concerning the ending of a pregnancy.

ABORTION

The facts of life include not only pregnancy and birth, but also abortion and pregnancy loss. Nearly half of all pregnancies which occurred in the world each year between 2015 and 2019 were unintended, and most of them (61%) ended in abortions (Guttmacher Institute 2022).

Abortion refers to the induced termination of a pregnancy. In contrast, medical practitioners use the term spontaneous abortion to describe a miscarriage or early loss of a pregnancy that occurs without intervention (see Chapter 3). As with contraception, people have long used a range of techniques in their attempts to discontinue or end pregnancies and thus manage whether and when they have children and how many of them. There are, of course, a host of reasons why people may decide they will not or cannot continue a pregnancy, even when they wish to have a child. The circumstances under which people make these decisions are often complex and shaped by intersecting structural inequities that make caring for a child challenging—ranging from a lack of supportive state policies to forms of racial, gendered, and sexual oppression asserted against women and birthing people. A pregnancy itself may pose risks for the pregnant person's life, health, or future fertility. Prenatal tests and screenings may provide expectant parents with diagnoses of serious conditions that may end an expected child's life shortly after birth or result in disabilities requiring intense and prohibitively expensive life-long care and support (see Chapter 4). Even when we talk and think about these decisions as those of individuals, anthropologists recognize people as always already embedded in social relations. For example, an individual person is also someone else's partner, parent, child, or sibling. Our relationality powerfully shapes what we feel we owe to each other and ourselves as well as whether we can fulfill these responsibilities.

What differs today is not the need or want for abortion, but the development of methods and means that better serve people who do not intend to continue a pregnancy. Equally important are the conditions which allow or deny people access to abortion services including the policies, laws, and practices of national governments. In the United States today, in the aftermath of the Supreme Court's 2022 decision overturning the legal recognition of an individual's right to access abortion that had stood for almost 50 years, there has been renewed concern about the harm and injury to people attempting to end pregnancies without needed care—which has been and is a continuing fear and worry for many people around the world. A critical insight of anthropologists and others invested in reproductive justice is that restrictions of policy, law, and practice do not reduce the demand for abortion, but only make it less safe for people's bodies, health, and lives (Mishtal and De Zordo 2022; Unnithan et al. 2024). Access to safe abortion is also highly stratified, or unequal. Low- and middle-income countries account for 88% of abortions and almost all (97%) of unsafe abortions (Allotey et al. 2021). Unsafe abortions are estimated to cause 8–11% of maternal deaths globally, mostly in low- and middle-income countries (The Lancet 2018).

The evidence of abortion in the past can be found in various forms (Riddle 1992). For example, in a given population, the number of children that a woman had and the spacing between each of these births might suggest the use of birth control and possibly also of abortion. Medical texts from ancient China, Egypt, and Rome allude to a range of different techniques that were known and used in these societies. *De Materia Medica*, known today as one of the oldest known written texts of Western pharmacology (dating 50 to 70 CE), described various plant-based abortifacients, or substances which can bring about the end of a pregnancy, typically by stimulating uterine contractions. Various plant ingredients might be prepared in the form of medicinal "wine" or tea or for application directly to the cervix (the opening of the uterus), as in a vaginal suppository or pessary. There are written documents also of various simple tools, like pointed sticks of wood, which have been used to induce miscarriages; a tenth century Persian text offers instruction on the use of instrumented abortion (Joffe 2009). Massage abortion is depicted in twelfth century bas-relief sculptures adorning the walls of the Angkor Wat temple complex in Cambodia. Its continuing practice is documented in contemporary Southeast Asia, including in Myanmar, Thailand, Malaysia, Indonesia, and the Philippines, particularly in rural areas (Potts, Graff, and Taing 2007). The massages typically involve pressure on a woman's abdomen (without vaginal manipulation). The technique has been one that traditional birth assistants, like midwives, might have learned and practiced as part of their training.

Today, the most common techniques of abortion available in formal healthcare systems are surgical abortion and medical or medication abortion. A surgical abortion during the first trimester (12 weeks) of pregnancy is typically performed by a trained practitioner using a vacuum aspiration machine to remove tissue from the uterus; the patient receives sedative and pain relief medication. The procedure itself does not require a hospital stay and individuals can leave the clinic or office where the abortion is performed after a few hours of recovery. Medication abortion involves the use of pre-scribed drugs during early pregnancy; taken most frequently today is a combination of mifepristone (which blocks the pregnancy hor-mone progesterone) and misoprostol (which causes uterine cramp-ing). The World Health Organization (WHO) includes mifepristone in its list of essential medicines and recognizes it as safe and effective enough for individuals to self-manage its use (www.who.int/publications/i/item/WHO-SRH-22.1). Access to medi-cation abortion has been essential for reproductive care during health emergencies. During the Zika outbreaks in 2015 and 2016, the online requests for pills doubled from women in Brazil and increased by more than 30% in El Salvador; both countries severely restrict abortion (Wenham et al. 2019). Many people in places like the US turned to medication abortion during the COVID-19 lockdown measures that prevented them from accessing abortion care in person. In June 2024, the US Supreme Court knocked down an effort to have the regulatory approval of mifepristone revoked, affirming its continuing availability for now, but it remains inaccessible in many abortion-restrictive states and its future is threatened (see Chapter 6). Medication abortion now accounts for at least half of abortions in 24 high-income countries, and 90% of them in Finland, Sweden, and Norway (Sedgh and Taqi 2023). Access to medication abortion, however, remains highly stratified, with its availability limited in low- and middle-income countries, even when the law allows it.

How laws allow or disallow abortion varies (Unnithan et al. 2024). Restrictions may target the people seeking abortions, the people providing them, the conditions in which the procedures can be performed, or a combination of any or all of the above. There may be mandatory counseling or waiting periods, which mean more or longer absences from home that may be more dif-ficult to explain or conceal as needed, not to mention the added expenses. These delays also put people at risk against gestational age limits, especially when access to abortion is restricted to the first trimester only. Many countries no longer require parental notification of adolescents seeking abortion or spousal authoriza-tion for married women, but a number until recently did and some still do (Center for Reproductive Rights n.d.). Some laws prohibit abortion, but also offer exceptions—for example, to save a woman's life or to discontinue a pregnancy resulting from rape; however, these exceptions often require approval from a third party such as a medical committee or a judge which, again, may delay or ultimately entirely obstruct urgently needed care.

BOX 2.1   ABORTION, DELAYED CARE, AND CRIMINALIZED PREGNANCY LOSS

Bans and restrictions on abortion can cause myriad harms, as observed around the world. Even when a ban includes an exception for the life and health of a pregnant woman, she is required then to receive the permission of a medical committee or the ruling of a judge, so that her access to urgently needed care is delayed. Women seeking abortions under these conditions can also be denied abortions, which led to a 2023 lawsuit filed by 20 women against Texas; in 2024 the state's highest court ruled against the women, upholding the state's near-total ban. The restrictions have impacts on care for spontaneous pregnancy losses more generally. In cases of incomplete miscarriage, not all of the pregnancy tissue has been passed from a person's body, posing risks for severe bleeding or sepsis (infection). An incomplete miscarriage may require a surgical procedure to remove tissue from the uterine lining, called dilation and curettage or D&C, but people have experienced delays or even been denied this care (Ranji et al. 2024).

Laws making it a crime for women to obtain abortions also put them at risk of being unjustly accused of criminally inducing a miscarriage or stillbirth. El Salvador is infamous for having among the world's harshest anti-abortion policies, banning it in all circumstances with no exceptions (see Further Exploring). Since the ban's implementation in 1998, more than 180 women have been convicted for inducing their own pregnancy losses and 50 of them have been incarcerated (Shoichet 2023). In some of these instances, women were arrested at a hospital where they had gone to seek emergency care.

In the United States, a federally protected right to access abortion care was undone after 50 years as settled law by the country's highest court in 2022. Over the years, in fact, opponents of abortion had been mounting legislative attacks on not only people obtaining care, but also people offering it, with targeted regulation of abortion providers (TRAP) laws aimed at clinics and doctors. Alongside these measures was the application or revision of already existing laws intended to protect children, but weaponized against women with histories of substance abuse or untreated mental health problems. These women were prosecuted for causing their own miscarriages and pregnancy losses, accused of violating child abuse and neglect laws. A disproportionate number of them were poor as well as people of color and lacked access to basic resources and healthcare.

The pursuit of legal recognition for fetuses and embryos has been part of the effort to remove access to abortion. In 2024, the state of Alabama's highest court legally recognized embryos as "children," extending the reach of a state law, passed in 1872, concerning the wrongful death of minors. So-called fetal assault or fetal protection laws have been enacted in 38 US states under the guise of protecting children, and while many exclude the prosecution of pregnant people, they have been weaponized against them (ACOG 2020). The Alabama court's ruling inadvertently criminalized the routine activities of in vitro fertilization providers who immediately halted their services, initially creating chaos and dismay for people being treated for infertility (see Chapter 3). Laws to protect providers were quickly passed in Alabama so that fertility treatments could resume, but in June 2024, Republicans in the US Senate blocked a bill to ensure availability across the country. Additionally, the legal recognition of embryos further complicates whether people can decide for themselves how to proceed with their own fertility journeys, such as what to do with frozen embryos that were created, but not used. These embryos may be donated for scientific research or even "adopted" through agencies established by evangelical Christian organizations (Cromer 2018).

In sum, anti-abortion measures have proliferating impacts that include criminalizing pregnancy loss as well as compounding already existing injustices.

One consequence of these restrictions is that people will travel out of their communities and even out of their countries to access care (Mishtal and De Zordo 2022). Spain, England, and the

Netherlands have been destinations of abortion travel, receiving people from elsewhere in the European Union as well as from abroad. In the United States, the Society for Family Planning reported in 2023 that while states that imposed bans had decreased if not eliminated the number of abortions recorded by providers, the total number of abortions increased, with surges in the numbers recorded by providers in states like Illinois, where abortion remains legal with no new restrictions and which border other states with bans (Society for Family Planning 2023). Even before the overturning of Roe v. Wade in 2022, there were many states and regions of the country where people had little or no access to abortion care, forcing them to travel. States like Mississippi had effectively blocked access to abortion by adopting TRAP laws which created a number of requirements that went well above and beyond existing ones for other surgical procedures, even specifying the dimensions of the rooms where abortions can be performed. Since 2022, in states like Texas, abortion practitioners now risk arrest and prosecution.

Whether looking at the present or the past and at the reproductive experiences of people around the world, we can find accounts of the horrifying injuries to and deaths of women who attempted to end their pregnancies under restrictive conditions, forcing them to turn to people who were ill equipped and underprepared, not to mention biased and harshly judgmental, and sometimes to self-induce miscarriages from physical traumas of "overwork" or jumps and falls. Not surprisingly, they or others around them may have been reluctant to seek needed care afterward; however, to avoid unwanted attention (including from authorities), they also became further imperiled. The secrecy under which women sought abortions also has shaped and continues to shape the conditions in which even the most experienced, skilled, and conscientious practitioners can offer their help (see Solinger 2019 [1994]).

Many people may feel strongly sympathetic and supportive of access to safe and legal abortion and at the same time also feel troubled about the moral and ethical questions it raises for them, particularly in the context of religious teachings. Yet, religions are, in fact, not all entirely absolutist. In many if not most of the world's religions, offering compassionate aid to a person who is suffering is a moral imperative that may be interpreted to allow for ending a pregnancy. Written into policy and law in the United States and elsewhere is the right for health workers to not provide abortion care on the grounds of religious or conscientious objection. While conscience is frequently invoked to describe, explain, and justify anti-abortion refusal, historian Sara Dubow (2022) notes also that moral conviction significantly motivates abortion providers. During the 1960s, a group of US Christian ministers, Catholic priests and nuns, and Jewish rabbis formed the Clergy Consultation Service to refer women to safe abortion providers.

Even among people whose objections to abortion are religiously influenced, there is a range of beliefs. US anti-abortion activists became organized around a "pro-life" stance, drawing from Christian and specifically Catholic theological claims that life begins at conception and abortion is the taking of a human life. Activists also argued that a fetus is a person whose rights should be protected (see Chapter 3), employing images of fetuses evocative of babies and even sound recordings of fetal heartbeats (Howes-Mischel 2018). The assertion of fetal personhood has been part of a larger political and legislative strategy (see Box 2.1) and a campaign to win popular opinion. Most Americans support legal access to abortion care, with a 2024 survey reporting that 63% of respondents agreeing it should be legal in all or most cases (Pew Research Center 2024). Religiously affiliated anti-abortion groups also operate so-called crisis pregnancy centers that promised free or low-cost healthcare services, but have the aim of dissuading or preventing people from receiving abortion care (Montoya et al. 2022).

US Christian beliefs about life and especially fetal life were not shared by Russian Orthodox anti-abortion activists, with whom Sonja Luehrmann (2018) conducted ethnographic research between 2008 and 2014. For the Russian Orthodox activists, US Christians were overly concerned with biological life, like fetal heartbeats, distracting them from focusing on the eternal life of souls. Luehrmann's account reminds us again to look at the specific context of people's behaviors and beliefs, which in the case of Russian Orthodox anti-abortion activists included not only the religious teachings of their church, but also their lived experiences in post-Soviet Russia. Faye Ginsburg (1989), conducting fieldwork with US anti-abortion activists in North Dakota during the 1980s, came to understand how their locally grounded lived experience had shaped their motivations. US political observers often say the rhetoric of national politics does not necessarily translate into the conduct of local government. More than 40 years after Ginsburg's research, however, national politics have infiltrated into local politics. With the striking down, in 2022, of constitutional protections ensuring abortion access, one wonders how much common ground still exists and what can be done to rebuild it.

In recent years, activists around the world have successfully pushed countries to decriminalize abortion. Notably, women across Latin America formed the Green Wave or marea verde movement, which celebrated landmark wins in the highest courts of Mexico (2023), Colombia (2022), and Argentina (2021). While these more liberal laws do not necessarily make abortion more equitably accessible and remain key sites of struggle (see also Chapter 6), they still represent important, meaningful, and necessary movement toward reproductive justice.

SUMMARY

- Reproduction includes the experiences of not having children as well as those of having them.
- How people talk about menstruation, whether positively or negatively, gives us insight into what they think about the people who menstruate. The ability for girls, women, and people on their periods to care for themselves is also a matter of reproductive justice.
- Humans have longstanding concerns with managing their fertility, as we learn from archaeological and historical evidence of the various means and methods of birth control, restoring regular menstruation, and induced abortion that people have devised and used.
- Both denying access to wanted contraception and coercing or forcing its use against people's wishes are reproductive injustices that have particularly impacted poor and Black or Brown women globally. These are direct outcomes of racist colonial and postcolonial policies and practices that aim to assert control over reproduction.

- In the United States, incidents of involuntary sterilization have been documented recently as well as historically.
- Around the world, restricting access to contraception and abortion care makes reproduction less safe for everyone and restoring access to both are matters of reproductive justice.

FURTHER EXPLORING

MENSTRUATION

See *The Routledge Handbook on Anthropology and Reproduction*, edited by Sallie Han and Cecília Tomori (2022), for chapters by Karen Kramer, Amanda Veile, and Paula Ivey Henry (2022); Elisha P. Renne (2022); Mary P. Rogers-LaVanne and Kathryn B.H. Clancy (2022); and Lynnette Seidy Sievert and Subho Roy (2022). See the references for more information.

The significance of a Karuk girl's coming-of-age Ihuk, or flower dance ceremony for a girl, her family, and their larger community is explored in "Long Line of Ladies," a 2022 short documentary film co-directed by Rayka Zehtabchi and Shaandiin Tome. The 22-minute film can be streamed on *The New York Times* website: www.nytimes.com/2022/11/01/opinion/karuk-indigenous-celebration-menstruation-ceremony.html.

"PERIOD" podcast, hosted by Kate Clancy, a biological anthropologist whose research is described in this chapter, examines a range of topics on menstruation, from the evolution of menstrual cycles to the gender politics of period to the history of tampons. Recorded between 2016 and 2020, each episode (about 48 minutes) features an interview with a researcher or advocate working in the field of menstrual health. All 38 episodes can be accessed (for free) at https://periodpodcast2.libsyn.com.

CONTRACEPTION

See *The Routledge Handbook on Anthropology and Reproduction*, edited by Sallie Han and Cecília Tomori (2022), for discussion of female sterilization in Puerto Rico in the chapter by Iris López (2022). See the references for more information.

On the topic of coerced sterilization, this web page for the PBS documentary series "Independent Lens" features film and video clips and links to books and other resources: www.pbs.org/indep endentlens/blog/unwanted-sterilization-and-eugenics-programs-in-the-united-states.

ABORTION

See *The Routledge Handbook on Anthropology and Reproduction*, edited by Sallie Han and Cecília Tomori (2022), for discussion of abortion travel in the chapter by Joanna Mishtal and Silvia De Zordo (2022). See the references for more information.

Jane was the name of a Chicago women's network referring and providing abortion services during the late 1960s. Their work was chronicled in the 2022 documentary "The Janes," streaming on Max as well as in the 1996 documentary "Jane: An Abortion Service," streaming on Kanopy.

In El Salvador, Teodora Vásquez was sentenced to 30 years in prison after suffering a stillbirth and being accused of having an abortion, which is a crime there. Her story is told in a 2021 documentary, "Fly So Far: When Miscarriage Is a Crime," in Spanish with subtitles, streaming on Kanopy. More information and a trailer can be found here: www.wmm.com/catalog/film/fly-so-far.

REFERENCES

ACOG. 2020. *Opposition to Criminalization of Individuals During Pregnancy and the Postpartum Period*. www.acog.org/clinical-information/policy-and-posi tion-statements/statements-of-policy/2020/opposition-criminalization-o f-individuals-pregnancy-and-postpartum-period.

Allotey, Pascale, T.K. Sundari Ravindran, and Vithiya Sathivelu. 2021. "Trends in Abortion Policies in Low- and Middle-Income Countries." *Annual Review of Public Health* 42: 505–518.

Appleton, Nayantara Sheoran. 2024. "Hormonal Contraception: From Demographic Histories to Pleasurable Futures?" In *A Companion to the Anthropology of Reproductive Medicine and Technology*, edited by Cecilia Coale Van Hollen and Nayantara Sheoran Appleton, 332–348. Hoboken, NJ: John Wiley & Sons.

BBC. 2018. "India Scraps Tampon Tax After Campaign." *BBC*, July 21. www.bbc.com/news/world-asia-india-44912742.

Bobel, Chris and Breanne Fahs. 2020. "The Messy Politics of Menstrual Activism." In *The Palgrave Handbook of Critical Menstruation Studies*, edited by Chris Bobel *et al.*, 1001–1018. New York: Palgrave Macmillan. doi:10.1007/978-981-15-0614-7_71.

Boydell, Victoria, Robert Dean Smith, and Global LARC Collaborative. 2023. "Hidden in Plain Sight: A Systematic Review of Coercion and Long-Acting Reversible Contraceptive Methods (LARC)." *PLOS Global Public Health* 3(8): e0002131.

Browner, Carole and Carolyn Sargent. 2022. "Reproduction and the State." In *The Routledge Handbook of Anthropology and Reproduction*, edited by Sallie Han and Cecília Tomori, 87–105. Abingdon and New York: Routledge.

Buckley, Thomas and Alma Gottlieb. 1988. *Blood Magic: The Anthropology of Menstruation*. Berkeley, CA: University of California Press.

Center for Reproductive Rights. n.d. *Law and Policy Guide: Third-Party Authorization*. https://reproductiverights.org/maps/worlds-abortion-laws/law-and-policy-guide-third-party-authorization/.

Chalabi, Mona. 2015. "How Many Women Don't Use Tampons?" *FiveThirtyEight*, Oct. 1. https://fivethirtyeight.com/features/how-many-women-dont-use-tampons/.

Choi, Hansol, Nam-Kyoo Lim, Heeja Jung, Oksoo Kim, and Hyun-Young Park. 2021. "Use of Menstrual Sanitary Products in Women of Reproductive Age: Korea Nurses' Health Study." *Osong Public Health and Research Perspectives* 12(1): 20–28. doi:10.24171/j.phrp. 2021.12.1.04.

Colen, Shellee. 1995. "'Like a Mother to Them': Stratified Reproduction and West Indian Childcare Workers and Employers in New York." In *Conceiving the New World Order: The Global Politics of Reproduction*, edited by Faye Ginsburg and Rayna Rapp, 78–102. Berkeley, CA: University of California Press.

Cooper, Danielle B. and Preeti Patel. 2024. "Oral Contraceptive Pills." *StatPearls*, Feb. 29. www.ncbi.nlm.nih.gov/books/NBK430882/.

Courinho, Elsimar. 1999. *Is Menstruation Obsolete?* Oxford and New York: Oxford University Press.

Cromer, Risa D. 2018. "Waiting: The Redemption of Frozen Embryos through Embryo Adoption and Stem Cell Research in the United States." In *The Anthropology of the Fetus: Biology, Culture, and Society*, edited by Sallie Han, Tracy K. Betsinger, and Amy B. Scott, 171–199. New York and Oxford: Berghahn Books.

Daniels, Kimberly and Joyce C. Abma. 2020. "Current Contraceptive Status Among Women Aged 15–49: United States, 2017–2019." In *NCHS Data Brief*, 388. Hyattsville, MD: National Center for Health Statistics.

Douglas, Mary. 1966. *Purity and Danger*. London: Routledge and Kegan Paul.

Dubow, Sara. 2022. "From Conscience Clauses to Conscience Wars." In *Abortion Care as Moral Work: Ethical Considerations of Maternal and Fetal Bodies*, edited by Johanna Schoen, 83–98. Lewisburg, PA: Bucknell University Press.

Eichner, Katrina. 2013. "*Intimate Identities: Archaeological Investigations of Nine-teenth-Century Sexuality.*" Paper presented at the Annual Meeting for the Society for Historical Archaeology, Quebec City,January 8–12.

Eichner, Katrina C.L. and Laurie A. Wilkie. 2015. "Contraception/Conception, Archaeology Of." In *The International Encyclopedia of Human Sexuality*, edited by Patricia Whelehan and Anne Bolin. Hoboken, NJ: John Wiley & Sons.

Ellis, Samuel, Daniel W. Franks, Mia Lybkær Kronborg Nielsen, Michael N. Weiss, and Darren P.Croft. 2024. "the Evolution of Menopause in Toothed Whales." *Nature* 627: 579–585. doi:10.1038/s41586-024-07159-9.

Elsesser, Kim. 2023. "States and Retailers Take a Stand Against the 'Tampon Tax.'" *Forbes*, May 18. www.forbes.com/sites/kimelsesser/2023/05/18/states-and-retailers-take-a-stand-against-the-tampon-tax/?sh=7d3d46944610.

Fennell, Julie Lynn. 2011. "Men Bring Condoms, Women Take Pills: Men's and Women's Roles in Contraceptive Decision Making." *Gender and Society* 25(4): 496–521.

Ginsburg, Faye D. 1989. *Contested Lives: The Abortion Debate in an American Community*. Berkeley, CA: University of California Press.

Gottlieb, Alma. 1988. "Menstrual Cosmology among the Beng of Ivory Coast." In *Blood Magic: The Anthropology of Menstruation*, edited by Thomas Buckley and Alma Gottlieb, 55–74. Berkeley, CA: University of California Press.

Gray, Peter B., Alex Straftis, and Kermyt G. Anderson. 2022. "Men and Reproduction: Perspectives from Biological Anthropology." In *The Routledge Handbook of Anthropology and Reproduction*, edited by Sallie Han and Cecília Tomori, 52–67. Abingdon and New York: Routledge.

Gutmann, Matthew C. 2007. *Fixing Men: Sex, Birth Control, and AIDS in Mexico*. Berkeley, CA: University of California Press.

Guttmacher Institute. 2022. *Unintended Pregnancy and Abortion Worldwide Fact Sheet*. www.guttmacher.org/fact-sheet/induced-abortion-worldwide.

Howes-Mischel, Rebecca. 2018. "The 'Sound' of Life: Or, How Should We Hear a Fetal 'Voice'?" In *The Anthropology of the Fetus: Biology, Culture, and Society*, edited by Sallie Han, Tracy K. Betsinger, and Amy B. Scott, 252–275. New York and Oxford: Berghahn Books.

Joffe, Carole. 2009. "Abortion and Medicine: A Sociopolitical History." In *Management of Unintended and Abnormal Pregnancy*, edited by M. Paul et al., 1–9. Malden, MA: Blackwell Publishing.

Joshi, Supriya and Yubraj Acharya. 2022. "Women's Extreme Seclusion During Menstruation and Children's Health in Nepal." *PLOS Global Public Health* 2(7): e0000355. doi:10.1371/journal.pgph.0000355.

Kimport, Katrina. 2018. "Talking about Male Body-Based Contraceptives: The Counseling Visit and the Feminization of Contraception." *Social Science and Medicine* 201: 44–50. doi:10.1016/j.socscimed.2018.01.040.

Kramer, Karen L., Amanda Veile, and Paula Ivey Henry. 2022. "Reproduction in Biological Anthropology." In *The Routledge Handbook of Anthropology and Reproduction*, edited by Sallie Han and Cecília Tomori, 19–35. Abingdon and New York: Routledge.

The Lancet. 2018. "Abortion: Access and Safety Worldwide," 391: 1191. doi:10.1016/S0140-6736(18)30624-X.

López, Iris. 2008. *Matters of Choice: Puerto Rican Women's Struggle for Reproductive Freedom.* New Brunswick, NJ: Rutgers University Press.

López, Iris. 2022. "Sterile Choices: Racialized Women, Reproductive Freedom, and Social Justice." In *The Routledge Handbook of Anthropology and Reproduction*, edited by Sallie Han and Cecília Tomori, 165–179. Abingdon and New York: Routledge.

Luehrmann, Sonja. 2018. "Beyond Life Itself: The Embedded Fetuses of Russian Orthodox Anti-Abortion Activism." In *The Anthropology of the Fetus: Biology, Culture, and Society*, edited by Sallie Han, Tracy K. Betsinger, and Amy B. Scott, 227–251. New York and Oxford: Berghahn Books.

Martin, Emily. 1987. *The Woman in the Body: A Cultural Analysis of Reproduction.* Boston, MA: Beacon Press.

Mishtal, Joanna and Silvia De Zordo. 2022. "Policy, Governance, Practice: Global Perspectives on Abortion." In *The Routledge Handbook of Anthropology and Reproduction*, edited by Sallie Han and Cecília Tomori, 150–164. Abingdon and New York: Routledge.

Montoya, Melissa N., Colleen Judge-Golden, and Jonas J. Swartz. 2022. "The Problems with Crisis Pregnancy Centers: Reviewing the Literature and Identifying New Directions for Future Research." *International Journal of Women's Health* 14, 757–763. doi:10.2147/IJWH.S288861.

Morgan, Lynn M., and Elizabeth F.S. Roberts. 2012. "Reproductive Governance in Latin America." *Anthropology & Medicine* 19(2): 241–254.

Mullings, Leith. 2022. "The Necropolitics of Reproduction: Racism, Resistance, and the Sojourner Syndrome in the Age of the Movement for Black Lives." In *The Routledge Handbook of Anthropology and Reproduction*, edited by Sallie Han and Cecília Tomori, 106–122. Abingdon and New York: Routledge.

Oudshoorn, Nelly, 2003. *The Male Pill: A Biography of a Technology in the Making.* Durham, NC: Duke University Press.

Pew Research Center. 2024. *Public Opinion on Abortion Views on Abortion, 1995–2024.* May 13. www.pewresearch.org/religion/fact-sheet/public-opinion-on-abortion/.

Planned Parenthood. n.d. *How Safe Is the Birth Control Pill?* www.plannedparenthood.org/learn/birth-control/birth-control-pill/how-safe-is-the-birth-control-pill.

Potts, Malcolm, Maura Graff, and Judy Taing. 2007. "Thousand-Year-Old Depictions of Massage Abortion." *Journal of Family Planning and Reproductive Health Care* 33(4): 233–234. doi:10.1783/147118907782101904.

Ranji, Usha, Alina Salganicoff, and Laurie Sobel. 2024. "Dobbs-Era Abortion Bans and Restrictions: Early Insights about Implications for Pregnancy Loss." *KFF*, May 2. www.kff.org/womens-health-policy/issue-brief/dobbs-era-abortion-bans-and-restrictions-early-insights-about-implications-for-pregnancy-loss.

Ren, Liqi, Denis Simon, and Jianfeng Wu. 2018. "Meaning in Absence: The Case of Tampon Use Among Chinese Women." *Asian Journal of Women's Studies* 24(1): 28–46. doi:10.1080/12259276.2017.1421291.

Renne, Elisha P. 2022. "Menstruation: Sociocultural Perspectives." In *The Routledge Handbook of Anthropology and Reproduction*, edited by Sallie Han and Cecília Tomori, 200–216. Abingdon and New York: Routledge.

Richards, Audrey. 1988 [1956]. *Chisungu: A Girls' Initiation Ceremony among the Bemba of Zambia*. London and New York: Routledge.

Riddle, John M. 1992. *Contraception and Abortion from the Ancient World to the Renaissance*. Cambridge, MA: Harvard University Press.

Roberts, Dorothy E. 1997. *Killing the Black Body: Race, Reproduction, and the Meaning of Liberty*. New York: Pantheon Books.

Rogers-LaVanne, Mary P. and Kathryn B.H. Clancy. 2022. "Menstruation: Causes, Consequences, and Context." In *The Routledge Handbook of Anthropology and Reproduction*, edited by Sallie Han and Cecília Tomori, 183–199. Abingdon and New York: Routledge.

Schwartz, Beth I., Benjamin Bear, and Anne E. Kazak. 2023. "Menstrual Management Choices in Transgender and Gender Diverse Adolescents." *Journal of Adolescent Health* 72: 207–213.

Sedgh, Gilda and Irum Taqi. 2023. "Mifepristone for Abortion in a Global Context: Safe, Effective and Approved in Nearly 100 Countries." *Guttmacher Institute*, July 21. www.guttmacher.org/2023/07/mifepristone-abortion-global-context-safe-effective-and-approved-nearly-100-countries.

Shaw, Malissa Kay. 2024. "Menstrual Materiality: Anthropological Mappings from Menstrual Taboos to the FemCare Industry." In *A Companion to the Anthropology of Reproductive Medicine and Technology*, edited by Cecilia Coale Van Hollen and Nayantara Sheoran Appleton, 301–316. Hoboken, NJ: John Wiley & Sons.

Shoichet, Catherine E. 2023. "These Women Say Their Babies Were Stillborn: Courts Convicted Them of Homicide in a Country with Harsh Abortion Laws." *CNN*, October 8. www.cnn.com/2023/10/08/health/el-salvador-abortion-homicide-convictions-cec/index.html.

Sievert, Lynnette Leidy and Subho Roy. 2022. "Menopause." In *The Routledge Handbook of Anthropology and Reproduction*, edited by Sallie Han and Cecília Tomori, 575–589. Abingdon and New York: Routledge.

Society for Family Planning. 2023. *#WeCount Report April 2022 to June 2023*. doi:10.46621/218569qkgmbl.

Solinger, Rickie. 2019 [1994]. *The Abortionist: A Woman Against the Law.* Berkeley, CA: University of California Press.

Strassmann, Beverly I. 1997. "The Biology of Menstruation in Homo Sapiens: Total Lifetime Menses, Fecundity, and Nonsynchrony in a Natural-Fertility Population." *Current Anthropology* 38(1): 123–129.

Sufrin, Carolyn. 2018. "Making Mothers in Jail: Carceral Reproduction of Normative Motherhood." *Reproductive Biology, Medicine and Society Online* 7, 55–65. doi:10.1016/j.rbms.2018.10.018.

Tone, Andrea. 2001. *Devices and Desires: A History of Contraceptives in America.* New York: Hill & Wang.

United Nations. 2019. *Contraceptive Use by Method.* doi:10.18356/1bd58a10-en.

Unnithan, Maya, Silvia De Zordo, Astrid Blystad, and Karen Marie Moland. 2024. "Anthropology of Abortion." In *A Companion to the Anthropology of Reproductive Medicine and Technology,* edited by Cecilia Coale Van Hollen and Nayantara Sheoran Appleton, 349–364. Hoboken, NJ: John Wiley & Sons.

Vostral, Sharra. 2017. "Toxic Shock Syndrome, Tampons and Laboratory Standard—Setting." *CMAJ* 189: E726–728. doi:10.1503/cmaj.161479.

Wenham, C., Arevalo, A., Coast, E.*et al.*2019. Zika, Abortion and Health Emergencies: A Review of Contemporary Debates. *Global Health* 15(49). doi:10.1186/s12992-019-0489-3.

Wentzell, Emily, Maral Erol, and Salih Can Aciksöz. 2024. "Anthropologies of Men, Masculinities, and Reproduction." In *A Companion to the Anthropology of Reproductive Medicine and Technology,* edited by Cecilia Coale Van Hollen and Nayantara Sheoran Appleton, 203–218. Hoboken, NJ: John Wiley & Sons.

World Health Organization. 2022. *WHO Recommendations on Self-Care Interventions: Self-Management of Medical Abortion, 2022 Update.* www.who.int/publications/i/item/WHO-SRH-22.1.

Zhu, Alex, Catherine S. Nam, Devon Gingrich, *et al.*2024. "Short-Term Changes in Vasectomy Consults and Procedures Following Dobbs v Jackson Women's Health Organization." *Urology Practice* 11(3): 517–525. doi:10.1097/UPJ.0000000000000528.

3

INFERTILITY, ASSISTED REPRODUCTIVE TECHNOLOGIES, AND REPRODUCTIVE LOSSES

People around the world invest a great deal into ensuring that marriages are made, women become pregnant, and children are born so that families and communities may continue. These reproductive trajectories are only part of the story. Pregnancies and the births of children can and do occur outside sanctioned relationships. The consequences may particularly affect mothers and their children, but also have ripple effects across the entire kinship network. Much attention in US anthropology has centered around the constraints that women experience in making reproductive decisions around fertility, focusing on access to contraception and to abortion when a pregnancy is not desired for any number of reasons. As always, structural inequities give form to the options that may or may not be available to people; how, whether, and what individuals may decide; and the consequences of these decisions.

Another side of the story is **infertility**, the inability to become pregnant, and still another includes **pregnancy losses**, or unintended endings of pregnancy in miscarriage and stillbirth. Anthropological attention to these experiences has grown over the past 30 years and they are the subject of this chapter. The first part of the chapter addresses infertility and the second highlights the **assisted reproductive technologies** (ARTs) that are increasingly used to address infertility and unwanted childlessness. The final part of the chapter focuses on pregnancy loss. By approaching these topics together and viewing them through an anthropological lens, we can see more clearly the interrelatedness of reproductive

DOI: 10.4324/9781003379416-3

trajectories that are typically regarded as disparate experiences. Additionally, we can observe how the experiences of reproduction—whether they follow the socially desirable trajectories or not—fit into local understandings of gender, kinship, and personhood, which in turn are shaped and influenced by religion, culture, and broader social contexts and structural inequities.

INFERTILITY, UNWANTED CHILDLESSNESS, AND THE "QUEST FOR CONCEPTION"

Infertility has been an experience that individuals may choose not to speak about openly even while their involuntary childlessness is quite visible to other family members and in their communities. This silence was reflected in the anthropology of reproduction. Infertility has since become one of the most generative areas of study, closely connected with the development and usage of ARTs.

Infertility is a major global health problem, with approximately one-sixth of the world's people experiencing infertility over the course of their lives (WHO 2023). Most people affected by infertility reside in the Global South. Many of them reside in countries that in fact have relatively high fertility rates. This fact, based on population statistics, does not make infertility any less a problem for the people affected by it. When the norm is to have many children, to have none at all or even only one can cause suffering. Ethnographic studies of infertility and unwanted childlessness document the devastating social, emotional, and physical effects for people who desire children, but cannot get pregnant or face long periods of infertility between pregnancies. Unfortunately, the places where the social expectation and pressure to have children is great are also the ones where people may have the least access to effective and accessible treatment options.

The causes of **primary infertility**, when no prior pregnancy has taken place, are diverse, driven by a wide range of determinants, from exposure to harmful chemicals via environmental exposure that may begin in utero, to diseases that arise later in life. **Secondary infertility**, after a previous pregnancy, may arise with aging or chronic disease and via other mechanisms, such as the impacts of untreated or inadequately treated reproductive tract infections or complications from previous pregnancies.

Infertility affects both men and women. Indeed, male infertility is the cause in over half of all cases. Yet, the causes are usually presumed to be located in women's bodies and women disproportionately bear the social consequences of infertility. The gendered experiences of infertility are a key thread across ethnographic work on this subject. Blamed for infertility, women may experience mistreatment, abuse, and other forms of violence and neglect from their spouses. They may be considered "useless," rejected, and abandoned. Infertility can be grounds for divorce or, in societies practicing polygyny, a reason for men to bring another spouse into the household who can provide children. Infertility can also cause hostilities and exclusions from relationships of kinship and family as well as broader social marginalization. The stigma of being "barren" and childless is such that infertile women may also be blamed for causing other women's infertility and excluded from their communities. Their acute marginalization can become a sentence of social death in a context where every aspect of a woman's status and material wellbeing depends upon her ability to have children.

A key insight of the anthropology of reproduction is not to collapse people's reproductive experiences into a single narrative. Importantly, although the gendered burden of infertility weighs particularly on women, ethnographies also document the instances of men remaining loving and supportive partners of women struggling with infertility. Men can and do play significant positive roles in negotiating infertility, including the pursuit of fertility treatment, and also accepting childlessness when ARTs do not work. When male-factor infertility is recognized to be the cause of a couple's childlessness, men may express deep sorrow and guilt over disappointing a partner's wishes for children and motherhood and being the cause of suffering for a cherished spouse. Interestingly, in these instances, women may choose to "cover" for their partners in order to protect them from public humiliation and private hurt. Documenting these diverse responses to infertility in relationships and families, while also attending to broader gendered power relations, is a key feature of anthropological research.

SEEKING SOLUTIONS FOR CHILDLESSNESS

Given the social and cultural significance of having children—and the costs of not being able to have them—it is not surprising that people will go to great lengths to resolve their infertility. These days, the solutions that receive the most attention, including that of anthropologists, involve seeking biomedical treatment and, especially, the use of ARTs. Yet, in fact, people have long pursued diverse and often creative ways to have children and make families. Before turning to new reproductive technologies of assisted conception, for example, these other forms of "old" reproductive technologies also deserve our attention.

The **adoption** of children is one way to establish kin ties and ensure the continuity of a family. Children may be adopted from kin networks or from strangers within the same nation or from different nations. Whether and how adoption is arranged depends greatly on local understandings of relatedness. In addition, the policies and laws concerning adoption vary from country to country, which is especially salient in transnational (cross-border) adoptions. Adoption is more readily acceptable in some settings than in others, particularly when it takes place within an already existing kin network. Infertility is, of course, not the only or even a primary reason for adoptions. Grandparents, particularly grandmothers, play an especially important role in raising their grandchildren, not uncommonly seen when the children's mother has died. This situation is particularly well documented in families in sub-Saharan Africa, where scores of children were orphaned by AIDS before broad access to antiretroviral therapies, which also use the acronym ART. Importantly, which grandmother may care for a grandchild can depend both on kinship configurations (e.g. whether the child resides in the mother's natal home or their spouse's) and on specific circumstances, as Ellen Block's (2022) ethnographic work in Lesotho shows.

Adoption has been an avenue of family making for LGBTQ+ people who may be fertile, but cannot conceive children on their own. Ethnographic research documents the desire of same-sex couples to have children. Yet, unlike their heterosexual counterparts who are presumed to have the right to do so, LGBTQ+ individuals find themselves being systematically questioned and being denied reproductive justice. Access to adoption has been fraught, even in settings that have legally begun to recognize the rights of LGBTQ+ people. A pervasive stigmatizing accusation leveled particularly at gay men was the threat of child sexual abuse. This moral panic prevented them from realizing their dream of having children via adoption until relatively recently. The legitimacy of LGBTQ+ families continues to go unrecognized in many regions of the world. Even in comparatively supportive settings, LGBTQ+ families continue to face many obstacles in accessing not only adoption, but also other, newer reproductive technologies as we will see below.

Additionally, ethnographic literature has highlighted pervasive inequities structuring the practices of adoption, wherein poor children are made available to more privileged families from the same setting or via transnational networks. There are particularly heart-wrenching examples of the lack of resources that families in the Global South face resulting in children being relinquished to wealthy, predominantly white families from the Global North. There is also critical work on transnational adoptees' lived experiences of disconnectedness from their communities of origin and of racism they confronted as people of color adopted into white families. These experiences should be understood as not isolated. Rather, they are representative of the larger political, social, and cultural context in which they occur. The international adoption of children from Korea, for example, results from a rejection of mixed-race "GI babies" born to Korean women and US soldiers in the context of the continuing US military presence (Oh 2015). These overseas adoptions also fit into the nationalist government's policies of anti-natalism and economic development (see Chapter 6). Today, we are living in a historical moment in which racism remains pervasive and far-right nationalist movements around the world exert increasing influence over immigration policy and in discourses and attitudes toward minority communities.

An important takeaway from anthropology is that adoption can and has allowed individuals to resolve their unwanted childlessness, but unlike the conversational claims that people can "just adopt" a child, it is not at all a simple solution. Adoption may not be culturally accepted. There are various restrictions and prohibitions on who is allowed to adopt and be adopted. As a practice situated in the larger local and global inequities that characterize reproduction as a whole, adoption is still fraught with challenges.

THE INFERTILITY TREATMENT JOURNEY

Historically and cross-culturally, women have sought the methods and means not only to prevent and end unwanted pregnancies, but also to become pregnant. Interestingly, there are overlaps between not becoming and becoming pregnant. In settings where the regularity of periods and even the characteristics of menstrual blood, like its quantity and color, are scrutinized as signs of health and fecundity, women may take plant-based **emmenagogues**, or remedies, to stimulate menstruation (Renne 2022; also see Chapter 2). Some of these compounds were used also to induce losses when the pregnancies were not wanted. Hormone-based contraception, like the pill, is based on the same scientific investigations of the mid-twentieth century that were undertaken to develop treatments for infertility.

Infertility treatments before the widespread use of ARTs have been shown to have a very wide range of quality and efficacy. These treatments included various medications and surgeries. In her classic ethnographic work, Marcia Inhorn documented that women in Egypt underwent painful and ineffective infertility treatments in the 1980s and 1990s in their hopes of having children (see Inhorn 2022 for an overview). Some of these treatments resulted in children; however, others were ineffective and even potentially damaging for these women's future fertility. Unfortunately, even after the dramatic expansion of ART services globally, many people around the world lack access to appropriate care and services for infertility. The places where infertility rates are high and people have the most need are also the ones disproportionately most affected by unmet needs for fertility treatment. Cost may prohibit people from accessing services. In addition, the laws regulating the use of ARTs vary, not only by country, but also by the forms of treatment and the individuals who are seeking to use them.

To overcome these barriers in access, people who can gather the means to do so will travel to obtain fertility treatment, a situation called **reproductive tourism**. There are a range of reasons for why people travel for reproductive care. All or specific forms of treatment may be unavailable in the home location of the individual or couple seeking care. Couples will travel, for example, to evade religious prohibitions on specific procedures such as gamete donation. Even when services are available, there may be legal restrictions locally on who can access them, so that single or unmarried individuals or LGBTQ+ couples are forced to cross borders for care. The experience of racial and ethnic discrimination also drives people to seek treatment elsewhere, as has been the case for Arab refugees in the United States (Inhorn 2018). These couples look for providers who share similar cultural and religious backgrounds and who will validate their desire for children and support them. In still other cases, the services may be available and accessible, but not high quality, and so those struggling with infertility may seek care where the rates of successful treatment are higher—even though it may cost more. Affordability, however, is an important motivation for many people who may travel from wealthier nations in the Global North to middle and low-income countries in the Global South where the differences in cost may be profound. In all of these narratives, there are profound inequities in being able to access treatment. Yet, because having children is so enormously important in most societies, people will spend enormous amounts of resources in accessing a range of reproductive technologies now used to treat infertility.

ASSISTED REPRODUCTIVE TECHNOLOGIES

A variety of technologies are now available to individuals seeking to address involuntary childlessness. Depending on the circumstances, one or multiple technologies may be used separately or in conjunction with each other over time as repeated attempts will likely be needed.

Anthropologists have carried out in-depth ethnographic studies across a wide variety of settings related to these technologies. A key lesson across this work has been that the technologies are incorporated into local understandings of kinship, gender, and religion, and they directly tie to state policies and approaches toward reproduction as well as existing inequities. For instance, states such as Israel encourage the use of reproductive technologies to ensure the reproduction of the nation and provide fertility treatment in national healthcare services or cover it in basic health insurance plans (Inhorn 2022). Reproductive technologies can serve as tools to achieve pronatalist and ethnonationalist visions of purity in reproduction. Producing the "right" kind of child can therefore play into broader reproductive projects of the state, once again demonstrating that reproduction is about the reproduction of power relations, not simply the production of children.

ARTs have increasingly become the main avenue for overcoming the devastation of infertility in people's lives. Whereas even a few decades ago access to these technologies was extremely limited, today over half of countries offer at least some of these services. Perhaps the most well-studied among these technologies is **in vitro fertilization** (IVF). Its use resulted in the birth of the world's first "test-tube baby" in 1978 and since been labeled a "hope technology" by Sarah Franklin (2022 [1997]) to reflect the possibility it provides to conceive children. In this procedure, the oocyte (egg) is fertilized with sperm in the lab. The fertilized egg is allowed to develop for a few days and is then placed inside the uterus of the person who hopes to become pregnant and eventually give birth to a child. This process allows clinicians to overcome many possible barriers to fertilization, including scarring or blockage in the fallopian tubes, and provides more opportunities to create embryos since the stimulation of ovaries usually produces multiple eggs and both eggs and sperm quality can be controlled. In the United States, about a third of women under 35 using IVF have successful pregnancies—a rate that declines with their age. A single cycle of IVF costs $15,000 to $20,000 in the US, but can vary widely across the country, with highly variable insurance coverage and out of pocket costs (Conrad 2023).

IVF has many other permutations and can be accompanied by a series of other technologies that may be used in tandem. For instance, embryos are usually screened for genetic diseases via **preimplantation genetic diagnosis** (PGD) (Schwennesen and Gammeltoft 2022). This technology, to which we return later, has itself given rise to a whole series of new considerations and ethical dilemmas since it can be used for much more than just to avert a fatal disease. (See Chapter 4.)

Importantly, **cryopreservation** (freezing) is an element of IVF that can provide for numerous possibilities. One is that it extends the temporal timeline of fertility. Eggs and sperm as well as fertilized embryos can be frozen and later thawed and used or implanted, keeping open the potential for pregnancies in future cycles and providing an opportunity to maintain a biogenetic relationship that may be desired between parents and children. IVF also makes possible the use of viable gametes from a donor when intended parents themselves do not have healthy eggs or sperm or when same-sex couples or a single parent require reproductive materials from the other sex. These gametes may be frozen and "banked," or stored and made available for intended parents' choosing.

Ethnographic studies demonstrate that these technologies of assisted conception have broadened the range of possibilities for heterosexual couples pursuing pregnancies (Twine and Smietana 2022). For LGBTQ+ families, these technologies have opened doors that were previously completely closed; however, they may be blocked from accessing ARTs in many settings due to discriminatory laws. These technologies also introduce new flexibilities into family making. While some gamete donors become incorporated into family networks, others are regarded, and choose to remain, as merely having provided the genetic material for conception.

Another major advance in assisted conception is the development of **intracytoplasmic sperm injection** (ICSI), which enables the selection of the best available sperm and injects it directly into the egg's cytoplasm (Inhorn 2022). ICSI can aid in cases of male infertility where sperm may not be sufficiently numerous (low sperm count) or do not move adequately (low motility). A common myth about male infertility links it to sexual potency and erectile dysfunction, so men who have no problems with sexual function may mistakenly assume they have no problems with infertility. Additionally, men may be reluctant to share their challenges with fertility due to fears that others would assume sexual dysfunction, a challenge to masculinity. By advancing the treatment of male infertility, ICSI may help to destigmatize it.

In a combination of old and new reproductive technologies, an embryo created with IVF or ICSI can be transferred to the body of a **surrogate** who carries the pregnancy (Whittaker 2022). The embryo may be created from the eggs and sperm of intended parents or from one or two donors; or it may be "adopted" from a donor. There are situations when a surrogate may also be the egg donor. These days, however, ova donations from a third party, or donor other than the surrogate, may be legally required or personally preferred by all of the individuals involved in the arrangement. The term gestational surrogacy is commonly used to describe this situation. These measures are responses to legal and personal concerns about who claims parentage of a child. Surrogacy, like the other reproductive technologies discussed here, brings with it new dilemmas about relationships and relatedness among all those who partake in this process.

ALLEVIATING THE GENDERED BURDEN OF INFERTILITY

For anthropologists, these many configurations can tell an array of stories. One is that ARTs can alleviate the gendered burden of infertility that disproportionately falls on women. This burden is carried by women whether the infertility is associated with them or even when it is linked to their male partners. For women able to carry the pregnancies themselves, the production of children from their own bodies makes visible to their communities that their reproductive goals have been achieved. What can remain concealed, however, is the use of donor eggs or sperm, which may or may not be acceptable in particular cultural contexts. For men, ICSI dramatically increases the possibility of using their own gametes. Ethnographic work suggests that when individuals have a better understanding of the causes of male-factor infertility as well as access to an effective solution to it, like ICSI, men may feel motivated and enabled to challenge the narratives that continue to locate blame in women. This can contribute to reframing gender roles and relationships within marriages, larger kin networks, and communities. The broader acceptance of ARTs may help destigmatize infertility for both women and men. There are enormous implications for marriage relationships between women and men. ARTs offer a chance for couples to remain together in settings where the social pressures on childless people may drive them apart. Their use can also strengthen the bonds between partners when they undertake the infertility treatment journey together and offer care for one another.

MARRIAGE, KINSHIP, AND RELIGION

Discourses on new technologies in general tend to be focused on innovation and emphasize the impacts on social norms and values. These presumptions about sweeping changes to culture and society may or may not be evidenced. Ethnographic studies of people's experiences with ARTs document how the uses of these technologies are both incorporated into existing notions of kinship and also invite reworkings in our understandings of relatedness.

Anthropological understandings of marriage and kinship are based on cross-cultural and historical observations that enable us to see patterns in human ideas and practices. What anthropologists have observed is that kinship should not be taken for granted as biogenetic relatedness, or determined by biological and genetic transmission, such as when people talk about family as individuals with the same blood or DNA. Because a person's status, identity, and rights—including claims to property and guidance on who should or should not marry—are connected to kinship and specifically lineage (tracing ancestry and descent), parentage is important and necessary knowledge in a society. In the context of cultures that assume or expect sexual relationships, particularly for women, between married partners only, marriage implies parentage. From this perspective, marriage is understood as an important and meaningful means of organizing kinship.

This context helps us to understand the range of concerns that people may have about whose gametes are used in assisted conception. In ARTs, parentage is treated as a known quantity in the form of eggs and sperm. The use of the intended parents' own gametes can be particularly important for ensuring relatedness in certain cultural and religious settings. The use of gametes from other than the intended parents, however, opens the door to other claims on relatedness that were unanticipated and may be unwanted. With the availability of genetic ancestry testing through commercial services like 23andme, for example, anonymity is no longer entirely guaranteed. Donors or children themselves may seek to identify and contact each other. Children may have genetically related siblings in other families (see Han 2022).

Depending on how kinship is configured in a given cultural or religious community, gametes are differentially important to the status and identity of an anticipated child. Claims of citizenship, for example, can be based on a genetic parent's nationality, although it may matter whether it is the father or mother. In Islam, paternity (father) may be significant for the purposes of identifying an heir. For Orthodox Jews, however, having a Jewish mother establishes her child as also Jewish, so the ova must come from a Jewish woman, who may be the intended parent or a donor.

Faith traditions around the world celebrate having children as a virtuous act or even delineating it as a moral obligation. Yet, the use of reproductive technologies, which could be used for people to fulfill their religious commitments, may or may not be permitted by the teachings of their faiths. There is also, however, considerable variation across religious groups and even within them. For instance, in Sunni Islam, third-party gamete donation is interpreted as *zina*, or adultery, and therefore not allowed (Inhorn 2006). In Shia Islam, however, donor gametes may be used with strict adherence to certain rules ensuring, for example, there is no risk of incest between the future children of the donor and the intended parents. Since the introduction of ARTs, religious considerations have been and continue to be actively discussed among faith leaders as the technologies themselves are further developed and social perceptions and norms change. ARTs are increasingly part of the everyday lives of people who themselves may experience a shift in their attitudes so that they choose to secretly work around religious prohibitions, for example by traveling to another location where the process is allowed.

Religion not only shapes access to certain forms of ARTs, but it is very much present within the laboratories and clinics themselves. Susan Kahn (2000) documented the measures taken in Israeli IVF clinics to adhere to the expectations for Orthodox Jewish couples, including the employment of religious observers who oversee the procedures to ensure that the correct egg and sperm are used. In Ecuador, a majority Catholic country, Elizabeth F.S. Roberts (2021) describes how clinicians, laboratory technicians, and people seeking treatment have embraced IVF despite the church's condemnation of it. Yet, they also continue to perceive IVF processes through a religious worldview, incorporating prayer into each step. They also espoused the belief that God's will shapes what happens to gametes and embryos that are not used in an IVF cycle. This case reminds us once again that ARTs and the outcomes of their use are negotiated locally. How reproductive technologies are perceived and incorporated into the lives of everyday people depends not on abstract ideological constructs, but on our experiences of kinship and care within our "local moral worlds" (Kleinman and Kleinman 1991).

TROUBLING KINSHIP RELATIONS

Reproductive technologies offer the prospect of making families whole by, ironically enough, breaking down people into the component materials and functions of reproduction. This separation of people from parts is seen particularly in the example of gamete donation. Daisy Deomampo (2022) describes how women traveling to India from South Africa discussed their motivation for egg provision primarily in terms of the financial benefits. In addition, they embraced the opportunity to travel, party, and enjoy themselves. These women perceived themselves as merely providing genetic material. They actively distanced themselves from the status of "parent" that they regarded as an entirely separate role, downplaying the importance of genetics in favor of the claims of intended parents. This is notable because in other situations, parents accessing reproductive technologies may insist on using their own gametes to confirm their kinship with children as one that is based in biogenetic relatedness. By paying attention to people's lived experiences, ethnographies demonstrate that kin making is in fact a flexible practice, even in societies that may presume biogenetic kinship is the truly legitimate form of relatedness.

In the same research, Deomampo also contrasted the experiences of the South African women who had traveled for egg provision with those of Indian women who also served as egg providers or as gestational surrogates. These women were under substantial financial stress, which motivated their involvement, and they perceived the process as painful and difficult. They were also generally compensated less than their South African counterparts due to the racialized value ascribed to them.

SURROGACY, KINSHIP, RACE/ETHNICITY, AND THE NATION

Reproductive technologies isolate reproduction into component parts such as gametes which may be frozen and donated, and processes notably including pregnancy and birth. Gestational surrogacy raises important and meaningful questions about parentage and kinship. Beyond biomedical explanations of conception, gestation, and parturition (birth), there are also various cultural understandings of children made through the co-mingling of father's and mother's bodily substances and the transformation of blood into the blood of the fetus. Similarly, breastfeeding represents another form of sharing substance that constitutes a physical connection of kinship. These cultural understandings may have implications for surrogacy and how it is perceived and experienced. In arrangements of transnational surrogacy, ethnographers have documented conflicting interpretations of what surrogacy means for the intended parents from the Global North and surrogates from the Global South (Deomampo 2022; Whittaker 2022). Among Indian surrogates, for instance, Deomampo found that they believed the processes of pregnancy, birth, and breastfeeding incorporated them into a kin relationship with a child. In contrast, the intended, or "commissioning," parents conceived of surrogacy as a commercial transaction. These different understandings of kinship and the refusal by intended parents to participate in the implied reciprocity and lasting connection expected in kin ties can leave surrogates bitterly disappointed. Gift exchanges and even close personal connections may develop between intended parents and surrogates, but long-term relationships are often limited by their geographic distance from each other, particularly in transnational arrangements.

In Western societies and cultures, sharp ideological divisions are frequently made between commercial and non-commercial exchanges, or between money and love. Yet, these distinctions are not universally made, as Andrea Whittaker has documented in her research on surrogacy in Thailand. Here, supported by Buddhist beliefs, the giving and receiving of money for paid surrogacy can comfortably co-exist and intermingle with other forms of gift exchange and extensions of care. Ethnographic work in Ukraine has documented similar co-mingling of these practices. Lance and Merchant (2016) documented how paid surrogacy fits into Ukrainian women's concepts of altruism and maternal duty and even their religious views of Mary as a surrogate for Jesus. Many women sought out the blessing of Ukrainian Orthodox priests to facilitate their arrangements.

There is a complex mix of relations between intended parents and the women serving as surrogates. Within high-income settings where commercial surrogacy is widely available to those who can afford these services, like in the United States, the emphasis may be on the contractual nature of these arrangements. In these cases, surrogates may downplay their relationship to the child and not claim kinship (Berend 2016). In still other cases, surrogates and intended parents develop much closer connections. Some Israeli intended parents even experienced bodily symptoms that mimicked those of the pregnant surrogate (Teman 2010). Surrogates emphasized the importance of helping another woman become a mother as they transferred kinship over to the intended parent, which Teman called the narrative of "triumphant sacrifice" (Whittaker 2022, 275). Of course, not every surrogacy arrangement resulted in close ties between intended parents and surrogates, and sometimes the inability to conform to this dominant narrative itself became a problem. These instances when kin ties are not made or are broken are as important and necessary to document as the instances when kinship is successfully made.

Teman's account of surrogacy in Israel also reminds us that reproduction is not only a private and personal matter for individuals and their families, but also a public and political concern of states. In Israel, surrogates often feel a strong sense of service not only to the families they help, but also to the state, which encourages and supports fertility treatment for Jewish women. The population policies of countries include or exclude people from access to surrogacy and other forms of fertility treatment as they fit into larger visions of who constitutes a nation's lineage and people. These ideologies link back to the racialized views of gamete donation discussed below.

ASSISTED REPRODUCTIVE TECHNOLOGIES AND IDEOLOGIES OF RACE AND NATION

Worth remembering here is that differences in skin color and other physical features that are used commonly to identify and mark "race" are not correlated with other human characteristics including cognitive abilities or intellectual capacities. This is why anthropologists tell us that there are no biological races, but one race of humans exhibiting variations in their appearance. Yet, just as people are socially ascribed unequal status based on perceptions about their "race," so, too, are their gametes racialized. Eggs, for example, may be unequally valued or devalued, creating a racialized hierarchy linked to how intended parents perceive the women who are egg providers. Intended parents may seek gametes they consider "pure," belonging to people whose own parentage is single race, not mixed race. Others may be influenced by the privileging of whiteness or by colorism, or the preference for lighter over darker skin. Consequently, Deomampo (2022) observed the racialized sorting of Indian women into lighter-skinned egg providers and those considered "only adequate" for surrogacy, which takes considerably more time and reproductive labor.

The uses of ARTs reflect the ideologies of race and nation that shape reproductive injustices. The Israeli state, for example, provides free access to IVF and ICSI services for Jewish families and recently lifted some of its local restrictions on gamete donation and surrogacy services so that LGBTQ+ people might access them. The generous provisions for fertility treatment are part of the state's pronatalist policies, which represent a response to the genocide of Jews in Europe during the Second World War. The specific aim is to ensure the reproduction of the Jewish people and the continuity of Israel as the lone Jewish state amidst neighboring Arab countries. Ideologies of Jewish ethnicity, race, and nation are observed to permeate the practices surrounding gamete donation, with Israelis rejecting sperm or eggs from Palestinians.

Notions of "purity" and "high quality" also shape the nationalist and pronatalist agendas taking shape in China. Once the world's most populous country that pursued its anti-natalist "one-child" policy for decades, China has pivoted toward efforts to raise its fertility rates. There are concerns with infertility caused by previously sanctioned practices, like the repeated mandatory abortions to which women were subjected under the one-child policy. In addition, there are worries about the environmental degradation resulting from intense economic development and especially, as Ayo Wahlberg (2018) has documented, the impacts on the quality or health of sperm, which is seen as vital to the continuity of the Chinese state. To ensure the quality of future generations, young men are identified as potential sperm donors through their state college exams and undergo a rigorous screening process that examines not only their physical health, but a range of intellectual, emotional, and other characteristics. In the end, only a few are chosen.

THE POLITICAL ECONOMY OF ASSISTED REPRODUCTIVE TECHNOLOGIES

Despite growing access, the political economy of ARTs continues to be situated in a profoundly unequal landscape that exemplifies what anthropologists call **stratified reproduction** (see Chapter 1). These technologies have been developed and promoted within a commercial market that has actively perpetuated these inequities. The number and expansion of fertility clinics is particularly notable in the United States, United Kingdom, and countries in Western Europe, as well as in India, Japan, China, and Brazil, which are the world's largest economies. Anthropological research on ARTs largely mirrors these inequities; however, there is substantial work in the Middle East (Gerrits 2022). There remain significant gaps in research on ARTs in Latin America and in Africa, where countries have high rates of infertility and demand for treatment.

One exception is the ethnographic research that Trudie Gerrits (2016) conducted in Ghana, highlighting the challenges of accessing and negotiating fertility treatment in the country's clinics, which at the time numbered 14. These clinics served those residing not only in Ghana, but also in neighboring countries as well as Ghanaians living abroad in Europe and the United States. Gerrits describes the distinctive features of IVF in Ghana. First, while clinics elsewhere have restrictions on age—IVF success rates decline for older women—there was none in Ghana, where clinics accommodated people who had been pursuing other forms of treatment or were forced to wait while accumulating sufficient funds to pay for the procedure. These delays also meant greater reliance on donor gametes, especially ova. Second, Ghanaian physicians recommended lengthier hospitalization for women after IVF. The justifications for the longer stays, often weeks-long, included the challenges of transportation and long distances and poor-quality roads that people might need to traverse to and from the clinic. Additionally, women who traveled to Ghana from other countries would have no access to follow-up treatment should any complications arise. These stays, however, added substantially to the treatment costs.

Even where there are fertility clinics, how the costs are financed also makes access to treatment uneven. In some countries, reproductive technologies are available, but remain very costly or the costs are only partially reimbursed by insurance. In others such as Turkey (Gürtin 2016), they are offered freely by the state. The widened access to ARTs alleviates some of the social burden of infertility that usually falls disproportionately on poor and marginalized communities and especially on women within these groups. These efforts mitigate the inequities in whose infertility is treated or not, but they are highly unusual. In most cases, the costs of treatment in the commercial market for ART services continue to make reproductive technologies virtually inaccessible to poor people.

While many who struggle with infertility continue to lack access, wealthy people's reproductive desires are being met through these markets. Cross-nation inequities remain enormous. Fertility treatment remains most available in rich nations like countries in Europe and the United States, where clinics may compete for business. Global reproductive tourism has made the bodies of women from the Global South available in the service of wealthier people from the Global North.

There is another element of the commercial market that perpetuates inequities: the results of fertility treatment are never certain. Even repeated cycles of treatment may not result in a pregnancy, let alone the birth of a child. For intended parents, it can be difficult to reconcile these odds against a strong and persisting desire to have children. Despite evidence that the treatments are not working, commercial fertility clinics may continue to nurture the hopes of intended parents, which can propel them to pursue additional cycles that become less and less likely to succeed over time. Indeed, some clinics blatantly push parents toward these repeat cycles, generating more profit and leaving intended parents in debt or impoverished as they sacrifice whatever they can to have a child.

BOX 3.1   FERTILITY PRESERVATION: BRINGING NEW HOPE OR REINFORCING OLD INEQUALITIES?

Egg freezing, or the cryopreservation of oocytes, has emerged as a topic of much interest among people to whom these services are promoted for the purpose of preserving their fertility as well as in studies of reproduction. Much of this work is once again centered on the uses of this technology in rich nations, but the practice is also gaining popularity among wealthier women in other countries.

Cryopreservation is recommended to people in their teens and 20s who are undertaking cancer treatment. It is also discussed with transgender people pursuing gender-affirming treatment. In both situations, the procedure is offered as an option due to the possibility that an individual's future fertility may be negatively affected. The promotion of fertility preservation to otherwise healthy people, notably women in their 20s, raises some concern. The larger context in which egg freezing has become developed and marketed is one that Lucy van de Wiel (2020) notes also includes clinical and commercial infrastructures, with capital investments into fertility start-up companies and the creation of specialized financial products like loans specifically for fertility treatments. The process typically involves a course of hormone injections to stimulate the development of oocytes, which are then retrieved, or harvested with a long needle. (The person undergoing the procedure is given general anesthesia.) The mature eggs are put through a process called vitrification, or rapid freezing in liquid nitrogen. In theory, the ova can remain frozen indefinitely, but fertility clinics in the United States charge up to $500 a year for storage. This is in addition to the costs of the retrieval ($4,500 to $8,000 for one cycle) and the hormone injections ($4,000 to $6,000 per cycle) (Blum and Stock 2022). In the United Kingdom, egg freezing has recently been the fertility treatment with the fastest rate of growth, with the number of egg storage cycles up 64% between 2019 and 2021; however, they still represent only 4% of all treatments (Bishop 2023). There remain questions about the pregnancy and birth outcomes with these eggs.

In popular discourses, women who decide to freeze their ova for later use have been criticized as overly career-oriented and selfish. They are accused of delaying children to prioritize their own personal success. In contrast, Marcia Inhorn's (2023) recent ethnographic research indicates that most of these women choose to preserve their eggs because they are unable to find a suitable partner with whom to have children. Inhorn suggests this situation is one result of a growing divide between men's and women's educational attainment. There are more highly educated women and fewer men who would be potential partners. In 2023, men represented 42% of students at four-year colleges, a share that has declined over the last decade; in 2011, men were 47% of college students (Fry 2023).

Inhorn's study also reveals that women are interested in parenting with partners and not, for instance, entering into single motherhood on purpose. By freezing their eggs, the hope is to extend the time that they have for finding a suitable partner with whom they can have a child and co-parent. Research conducted elsewhere also finds professional women making similar decisions. What they are seeking is a partner who will be supportive during lengthy educational training, not to mention the professional demands associated with certain careers. Although cryopreservation has the potential to help women with gendered challenges of managing education and career and having children, ethnographers like Deomampo (2022) have warned that it may also reinforce inequities as only wealthy women can access these options.

ASSISTED REPRODUCTIVE TECHNOLOGIES AS A REPRODUCTIVE JUSTICE ISSUE

The principles of **reproductive justice** assert that people have the right to have children when desired (see Chapters 1 and 6). Yet, the ability to exercise this right is denied to many people. Profound inequities systematically shape lack of access to reproductive technologies that might help people to realize their hopes of having children. They also create the conditions in which the bodies and reproductive labor of poor and racialized women become exploited. Movements for reproductive justice are essential for righting these wrongs.

REPRODUCTIVE LOSSES

People who wish to have children may be thwarted for a range of reasons. The term reproductive loss calls attention to the various experiences of reproduction that do not result, as people themselves may have wanted and intended, in the birth of a living child. People experience reproductive loss when they are unable to conceive (infertility) or to carry a pregnancy to term (miscarriage). The decision to end a wanted pregnancy is also a loss. The unrealized hopes of finding a partner with whom to co-parent and, over the course of time, the impacts of age on fertility represent reproductive losses. LGBTQ+ people may anticipate no or limited paths to parenthood, with access to adoption and ARTs legally restricted or financially prohibitive. Other queer reproductive losses include people's thwarted attempts to adopt children as well as their experiences of miscarriage and pregnancy loss and disease and sickness, including endometriosis and breast cancer in female bodies and prostate cancer in male bodies (Craven 2019; Falu 2022; Falu and Craven 2024). It is important for us to take note of these losses because they, too, are everyday experiences of reproduction.

PREGNANCY LOSS AND ITS MEANINGS

Pregnancies are uncertain and the experience of loss is not uncommon. About a quarter of known pregnancies end spontaneously in miscarriage before 12 weeks, with many more never progressing beyond conception or implantation (see Chapter 4). There is no treatment to stop these losses, which are likely to be due to problems with the embryo or conditions of the uterus, particularly the endometrial lining which supports the biological processes of growing and gestating the embryo. On the other hand, collectively as members of our communities, societies, and countries, we can demand changes in the practices leaving pollutants in the soil where we grow our food, the air we breathe, and the water we drink, which a growing number of studies are linking directly to miscarriages and preterm births (before 37 weeks of pregnancy).

Very early pregnancy losses may not be recognized as miscarriages because people may not even be aware that they are pregnant. Pregnancy tests were not invented until the identification of human chorionic gonadotropin, often called the pregnancy hormone, in the 1920s; affordable at-home tests using urine samples became available during the 1970s. Historically and cross-culturally, women relied on their bodily signs, which became familiar to them when they experienced more than one pregnancy and had multiple children. The absence of a period, they knew, was and is not a reliable indicator of a pregnancy. Indeed, in many settings, a pregnancy may not have been acknowledged, by an individual or by others, before quickening, or the sensation of movement or fluttering within the uterus. Yet, even then, women were careful not to take for granted that they were pregnant with a human child.

Pregnancy is understood in many communities as not only a biological process, but also a social and spiritual one. In some cultural and spiritual traditions, pregnancy may be attributed to supernatural forces and the contents of the womb regarded as mysterious and possibly other than human (Layne 2022; Renne 2022; van der Sijpt 2022). Consequently, the end of a pregnancy and the resumption of a menstrual cycle might be welcomed as a sign that maligning spirits no longer occupied a woman's body. Similarly, when a pregnancy is known, but not desired, its end may also be seen as a relief. A key anthropological insight is that whether a pregnancy is recognized at all as such and how it is perceived vary across cultural settings. Even within a given context, the meaning of a pregnancy may still vary with the specific circumstances of individual lives.

Relevant to the meaning of pregnancy, and especially pregnancy loss, is the concept of personhood. The status of personhood has been a politically contentious issue in the United States where attempts to ban abortion access have been made on the claims that a fetus is a person with legal rights. In 2023, the state of Alabama's highest court ruled that frozen embryos, produced in IVF procedures, should be recognized as children (Sharfstein 2024).

As anthropologists have demonstrated, however, understandings of personhood are both variable across contexts and flexible within them (Layne 2022). To be a person is to be recognized as a person, or as a member of human society, culture, and community. It is not simply a "natural" fact or biological state of existence, although it is made to appear so because the recognition of personhood is associated with pregnancy, birth, and the care and raising of children. The transitional life events celebrated as rites of passage, for example, are cultural and social activities marking and making personhood—for example, in the traditions of Christianity, a baptism is the symbolic birth of a new member of the church.

Religion as well as culture significantly shape how we talk and think about personhood. According to the cosmology of the Beng, a minority ethnic group in Côte d'Ivoire, every living person is a reincarnated soul and the birth of a child represents the return of an ancestral spirit (Gottlieb 2015 [2004]). In this context, newborns and infants are seen as suspended in liminality, or a state of transition, between the afterlife and the life we inhabit now. In other religions, too, because the dead exist outside of the present and the living, they may be acknowledged to exist as spirits or souls in some traditions, but they are not regarded as persons. Similarly, the unborn also exist, but they may or may not be recognized as persons. Because the outcome of a pregnancy is not taken for granted, the status of a fetus is also uncertain. In fact, they may not be considered fully human; in the Ecuadorean Andes, pregnant women referred to the *criaturas* in their bellies (Morgan 1997).

The ability to not only imagine but to image the fetus has been critically important in the construction of personhood during pregnancy. The sonogram is both a familiar routine of biomedical care during pregnancy and a ritual of family and kinship. Around the twentieth week, a fetal survey to observe and measure organ development is prescribed as a non-invasive prenatal screening, but expectant parents generally anticipate it as a special occasion to "see the baby" and get "baby pictures." It is at this scan that expectant parents may learn the sex of an expected child, setting into motion other rituals of pregnancy, like gender reveal parties and baby showers (see Chapter 4), which also act as rites of personhood. Significantly, these occasions also incorporate other practices of material culture, like shopping for baby clothes and giving and receiving toys and other items intended for an expected child. In the United States, the acquisition of consumer goods and the creation of a space for the future baby may signal the accrual also of personhood (see Han 2013; Tomori 2024). In situations of miscarriages and stillbirths, an expected child may be lost, but the things intended for the baby may remain. Linda Layne (2000) has written movingly of how meaningful these items become as keepsakes and the memorials that women create to remember the imagined children they have lost.

Alternately, studies of infertility and ARTs suggest that a pregnancy may be immediately endowed with personhood, extending into the period even before conception takes place. When people embark on a journey of fertility treatment, they may already envision a future baby who may already have a name that the expectant parents have chosen. Their intention to have a child may itself endow personhood to the gametes procured from donors and establish kinship with an embryo gestated by a surrogate. When the transfer of an IVF embryo does not become successfully implanted in an intended parent's or a surrogate's uterus or when a pregnancy ends in a miscarriage, the loss of an imagined child also compounds atop the experience of infertility.

Evidence from the past suggests diverse concepts of personhood (Scott and Betsinger 2022). Ideas about personhood can be inferred from the bioarchaeological examination of mortuary practices, such as how bodies were prepared for burial, where they were interred, and what or even who else was included in their graves. Archaeologists have documented fetal burials that were consistent with the burials of infants and children, suggesting their statuses were socially recognized as alike. When a grave contained only a fetus, it was taken as an indication that the mother did not also die; however, other graves included the remains of both a fetus and a female, suggesting they died together. Bioarchaeologists warn against imputing our historically and culturally conditioned emotions to the past. They also caution against making assumptions based only on the limited evidence available from mortuary practices and overgeneralizing from it.

Recent ethnographic studies also examine what happens to pregnancy materials after a loss (Kilshaw and Borg 2020). They demonstrate more generally how context shapes the interpretation and handling of these materials. There is a difference between the tissue resulting from an early loss experienced as a "late" period and the remains of a much later one. In the United States, the remains of a pregnancy loss after 24 weeks may be cremated or buried, with some parents arranging funeral or memorial services. Interesting to consider here is that mortuary practices and funerary rites are typically enacted when a socially recognized person passes from life. In this case, however, they create the personhood of an expected child who was not born. The cultural and social importance of these activities is they transform a lost pregnancy into a lost person so that the loss itself is recognized as a real one.

EXPERIENCING LOSS

The meanings of pregnancy and the makings of personhood are varied. So, too, are people's experiences of reproductive loss. In the Gbigbil communities of eastern Cameroon, ethnographer Erica van der Sijpt (2022) learned, the meaning of pregnancy shifts within the context of a pregnant woman's relationships with her partner and her co-wives—because this is a polygynous society—as well as their extended families. Pregnancy losses can have dramatic effects on marital and kin relationships. For a Gbigbil woman, a pregnancy can strengthen and stabilize her relationship with a man, leading to formal marital exchanges that link the two families of the partners together. In this situation, a pregnancy loss may result in a weakening of the relationship and even the threat of a woman's abandonment or replacement by a co-wife. A woman in a more precarious relationship, however, might wish to end a pregnancy. Jealousy and competition between co-wives for the support and attention of their partner may also be seen as the cause of reproductive loss, including accusations of witchcraft to block a woman's fertility.

When a pregnancy has been long wished for and awaited, each passing day and week may represent another step closer to the desired outcome in the birth of a much-wanted child. For people pursuing treatment for infertility, the dates of fertilization and implantation are known—a precision that lends a sense of certainty—and every stage of the process is closely monitored by clinicians, offering reassurance or at least an illusion of it. The spontaneous loss of these pregnancies can be a devastating experience made especially painful because reproductive losses remain stigmatized in many settings, despite significant changes in understanding of it over the last several decades. Women are often blamed for having caused their own miscarriages—and sometimes accused outright of having induced an abortion—and devalued for their inability to maintain a pregnancy, as in the case of infertility. As discussed above, relationships can be undermined by pregnancy loss and women can even be discarded and replaced by another wife, which has material consequences in addition to social ones. The gendered nature of this stigmatization cannot be missed. Just as with infertility, the attribution of blame for pregnancy loss falls on women even when men clearly have responsibility. In Bangladesh, for example, a study of women's experiences of intimate partner violence found that 25% of women who reported experiencing abuse also reported a miscarriage, stillbirth, or induced abortion (Afiaz et al. 2020). Many people may attempt to hide their pregnancy loss as a way to cope with its stigmatization, but it can also compound suffering by socially isolating individuals when they especially need emotional support. The stigmatization of pregnancy loss is often internalized and can cause acute suffering and undermine mental health. Even in settings where pregnancy loss is more openly discussed, other people may make insensitive or hurtful comments, leading once again to social isolation.

LOSING A PREGNANCY

In other cases, a pregnancy loss is not spontaneous, but rather is induced by a decision that itself is driven by diagnostic technologies. For people pursuing IVF and other fertility treatment, embryos are screened and tested for major disorders that may be inherited. Embryos are then selected for implantation while the others are discarded (Inhorn 2022; Schwennesen and Gammeltoft 2022). The preimplantation screenings also allow embryos to be sorted by sex, which is information that intended parents may wish to know. In various cultural settings, expectant parents may feel pressure to have a child of one sex or the other. The combination of a cultural preference for sons in China, the state's one-child policy, and access to sonograms enabling the identification of an expected child's sex created demands for sex-selective abortions there. Today, the sex ratio at birth is about 110 males to 100 females, one of the most imbalanced in the world.

In pregnancies outside of fertility treatment, prenatal diagnostic tests may be recommended to people based on their age or in markers observed in non- or less-invasive screenings of urine or blood samples as well as fetal ultrasound scans. Amniocentesis is among the most frequently performed procedures and involves the insertion of a needle into a pregnant person's uterus to extract a sample of amniotic fluid containing fetal cells. It carries a small but still real risk of miscarriage, which pregnant people weigh against what they see as the benefits of testing. To test or not to test is one in a series of decisions confronting expectant parents who become forced into the role of what Rayna Rapp (2004 [1999]) called "moral pioneers." Test results pointing to a serious condition may raise the question of whether to continue a pregnancy or seek an abortion to end it. There are serious conditions that mean a baby may not live long past birth or a child will have major disabilities requiring life-long intense care that may be prohibitive for families in terms of both financial and social support. These diagnoses represent reproductive losses for people whether they decide to continue a pregnancy or not. Even for parents who continue, the unanticipated prospect of disability may itself be initially experienced as the loss of an imagined child. Those who decide to seek an abortion also feel loss.

These already complicated decisions have been made even more fraught in the United States, where the right for people to have an abortion is no longer constitutionally protected. The decision was framed as "pro-life," with assertions that life begins at conception.

Although Dobbs does not specifically claim that the fetus is granted personhood status, these assertions have accompanied the expanded bans on abortion that have unfolded since Dobbs. Since the US Supreme Court's 2022 decision in Dobbs v. Jackson Women's Health Organization, 21 individual US states now are enforcing laws that ban or restrict access to this procedure earlier in pregnancy than had been allowed previously, rendering abortion services practically inaccessible (KFF 2024). This has caused harm and suffering inflicted in many different forms. This harm ranges from the inability to assert the basic human right of bodily autonomy and determining whether to have or not have a child, to the suffering imposed on people experiencing pregnancy complications and diagnoses of serious conditions who may be experiencing miscarriage, or excruciating decisions terminating a pregnancy to prevent the suffering of their future child or to protect their own health (see Chapter 2).

REPEAT LOSSES

Repeat losses may be also part of the reproductive experiences of people who are struggling with their fertility. In numerous cultural settings, a woman may be valued by her ability to bear children and multiple children are desired. The imperative to have children is so strong that it drives people to undertake repeated cycles of IVF even when the likelihood of getting pregnant and giving birth to a child is low. The result is that couples may also experience multiple losses, which include not only miscarriages, but "missed" implantations when the embryos placed in the uterus do not become successfully embedded. These losses can take an enormous toll on couples and their mental health. Even when pregnancy is finally achieved, it may be approached with anxiety and trepidation, shaped by previous experiences of pregnancy loss. Although both partners are certainly affected, the mental health impacts are amplified for women who undergo the embodied experience of losing a pregnancy.

Repeat losses may lead couples to end their fertility journey and accept that they will not be able to have a child or additional children, in the case of secondary infertility. This decision can itself be experienced as a loss as it has a finality that is different from the ongoing pursuit of a pregnancy.

REPRODUCTIVE LOSS AND REPRODUCTIVE JUSTICE

How we are enabled or not to navigate the complicated and uncertain trajectories of having a child is an issue of reproductive justice. Understanding this fact is itself an important starting intervention. It requires our awareness that the decisions around fertility are connected to complex cultural and specific social circumstances, which themselves may make a pregnancy desirable or undesirable, tenable or untenable at a given point. To exercise their right to have a child, people require access to both fertility treatment and abortion care. People who experience losses at any point, whether they were involuntary and unanticipated or conscientiously decided, should not bear their pain alone. Stigmatization is the direct outcome of larger structural and cultural forces that are manifest in and reproduced through people's thoughts and actions. We have the power to disrupt the reproduction of these inequities, question and change our minds, support systems and laws, and do differently to destigmatize reproductive losses.

SUMMARY

- Cultures around the world place great value on having children, and many people desire and expect to create families and have children. However, uncertainty and disruptions also shape reproductive journeys.
- Many people experience undesired infertility and childlessness and pursue a variety of solutions ranging from adoption to seeking infertility treatment. Access to these options and their negotiation is shaped by broader inequities and national policies as well as local cultural and familial circumstances.
- Infertility treatment globally has made use of a growing array of ARTs that have dramatically expanded hope for having children. These technologies are incorporated into the larger set of cultural, religious, and gendered norms for creating kinship and state policies that govern these practices.
- Reproductive losses are often part of the process of infertility treatment as well as the broader process of reproduction. How loss is interpreted and whether the fetus is endowed with personhood is contingent on both specific, and larger social and cultural, circumstances.

- While uncertainty and disruptions may be part of human reproductive trajectories, we have the power to destigmatize infertility, loss, and childlessness.

FURTHER EXPLORING

See *The Routledge Handbook on Anthropology and Reproduction*, edited by Sallie Han and Cecília Tomori (2022), for chapters by Daisy Deomampo (2022); Nessette Falu (2022); Trudie Gerrits (2022); Marcia C. Inhorn (2022); Linda Layne (2022); Nete Schwennesen and Tine M. Gammletoft (2022); France Winddance Twine and Marcin Smietana (2022); Erica van der Sijpt (2022); and Andrea Whittaker (2022). See the references for more information.

In this short video clip, scholar-activist Loretta Ross defines reproductive justice and explains reproductive futurism, which offers a critique of the inequities shaping access to ARTs and the limitations on whether technologies can deliver on their promise: www.youtube.com/watch?v=lsOKBLmvqGI.

Fertility Futures is a series of recorded conversations with feminist scholars examining people's lived experiences with ARTs. Find the episodes at this website: https://fertilityfutures.co.uk.

The rise of infertility due to chemical exposures is the topic of this June 2024 article: www.thenewlede.org/2024/06/new-test-finds-more-than-50-common-chemicals-ma
y-be-linked-to-infertility.

Marcia Inhorn has been a leading scholar in the anthropology of infertility and ARTs, with a commitment to documenting the experiences of women and men in the Middle East. Here are links to two recorded videos:

- "Health, Rights, and Resilience: Refugee Well-being and Infertility in Egypt" (December 2022): https://youtu.be/k6Y9fnrkfvY?si=UnhtoGxdiR28qXuO.
- "Cosmopolitan Conceptions: IVF Sojourns in Global Dubai" (April 2016): https://macmillanreport.yale.edu/videos/cosmopolitan-conceptions-ivf-sojourns-global-dubai.

Additionally, Inhorn is featured in this November 2023 episode of the *Finding Genius* podcast, "Egg Vitrification: Exploring the Social and Psychological Impacts of Egg Freezing": https://youtu.be/Xp QTAKWXia8?si=IkEcG4Q9Dvoqldyv.

The perspectives of egg donors and the commodification and racialization of eggs—with insights from anthropologist Daisy Deomampo—are examined in this episode of the NPR Network podcast, *Embodied*, from March 8, 2024: www.npr.org/podcasts/ 898634025/embodied.

India's surrogacy laws are the focus of this April 2023 episode of *Laws of the Land*, a video series of *The Print*, a news organization based in New Delhi, India: https://youtu.be/UM9Vhn6C218?si= RKi_KmO-3e4MsT5H.

The LGBTQ+ Reproductive Loss website was initially created by anthropologist Christa Craven as a companion site for her 2019 book, *Reproductive Losses*, and it continues to point people to resources they might find helpful. The link is: www.lgbtqrep roductiveloss.org.

REFERENCES

Afiaz, Awan, Raaj Kishore Biswas, Raisa Shamma, and Nurjahan Ananna. 2020. "Intimate Partner Violence (IPV) with Miscarriages, Stillbirths and Abortions: Identifying Vulnerable Households for Women in Bangladesh." *PloS One* 15(7): e0236670. doi:10.1371/journal.pone.0236670.

Berend, Zsuzsa. 2016. *The Online World of Surrogacy*. New York and Oxford: Berghahn Books.

Bishop, Katie. 2023. "The Proactive Fertility Care Industry Is Soaring: Is That a Good Thing?" *BBC*, June 12. www.bbc.com/worklife/article/20231206-the-p roactive-fertility-care-industry-is-soaring-is-that-a-good-thing.

Block, Ellen. 2022. "The Shifting Role of Grandmothers in Global Reproduction Strategies." In *The Routledge Handbook of Anthropology and Reproduction*, edited by Sallie Han and Cecília Tomori, 590–603. Abingdon and New York: Routledge.

Blum, Dani, and Nicole Stock. 2022. "What to Know Before You Freeze Your Eggs." *The New York Times*, December 12. www.nytimes.com/2022/ 12/23/well/family/egg-freezing-risks-cost.html.

Conrad, Marissa. 2023. "How Much Does IVF Cost?" *Forbes* www.forbes. com/health/womens-health/how-much-does-ivf-cost/.

Craven, Christa. 2019. *Reproductive Losses: Challenges to LGBTQ Family-Making*. Abingdon and New York: Routledge.

Deomampo, Daisy. 2022. "Eggs." In *The Routledge Handbook of Anthropology and Reproduction*, edited by Sallie Han and Cecília Tomori, 257–270. Abingdon and New York: Routledge.

Falu, Nessette. 2022. "Invisible Hands: The Reproductivities of Queer(ing) and Race(ing) Gynecology." In *The Routledge Handbook of Anthropology and Reproduction*, edited by Sallie Han and Cecília Tomori, 305–320. Abingdon and New York: Routledge.

Falu, Nessette, and Christa Craven. 2024. "Queer Reproductive Futures." In *A Companion to the Anthropology of Reproductive Medicine and Technology*, edited by Cecilia Coale Van Hollen and Nayantara Sheoran Appleton, 219–233. Hoboken, NJ: John Wiley & Sons.

Franklin, Sarah. 2022 [1997]. *Embodied Progress: A Cultural Account of Assisted Conception*. Abingdon and New York: Routledge.

Fry, Richard. 2023. "Fewer Young Men Are in College, Especially at 4-Year Schools." *Pew Research*, Dec. 18. www.pewresearch.org/short-reads/2023/12/18/fewer-young-men-are-in-college-especially-at-4-year-schools/.

Gerrits, Trudie. 2016. "Assisted Reproductive Technologies in Ghana: Transnational Undertakings, Local Practices and 'More Affordable' IVF." *Reproductive Biomedicine & Society Online* 2: 32–38.

Gerrits, Trudie. 2022. "Global IVF and Local Practices: The Case of Ghana." In *The Routledge Handbook of Anthropology and Reproduction*, edited by Sallie Han and Cecília Tomori, 233–256. Abingdon and New York: Routledge.

Gottlieb, Alma. 2015 [2004]. *The Afterlife Is Where We Come From*. Chicago, IL: University of Chicago Press.

Gürtin, Zeynep B. 2016. "Patriarchal Pronatalism: Islam, Secularism and the Conjugal Confines of Turkey's IVF Boom." *Reproductive Biomedicine & Society Online* 2: 39–46.

Han, Sallie. 2013. *Pregnancy in Practice: Expectation and Experience in the Contemporary United States*. New York and Oxford: Berghahn Books.

Han, Sallie. 2022. "Spectacular Reproduction Revealed: Genetic Genealogy Testing as a Re(Tro)Productive Technology." In *Integrating Reproductive Technologies*, edited by Victoria Boydell and Katharine Dow, 131–147. London: Emerald.

Inhorn, Marcia C. 1994. *Quest for Conception: Gender, Infertility and Egyptian Medical Traditions*. Pennsylvania, PA: University of Pennsylvania Press.

Inhorn, Marcia C. 2006. "Making Muslim Babies: IVF and Gamete Donation in Sunni Versus Shi'a Islam." *Culture, Medicine and Psychiatry* 30: 427–450.

Inhorn, Marcia C. 2018. *America's Arab Refugees: Vulnerability and Health on the Margins*. Palo Alto, CA: Stanford University Press.

Inhorn, Marcia C. 2022. "Infertility, in Vitro Fertilization, and Fertility Preservation: Global Perspectives." In *The Routledge Handbook of Anthropology and Reproduction*, edited by Sallie Han and Cecília Tomori, 217–232. Abingdon and New York: Routledge.

Inhorn, Marcia C. 2023. *Motherhood on Ice: The Mating Gap and Why Women Freeze Their Eggs*. New York: NYU Press.

Kahn, Susan Martha. 2000. *Reproducing Jews: A Cultural Account of Assisted Conception in Israel*. Durham, NC: Duke University Press.

KFF. 2024. *Abortion in the United States Dashboard*. www.kff.org/womens-health-policy/dashboard/abortion-in-the-u-s-dashboard/.

Kilshaw, Susie, and Katie Borg, eds. 2020. *Navigating Miscarriage: Social, Medical and Conceptual Perspectives*. New York and Oxford: Berghahn Books.

Kleinman, Arthur, and Joan Kleinman. 1991. "Suffering and Its Professional Transformation: Toward an Ethnography of Interpersonal Experience." *Culture, Medicine and Psychiatry* 15(3): 275.

Lance, Delphine, and Jennifer Merchant. 2016. "Surrogacy in Context: Ukraine and the United States." In *Assisted Reproductive Technologies in the Global South and North*, edited by Virginie Rozé and Sayeed Unisa, 149–164. Abingdon and New York: Routledge.

Layne, Linda. 2000. "'He Was a Real Baby with Baby Things': A Material Culture Analysis of Personhood, Parenthood and Pregnancy Loss." *Journal of Material Culture* 5(3): 321–345.

Layne, Linda. 2022. "'Personhood' in the Anthropology of Reproduction." In *The Routledge Handbook of Anthropology and Reproduction*, edited by Sallie Han and Cecília Tomori, 323–338. Abingdon and New York: Routledge.

Morgan, Lynn M. 1997. "Imagining the Unborn in the Ecuadoran Andes." *Feminist Studies* 23(2): 323–350.

Oh, Arissa. 2015. *To Save the Children of Korea: The Cold War Origins of International Adoption*. Palo Alto, CA: Stanford University Press.

Rapp, Rayna. 2004 [1999]. *Testing Women, Testing the Fetus: The Social Impact of Amniocentesis in America*. Abingdon and New York: Routledge.

Renne, Elisha P. 2022. "Menstruation: Sociocultural Perspectives." In *The Routledge Handbook of Anthropology and Reproduction*, edited by Sallie Han and Cecília Tomori, 200–216. Abingdon and New York: Routledge.

Roberts, Elizabeth F.S. 2021. *God's Laboratory: Assisted Reproduction in the Andes*. Berkeley, CA: University of California Press.

Schwennesen, Nete, and Tine M. Gammeltoft. 2022. "Prenatal Screening and Diagnosis." In *The Routledge Handbook of Anthropology and Reproduction*, edited by Sallie Han and Cecília Tomori, 339–350. Abingdon and New York: Routledge.

Scott, Amy B., and Tracy K. Betsinger. 2022. "Reproduction in the Past: A Bioarchaeological Exploration of the Fetus and Its Significance." In *The Routledge Handbook of Anthropology and Reproduction*, edited by Sallie Han and Cecília Tomori, 365–380. Abingdon and New York: Routledge.

Sharfstein, Joshua. 2024. *The Alabama Supreme Court's Ruling on Frozen Embryos*. Johns Hopkins Bloomberg School of Public Health. https://publichealth.jhu.edu/2024/the-alabama-supreme-courts-ruling-on-frozen-embryos.

Teman, Elly. 2010. *Birthing a Mother: The Surrogate Body and the Pregnant Self.* Berkeley, CA: University of California Press.

Tomori, Cecília. 2024. *Nighttime Breastfeeding: An American Cultural Dilemma.* 2nd ed. New York and Oxford: Berghahn Books.

Twine, France Winddance, and Marcin Smietana. 2022. "The Racial Contours of Queer Reproduction." In *The Routledge Handbook of Anthropology and Reproduction*, edited by Sallie Han and Cecília Tomori, 289–304. Abingdon and New York: Routledge.

Van de Wiel, Lucy. 2020. *Freezing Fertility: Oocyte Cryopreservation and the Gender Politics of Aging.* New York: NYU Press.

van der Sijpt, Erica. 2022. "Navigating Reproductive Losses." In *The Routledge Handbook of Anthropology and Reproduction*, edited by Sallie Han and Cecília Tomori, 351–364. Abingdon and New York: Routledge.

Wahlberg, Ayo. 2018. *Good Quality: The Routinization of Sperm Banking in China.* Berkeley, CA: University of California Press.

Whittaker, Andrea. 2022. "Surrogacy." In *The Routledge Handbook of Anthropology and Reproduction*, edited by Sallie Han and Cecília Tomori, 271–286. Abingdon and New York: Routledge.

World Health Organization. 2023. *Infertility Prevalence Estimates, 1990–2021.* www.who.int/publications/i/item/978920068315.

PREGNANCY AND BIRTH

Today, many people have come to regard pregnancy and birth as matters of biology and medicine. You might have been taught that being pregnant is like having a sickness or condition which requires constant monitoring. Or you might have learned to think that giving birth is painful, risky, and best managed in a hospital. These particular ideas and practices represent the **biomedicaliza-tion** of reproduction, or the historical shift from seeing pregnancy and birth, along with all aspects of reproduction, as normal life events to treating them as abnormal biological ones requiring specialized intervention. This view of pregnancy and birth is now globally dominant.

Given its importance, a biomedicalized perspective on pregnancy and birth ought to be critically examined. To critique the biomedicalization of reproduction is not to reject biomedicine or technology and science more generally. Instead, an aim is to become more thoughtfully aware of how and why we experience pregnancy and birth as we do today, specifically the inequalities shaping and influencing reproduction. This critical understanding is arguably even more important for practitioners of biomedicine, including doctors and nurses, who in their work come face-to-face with people bearing the consequences of historical injustices.

It is worth remembering that pregnancies and births are common occurrences, bringing all of us into this world. When pregnant or birthing, people have sought and received attention and support from their communities. Doctors themselves acknowledge that not every intervention introduced by biomedicine is necessary or helpful to pregnant and birthing people—for

DOI: 10.4324/9781003379416-4

example, they question why procedures initially used in high-risk pregnancies have become widely adopted in routine and standard care. We need to ask who does or does not have access to the resources needed in pregnancy and childbirth, how the lack of access itself bears directly upon who does or does not have children, and how access to needed interventions or inappropriate use of interventions in birth may contribute to further inequities—all of them manifestations of **stratified reproduction**.

Importantly, we should recognize that biomedicine became ascendant not only because of what it could do *for* people, but also what it did *to* them. The biomedicalization of birth is based directly on a troubling history involving the exercises of power over women, particularly Black and Indigenous women and in societies of the Global South. The historical traumas of racism and colonialism continue to be felt in people's experiences of pregnancy and birth in these communities. An aim of **reproductive justice** is to think, talk, and act inclusively of people who have been marginalized by histories of colonialism and racism and whose rights to have children have been denied, restricted, and undermined.

In this chapter, and throughout this book, we argue for a **holistic** understanding of human reproduction that is encompassing and integrating of the broad range of people's experiences as they have been shaped historically and evolutionarily. One of the insights guiding the anthropological study of pregnancy and birth is that human reproduction is always simultaneously sociocultural *and* biological. Pregnancy and birth are, of course, intricate processes involving genes, cells, hormones, organs, and bodies. Yet, people are more than the sum of their genetic and biological parts. In our everyday lives, we experience pregnancy and birth as occasions of important and meaningful change when individuals and relationships are reinvented and redefined. People take on new or additional roles, statuses, identities, and responsibilities in relation to the new and existing members of their kin and family. Human reproductive experiences are human *relational* experiences by which we make not only babies, but also kinship: parents as well as grandparents, siblings, and so on. These transformations occur within households, communities, and other groups, institutions, and nations—for example, when citizenship is conferred to children at birth.

A **feminist** analysis, or one that centers on the unequal status of women based on the social construction of gender, helps us understand how and why the experiences of pregnancy and birth significantly shape the lives of women especially, including those who do not have children. A critique of gender is an important lens to view the reproductive lives of not only women, but also men and trans and queer people. The language we use in this chapter is guided by this perspective. We refer to women and mothers or men and fathers to reflect both the terms used originally in the research we cite and the specifically gendered expectations which become introduced and intensely felt during pregnancy and birth. We refer to people and parents when discussing the experiences of pregnancy and birth in general, reflecting our current understandings of gender as not defined by sex.

This chapter is organized into sections on pregnancy and on birth. The theme of biomedicalization will be considered in both sections, with a discussion of biomedicine, racism, and colonialism providing historical context on past and present inequities of reproduction.

PREGNANCY

The modern English word pregnant comes from Middle English and translates as "before being born." Yet, as we will discuss in this section, it is a mistake to approach pregnancy as merely the nine-month preamble to birth. Another less commonly used word for pregnant is gravid, which originates in the Latin word gravis, or heavy. Indeed, pregnancy is gravid, or weighted with significances that are varied and contradictory. It has particular importance and meaning for women, especially in sociocultural contexts in which being and becoming mothers define their status—which is a reason why infertility is experienced as a problem within marriage, family and kin, and community (see Chapter 3). Pregnancy is also widely understood as a metaphor for human creative processes. Pregnant bodies have long stood as symbols of nature, femininity, and the hope and promise we project onto future generations. Yet, they have also been portrayed as passive "vessels," which is not only an indication of what was known and not known about pregnancy, but also a reflection of how women were valued or not.

How we talk and think about pregnancy shapes and influences how we act and how we treat pregnant people in real life (Han 2022). In biomedicine, for example, human pregnancy has been described as a maternal-fetal conflict or competition. These terms suggest pregnancy is a contest of dueling interests. More recently, there has been a turn toward using terms like dyad which emphasize the alignments required in pregnancy and the exchanges occurring between pregnant person and gestating fetus. One example is that the cells of human offspring can be found in the bodies of their biological mothers, even long after pregnancy. Discovered in the 1990s, this phenomenon, called *microchimerism*, challenges a fundamental understanding in the biological sciences that one's own body is composed exclusively of one's own cells.

From the perspective of the biological sciences, pregnancy requires the complex harmonization of various overlapping processes which gestate a new human from a single cell as well as sustain the already existing one (the biological mother). Human pregnancy is described as normally occurring over 40 weeks, which biomedical clinicians and researchers also describe in terms of trimesters of the first 12 weeks, the second 12 weeks, and the third 12 and more weeks. For the purpose of calculating a date of delivery, biomedical care providers typically use the first day of a pregnant person's last menstrual period, then estimate a "due date" 280 days later. In fact, what occurs during the early weeks of the first trimester are two processes which create the biologically necessary preconditions for pregnancy. The first is *conception*, or the union of egg and sperm producing a unicellular zygote that divides and differentiates into a multicellular blastocyst. The second is the *implantation* of the blastocyst into the endometrial lining of the uterus. It is implantation, not conception, that triggers the production of human chorionic gonadotropin (hCG), which is often called the pregnancy hormone. One team of fertility researchers estimates that 30% of conceptions and 30% of implantations develop no further, making very early pregnancy loss a "default outcome" of human biological reproduction (Annual Capri Workshop Group 2020). Up to 25% of known pregnancies may end spontaneously before they are viable (see Chapter 2 and Chapter 3). In addition to the vagaries of biology, there are also the contingencies of lived experience shaping and influencing people's decisions about whether and when to have children and how many of them.

The identification of hCG in the 1920s led to the development of modern pregnancy tests, which required a blood sample. In the 1970s, tests using urine samples became available in the United States. There is, in fact, a long history of attempts to "diagnose" a pregnancy by examining urine. Written records from ancient Egypt describe testing urine on wheat and barley seeds—if they sprouted, then a pregnancy was confirmed. Today, pregnancy tests are widely available for purchase at pharmacies, and include instructions on interpreting the results (e.g., two lines indicating the detectable presence of hCG means pregnant and one line means not pregnant). The blood tests performed by healthcare providers are more sensitive and therefore considered more accurate even when used quite early, not long after implantation, but the at-home tests are also reliable.

THE PARADOXES OF PREGNANCY

For anthropologists, it says a lot about a culture or society to observe how people approach pregnancy and birth. These processes represent both continuity and change from one generation to another. They are paradoxically ordinary and extraordinary experiences.

The varied perceptions of pregnancy can be observed in the practices of everyday life (Han 2013). Some people choose not to disclose their conditions until their pregnancies have progressed without signs of complications. They may have concerns about avoiding awkward and distressing situations with family and friends. In some communities, open discussion of pregnancy may be interpreted as showing immodest interest in a woman's personal and private matters (e.g., her body and sexuality). Pregnant people themselves might make efforts to conceal or minimize the visibility of their pregnancies by wearing loosely fitted clothing—or they might be expected to practice seclusion. Historically, in the United States, confinement became equated with refinement and acted as a marker of privilege, with wealthier women withdrawing not only from public life, but also a range of activities deemed too physically strenuous for their female constitutions. Some women objected to these restrictions on their freedom of movement and the characterization of pregnancy (and of femininity) as a sickly condition. Many other women, particularly in poor and working (and Black and immigrant) households, had no choice but to continue their labor even when it was indeed strenuous. This difference of practice is not a cultural one, but one shaped by economic and social stratification.

Tsipy Ivry (2010) describes two contrasting "cultures of pregnancy" in Japan and Israel in the late 1990s and early 2000s. In Japan, pregnancy is described as a time of watchful anticipation when pregnant women are encouraged to bond with their babies. In Israel, however, pregnancy is experienced as an anxious time of screening, testing, and monitoring for anomalies, so that pregnant women maintain a tentative distance from what they talk and think about as fetuses, not babies. Japanese women purchase clothes and prepare other items for their babies in advance of their births while Jewish-Israeli women refrain from these activities. To observe these different responses is not to claim that Japanese women worry less and Israeli women worry more. Rather, we can understand that in each setting, there are distinct culturally patterned responses to uncertainty more generally and to uncertainty about pregnancy more specifically. In addition, we need awareness of their broader historical contexts. Both Japan and Israel are non-Western, industrialized, democratic countries where pregnant people receive healthcare within highly technologized systems of biomedicine. Both societies are also described as pro-natal, or promoting births. In Japan, however, the concern is the declining number of births set against an aging population, while in Israel, there is a perceived imperative to grow the population of a lone Jewish state situated among Arab nations. The anthropological study of reproduction reminds us that pregnancies and births are concerns which are both private and public, individual and social, and cultural and political.

In their study of the pregnancy experiences of Haredi ("ultra-Orthodox" Jewish) women in Israel and the United States, Elly Teman and Tsipy Ivry (2022) interviewed women who were mothers of between two and twelve children. They described pregnancy as "a way of life—not a one- to two-time 'out of ordinary' event" (385). Interestingly, Teman and Ivry found that the commonness of pregnancy did not necessarily make it less uncertain for the women in their study.

The perspectives of Haredi women are distinctive, as their pregnancies are experienced in terms of the specific ideas and practices of their religious devotion. Yet, they are also instructive for all of us, offering comparisons or contrasts to other experiences and expectations of pregnancy and birth. Many of the studies that have shaped the anthropology of reproduction were conducted either in countries where people on average have fewer children or by researchers who were trained at universities in these places (or both). These countries include the United States, which recorded a fertility rate of 1.62 in 2023, and the United Kingdom, which had a rate of 1.75. Israel had a rate of 2.93. These numbers represent the average number of children born to women in the national population. The number of children is not the same as the number of births or pregnancies, but it provides insight into the larger context of reproductive experience and expectation.

What assumptions do we bring into discussions about pregnancy and birth when we come from communities where smaller (or larger) families are the norm? What are the resulting blind spots in the anthropological study of reproduction? Critically examining our biases about the "ordinariness" of pregnancy is an insightful exercise in pursuit of understanding human reproduction.

PREGNANCY AS AN OCCASION FOR RITUAL

Rituals are activities that are performed to express or symbolically demonstrate a community's beliefs and values. Rituals are also recognized to have important and meaningful psychological effects, creating a sense of belonging and comfort in moments of change and uncertainty. Important and meaningful insights can be gleaned from examining rituals that otherwise may not seem especially serious. The examples of gender reveal parties and baby showers illustrate this point. Core beliefs and values concerning gender and class are featured centrally in both rituals, which are associated with the visibility of pregnancy in the United States today.

The gender reveal party is a recently invented tradition, with media coverage noting it as a trend in the late 2000s and early 2010s. The gatherings themselves may range in size and formality. The focus of the party is on the moment of the "reveal" itself, or an announcement of the biological sex of an expected child.

Typically, this information is obtained during a sonogram (discussed below). In the past, it might not have been known widely, but today, social media both enables the sharing of this announcement and encourages its creative staging. Videos on YouTube, for example, show expectant parents cutting into a cake that reveals pink icing for a girl or blue for a boy or opening a box of floating pink or blue balloons. In recent years, however, there has been some backlash against gender reveal parties, especially in the wake of serious injuries, deaths, and even a catastrophic wildfire in 2020 in California which resulted from the use of fireworks and confetti "cannons." Some of the criticism expresses disapproval of the perceived excesses of consumerism, so-called influencer culture, and social media more generally. Other criticism, coming from parents of non-binary and transgender children among others, is directed toward correcting the assumption that gender and sex are the same.

Baby showers appear to have become a popular ritual activity in some US communities in the second half of the twentieth century, with the public visibility of pregnancy and pregnant women becoming more accepted. Back then, baby showers typically were small parties hosted by a female relative for other family and friends. Nowadays, a baby shower may be a gathering of a pregnant person's workplace colleagues, including male co-workers. Or a celebration might be held for an expectant father. It was and still is customary for guests to bring clothing, toys, books, and other gifts intended for an expected child. If, as anthropologists observe, a ritual is a display of a community's most important values, then the giving and receiving of gifts are meaningful gestures of creating and maintaining social ties among people—an idea that is known as gift theory in anthropology. Yet, there have been shifts in practice that also suggest shifts in ideas. These days, guests at a baby shower may be asked to select their gifts from a chain store's baby registry or an online wish list or to directly contribute money to an account collecting funds for a larger purchase or savings. In addition, circulating on social media these days are images of lavish baby showers staged by celebrities and influencers and the extravagant gifts that are given and received. These practices communicate the importance of consumption, which is not surprising in the larger context of today's US culture and society, where the status and inclusion of individuals depends on what they do or do not have.

The performance of rituals during pregnancy, like gender reveal parties and baby showers, is insightful to consider in the study of reproduction. In addition, we can apply ritual analysis to pregnancy itself, examining it as a condition of **liminality**, or a state of transition. Particularly for people who are not already parents, pregnancy is a moment of transformation when individuals take on new roles and responsibilities in their community. Within this context, baby showers are rituals which socially recognize these changes in identity and status, or **rites of passage** from pregnant person to parent. New roles and responsibilities also require new knowledge, so that in ritual analysis, liminality is associated with learning. Pregnancy is a time when people actively seek information for themselves—or are given advice, wanted or not—from sources ranging from their peers to elders to other experts. Indeed, reading itself is a meaningful practice and important ritual of pregnancy.

Anthropologists have observed that the performance of ritual is one response of communities to moments of change and uncertainty. Pregnancy rituals were recorded by ethnographers dating back to Bronislaw Malinowski, who detailed Trobriand ceremonies surrounding the social recognition of a woman's first pregnancy. Among these customs were the presentation of a pregnancy robe that has been endowed with beautifying magic, and the ritual bathing of the pregnant woman. Other ritual practices include curtailments on the activities of pregnant women, which range from restrictions on which foods they may eat to **taboos**, or ritual prohibitions, on sexual intercourse. These bans, however, are not universally practiced. From the perspective of the Barí, an Indigenous group in Venezuela, intercourse "feeds" a gestating fetus—and its hunger may require a pregnant woman to maintain a relationship with an additional partner, or "secondary father" (Small 2003). Some communities abstain from mentioning a pregnancy for the purpose of protecting a pregnant woman and the child she is gestating from the unwanted attentions of supernatural forces—or of other people whose jealousy or displeasure could cause harm (see also Chapter 3).

In anthropology, there is a long history of fascination with the ritual involvements of men in pregnancy and birth, called **couvade**. A range of behaviors were documented in societies around the world, from men's participation in ritual seclusion to their experiences of food cravings during a partner's pregnancy and even pain during birth (Powis 2022). Couvade in Indigenous cultures attracted the interest of nineteenth-century evolutionist E.B. Tylor, who claimed that these male birthing rites were developed in prehistoric matriarchal societies in order for fathers to assert their rights over children. Twentieth-century psychiatrists concerned themselves with the medical and psychological dimensions of what they termed male sympathetic pregnancy, which caused men to experience bodily changes in tandem with their pregnant partners, such as weight gain.

What is perceived as men's overinvolvement in pregnancy and birth, as represented by couvade, is regarded as a problem, even a pathology, of masculinity. So, too, is the perception of men's under-involvement. In Senegal, involving men and fathers is an explicit goal in maternal and child health initiatives of non-governmental organizations (NGOs) based in countries of the Global North. Here and elsewhere in the Global South, men participate in ways which are consistent with local expectations of fathers by, for example, "finding the money" (Powis 2022, 418). Yet, these activities are overlooked or ignored because they do not fall in line with understandings of care held by donors in the United States and Europe who fund these NGO initiatives. Additionally, in a less than robust economy or in times of political instability, jobs may be scarce, limiting men's efforts to earn money. Men and fathers may feel their manhood challenged by the constraints on their ability to provide for their partners and children.

BOX 4.1 MEN, PREGNANCY, AND BIRTH

In discussions of pregnancy and birth, significantly less is said about men than women. How should we interpret this situation? One set of claims is that biological males, aside from contributing their gametes, have little to do "naturally" with these processes, which in turn shape the distinct roles and responsibilities of men as fathers in comparison with women as mothers. Anthropologists approach this topic rather differently, based on understandings both that biological sex differences matter in reproduction and that expectations about what these differences mean in our lived experiences are socially and culturally patterned. Men, women, fathers, mothers—these are terms we use for the identities and statuses we *ascribe* (assign) to people. There have been historical shifts and cross-cultural differences in what is associated with gender. Anthropologists contend that, in fact, men have been underacknowledged in reproduction due to social and cultural perceptions of masculinity and femininity. Men have had more to do in pregnancy and birth than has been generally recognized. This observation holds in terms of genetics, biology, and evolution as well as in the lived experiences of pregnancy and birth.

In biological anthropology, for instance, there have been long-standing interests in men's reproductive behaviors examined in terms of mating opportunities (selecting partners and maintaining relationships with them) and parental efforts or investments (activities to offer various forms of care to children). The evolution of human fathers is as important to consider as the evolution of human mothers. In addition, questions about the impacts that reproduction has on men themselves have become an area of especially active interest in the last 20 years (Gray, Straftis, and Anderson 2022, 60–66; Hrdy 2024). News media in the United States reported widely on research pointing to decreased levels of testosterone in men with new babies. These findings attracted so much attention not because they demonstrate any effects on men's (or babies') health, which remain unknown, but because testosterone itself is interpreted as a sign of masculinity.

From the perspective of sociocultural anthropology, what men do during pregnancy and birth is significantly *relational*, or in other words, they engage in activities and behaviors that support their relationships and the making of kinship with pregnant partners and expected children (Han 2013). These practices also enact the transformation of their own status from men to fathers. In the United States today, men may take on more tasks at home, like cooking meals or cleaning, to relieve their pregnant partners of these burdens or at least share them. They may undertake house improvement projects like painting the room that is planned for a new baby or even building an addition. Others take on more responsibilities at work to earn more money or to cover time off from their jobs after the birth. (There is no system of paid parental leave in the United States, unlike in other countries in the Global North and the Global

South.) Men are expected also to accompany their partners to healthcare appointments, for the purposes of supporting their partners and of "bonding" with a baby, or becoming invested in an expected child. The 20-week fetal scan is recalled by expectant fathers as a special occasion when the pregnancy became "real." Additionally, men in the United States may engage in "belly talk," or conversational interactions directed to an imagined and expected child (Han 2013, 2022). In Senegal, the prevailing gendered expectation is that men most importantly should work, enabling them to pay for the expenses associated with their pregnant partner's care. At the same time, Richard Powis (2022) found that men were capable and willing to take on the roles and responsibilities of emotional support and domestic tasks which by custom are performed by a pregnant woman's female relatives. Interestingly, however, women themselves resisted men's efforts, which they viewed as encroachment into women's space.

PRENATAL BIOMEDICAL CARE AND DIAGNOSTIC TESTING

These days, many of us take for granted that early and regular prenatal care is important and necessary for the health of pregnant people and their expected children. Yet, biomedical care during pregnancy cannot ensure or improve the outcomes for pregnant and birthing people whose wellness has not been supported over the life course. Typically, prenatal care entails the monitoring of pregnant people by biomedical doctors who acknowledge not every uncertainty during pregnancy can be addressed or treated— for example, there are no interventions to prevent or stop miscarriages. Biomedical care during pregnancy, as with other resources, is not equally accessible for everyone who needs or wants it, which is a concern in the high-income nations of the Global North and the low-income nations of the Global South. In the United States, access to reproductive healthcare is an obstacle for communities of color, including Black, Latine, Indigenous, and Asian people contending with poverty and racism. In Cuba, however, free and accessible healthcare is spotlighted as a symbol of the country's egalitarianism (Andaya 2022). Additionally, the invisibility of LGBTQ+ reproduction has a range of consequences for individuals during pregnancy and birth, such as women in same-sex couples navigating institutions that assume expected parents will be male-female (heterosexual) couples. Trans people who have a uterus and ovaries, whether they identify as female or not, also become pregnant, intended or not. Yet, they frequently suffer from poorer health and receive lesser quality care—or they may be denied care or simply do not seek it—because their situations are stigmatized or not recognized at all (Kirczenow MacDonald et al. 2020; Moseson et al. 2021; Stroumsa et al. 2023).

A particular focus of biomedical care during pregnancy is on prenatal diagnostic tests to screen for genetic disorders which may affect an expected child. In the last decade, non-invasive prenatal testing has come into wider use, although its availability remains limited globally (Jayashankar et al., 2023). Blood samples taken from a pregnant person contain fetal cell-free DNA that is examined for chromosomal anomalies, including the ones associated with Down syndrome and other disorders.

The sonogram, or fetal ultrasound imaging, has become adopted as a routine of biomedical care during pregnancy and embraced as a ritual of kinship and family. The scan is experienced as a highly meaningful occasion when expectant parents can "see the baby." In cultures, as in the United States, where seeing is believing, these "baby pictures" have clear sentimental value. Yet, sonograms do not necessarily provide diagnostic certainty, so that additional testing may be recommended. Unlike other tests which may be performed during pregnancy, a sonogram is non-invasive, meaning it requires no cutting into the skin. Instead, it uses a device, called a transducer, which is held against a pregnant person's abdomen and emits sonar waves producing visual images of the fetus. A fetal survey, examining the development of the fetus with particular attention to its organs, is typically performed around the 20th week of pregnancy. It is at this scan that expectant parents may learn the sex of an expected child.

Amniocentesis remains among the most frequently performed procedures despite its invasiveness and small but still real risk of miscarriage. It requires the insertion of a fine, long needle through the wall of a pregnant person's uterus to extract a small sample of amniotic fluid containing fetal cells.

When amniocentesis came into routine use in the United States during the 1980s, sociologist Barbara Katz Rothman (1986) raised concerns about the impacts that it and other forms of prenatal diagnostic tests had on the experiences of women, who regarded their pregnancies as "tentative." People look to prenatal diagnostic tests seeking clarity and reassurance about a pregnancy and an expected child. Yet, anthropologist Rayna Rapp (1999) observed they are made into "moral pioneers" forced to confront difficult questions. Existing therapies may help individuals manage their health; however, they may also be prohibitively expensive for families even when they have means, or simply unavailable where access to biomedical care is restricted, reflecting inequalities existing within and across societies of the Global North and Global South. Prenatal diagnostic testing presents these difficult questions to individuals as their "choices" when in fact they also reflect and reproduce larger existing cultural, social, and economic constraints on how and what they can decide (Schwennesen and Gammeltoft 2022). As Tine Gammeltoft (2015) learned from expectant parents in Vietnam, the decision to end a pregnancy reflects painful acknowledgments that all their best efforts at care, including their financial expenditures, will fall short of their parental desire and obligation to raise a child who will be accepted socially as a "full" person (see Chapter 3).

In the past, children with severe disabilities might not have lived into adulthood and babies with serious conditions might not live long past birth. Today, with improved resources including medical technologies, many children can have longer and more meaningful lives, but their families feel frustrated by a lack of information from doctors and genetic counselors who may indeed not be disability-sensitive or supportive (Ginsburg and Rapp 2024). Given the broad range of conditions and anticipated needs to care for children, there may be few clear answers. While prenatal diagnostic tests seem to promise reassurance and certainty about a pregnancy, they create other uncertainties.

IMPERFECT WOMAN, PERFECTIBLE PREGNANCY

The critique of biomedicalization owes much to feminists challenging the marginalization of women's experiences of reproduction. Building on the women's movement of the 1960s and 1970s, or what is known as the "second wave" of feminism, feminist anthropologists questioned how and why human biological reproduction had come to be used as a justification for the subjugation, or domination, of women. The unequal status of women is not determined by the unchanging "nature" of biological reproduction, but in fact is decided from the ideas and practices of society and culture.

The standardized care of biomedicine is based on an understanding of the human body as essentially a machine. A pregnancy is assumed to last no less and no more than 40 weeks. A pregnant person's weight is monitored to check not only how much is gained, but also the pace at which it is added. Human bodies, of course, are not machines and rarely operate with mechanical preciseness. Yet, women's bodies, like women themselves, have been variously described as flawed, unpredictable, and unruly, which has drawn them under gendered scrutiny during pregnancy and birth.

There is almost no end to the advice and information that pregnant women can seek—or become subjected to—on what to expect, eat, wear, and avoid. In the past, the advice was oriented toward protecting a pregnancy and, by extension, an expected child. Notable in the United States and other societies in the Global North, however, has been a recent shift toward having a "perfect" pregnancy and a "perfect" child. There is a concern with not only prenatal care, but also preconception care, so that women are treated as always potentially pregnant bodies. Underlying pregnancy advice and information is the assumption that responsibility for the health and wellbeing of pregnant people and their children lies primarily if not entirely with individual women. This assumption is one that scholars and advocates for reproductive justice are arguing vehemently against, particularly as new science on "maternal effects" becomes applied to old-fashioned blaming of women and mothers.

The shaping of health within the ecologies that humans inhabit is a central question for biological anthropologists and other researchers in health sciences (Kramer, Veile, and Ivey Henry 2022). It has long been understood that environments influence the health of a pregnant person that in turn influences the health of a fetus. This observation is one of the founding ideas of the area of research called **developmental origins of health and disease** (DOHaD), which has flourished over the last 30 years. The in utero conditions in which fetuses develop and grow have been demonstrated to have effects not only on these individuals in later life, but also on the offspring, or children of these individuals. In other words, what happens during people's pregnancies has long-lasting and intergenerational consequences. These findings point to the importance and necessity of supporting the health of pregnant people. While advocates for reproductive justice approach health as a collective project requiring societal effort and investment, other policy makers continue to promote initiatives targeting women and, for example, educating them to make healthier decisions, sometimes with little regard for the inequities that constrain these decisions.

In utero exposures result from individual behaviors, but these so-called lifestyle choices are not easily separable from the social environments in which people live. People may be limited in their ability to make decisions which will have real, material effects in their lives. DOHaD research examines the links between chronic diseases, like diabetes, or other cardiovascular and neurological disorders, and the lived experiences of poverty and discrimination (Thayer and Gildner 2022). These social conditions have biological effects on people, like nutrient deficiencies and elevated cortisol (a physiological marker of stress), with health impacts that are felt over generations and across communities. Making the desired changes to support healthier pregnancies and healthier people requires not only educating individuals to make different lifestyle choices, but also cultivating environments where these decisions are enabled and have real effects. Pregnant people may be advised that they can avoid toxic exposures, for instance, by selecting cookware free of forever chemicals. People in marginalized communities, however, have little control over these chemicals contaminating their water and may not be able to purchase more expensive cookware or water filters. A better approach would be to address underlying causes, such as regulations that would prevent the use of these toxic chemicals and create safer environments for everyone.

Today, DOHaD research also examines **epigenetic** effects, or changes to genes resulting from environmental exposures which then become transmitted to offspring and future generations. There are paternal effects as well as maternal ones. In Native American communities, for instance, elevated risks of diabetes, arthritis, and other conditions of chronic poor health have been observed in the children of men who were removed from their families to attend boarding schools—an "assimilation" policy of the

US government into the twentieth century (Brave Heart 1999; Running Bear et al. 2019).

BIRTH

Across historical, social, and cultural contexts, neither the course of pregnancy nor its end in the birth of a living human child nor the survival and continuing health of a birthing parent has been taken for granted as predictable or inevitable (see Chapter 3). People differ in how they respond to the uncertainties of pregnancy and birth, which they may experience as moments of wonder and mystery as well as of vulnerability or risk. Although the physiology of birth is the same for evolutionarily modern humans, the social ideas and practices surrounding it are diverse, as anthropologist Brigitte Jordan (1993) noted in *Birth in Four Cultures*. First published in 1978, her pioneering work lays out a framework for comparative studies of birth by examining who is present at a birth, including who may assist or attend birthing people, and where it takes place. Jordan noted that control over the tools of birth, especially with historically intensified reliance on technologies, has defined who holds **authoritative knowledge**, or the knowledge that is socially recognized to matter most, over reproduction.

Human birth, or parturition, can be difficult and for the birthing person, it may be an intense experience of bodily pain and sensation as well as a host of emotions which may include fear, worry, and distress. The difficulty or painfulness of the experience, however, varies by birth systems and individuals within them (see below). Birth usually occurs around the 40th week of pregnancy. Initially undetected are hormonal changes in the pregnant person's body which initiate the processes of normal (vaginal) birth. Increases in estrogen, oxytocin, and prostaglandin stimulate contractions in the muscles of the uterus and the dilation (opening) and effacement (thinning) of the cervix, or neck of the uterus, connecting it to the birth canal, or vagina. As the contractions become stronger, longer in duration, and more frequent, people in labor feel increasing pain. A baby is normally born head–first and as it begins to emerge, or crowns, the birthing person feels a burning sensation. After the baby has emerged, the contractions continue until the placenta has been delivered as well.

BIRTH, CULTURE, AND SOCIAL SUPPORT

Birth is also a **biocultural** experience: a biological process that is deeply intertwined with local cultural practices and requires social support (see Box 4.2). In the past, and still to this day in many communities, birthing women have looked to other women, including family and friends, nurses, and midwives or birth attendants. Depictions of birth can be found in historical documents and works of art as well as in archaeological evidence (Nowell, Mitchell, and Kurki 2002). A 3,700-year-old birth brick, or meskhenet, was unearthed at a site in Egypt. It was painted with a scene featuring a female figure, presumably a new mother, and newborn and two others, including one kneeling in front of the mother (interpreted as a midwife), and images of the goddess Hathor, associated with birth (Wegner 2006).

Across various historical and cultural settings, birth has been understood as the concern of women. Men were not expected to be present at births—a reason why male doctors were resisted—but they might be expected to provide food, drink, gifts, and payments necessary for the occasion. In Mexico's Yucatan region, Indigenous Maya midwives involved husbands or male partners during birth because they should "see how a woman suffers" (Jordan 1993, 33). In the mid-twentieth century, a "men's movement" to allow expectant fathers into labor and delivery rooms initially met opposition in hospitals amid concerns about their uninformed interference. Today, men's attendance at birthing classes has itself become a rite of passage into fatherhood (Reed 2005).

Birthing people are helped as much by emotional support as by direct assistance with delivering a baby. They were generally left isolated, however, in the historical shifts from midwifery to biomedicine and from home to hospital—a transition that became dominant in the Global North in the early to middle part of the twentieth century and has expanded elsewhere since. Midwife-attended births at home were intimate experiences of kinship; doctor-attended hospital births followed standard procedures which in the past restricted labor and delivery rooms to doctors and nurses. The emergence of **doulas**, or birth companions, is a response to the isolating conditions of US hospital births. Doulas are non-medical carers who offer support before, during, and after birth. They also may have knowledge and skills in areas like breastfeeding which often fall outside of biomedical expertise. A birthing person's fear and stress are associated with longer labor and contractions that are less effectual for delivering a baby and are relieved with emotional support, such as the help of doulas. This fact has come to be more fully recognized with biomedical research demonstrating that birthing people have shorter labor and fewer biomedical interventions when they receive continuous emotional support during birth (Hodnett et al. 2013). With emotional support, birthing people seem less likely to require pain medication, typically given through epidural catheter inserted into the spine, and **Cesarean section**, which is a surgery to deliver a baby through an incision into the birthing person's abdomen and uterus.

Given the human need and want for social support, it is not surprising that few cultures have an expectation of **solitary birth**, or one in which individuals do not seek the presence or assistance of others. Solitary birth has been a customary practice for the Bariba in rural Benin and the Tarahumara in the Sierra Madre region of northern Mexico. In these communities, birth in isolation from others is idealized as a demonstration of women's valor or an enactment of the cultural value of self-sufficiency. The story of a solitary birth opens the book, *Nisa: The Life and Words of a ! Kung Woman*, by Marjorie Shostak (1981), which presents an ethnographic account of the Ju/'hoansi (formerly called !Kung) through the life story of one woman. Nisa leaves her hut, walks a short distance from her village, and gives birth quietly while leaning against a tree.

BOX 4.2   BIRTH AND HUMAN EVOLUTION

The topic of birth is essential to our understanding of the evolution of our species. To answer important questions about how and why humans are born this way, biological anthropologists have investigated distinctive features of human birth, specifically the size of a baby's head in comparison with the size and shape of the pelvis, its outlet. The close fit and tight passage are believed to explain why humans experience pain in birth and why human babies are born head-first and facing a birthing person's spine. This position is understood to facilitate a human baby's emergence without injury to their neck or spine, but delivering the baby also may require direct assistance from people other than the person giving birth—a circumstance that is described as **obligate midwifery**.

Specialists in paleoanthropology examine the human fossil record—which includes both modern and extinct humans, or hominins—for differences in the bones of the pelvis and the cranium (skull) which may suggest changes in the mechanisms and behaviors concerning birth. Specialists in primatology compare births in humans and other primates, including apes and monkeys. Most hominin fossils are incomplete, but the available evidence suggests Neanderthal births were similarly difficult, so that birthing individuals may also have required support and assistance (Rosenberg and Trevathan 2022). Birth in non-human primates had not been well studied until recently and it was assumed to occur in isolation. In the last 30 years, however, primatologists have amassed evidence that individuals of other primate species are not solitary in birth, but in the presence of other individuals. We are now learning that humans and other primates may be a lot more alike than we were previously taught to think.

These findings illustrate how scientific inquiry about birth and evolution has been influenced and informed by human exceptionalism, or the assumption that our species is uniquely complex. In keeping with this unexamined logic, the **obstetric dilemma** remains a popular explanation for why human birth is difficult and why human babies require so much care and attention. Proposed in 1960, it posits a mismatch between our brain size, which is large relative to our bodies, and our bipedalism, or ability to stand upright and move on two feet. Based on the presumption that the male pelvis is the optimal anatomy for standing, walking, and running, the obstetrical dilemma hypothesis contends the female pelvis represents an evolutionary compromise between the requirements of bipedalism and of birth. It also claims these uniquely human problems of birth are solved by the "early" end of gestation for human babies who are born "underdeveloped" and "immature" when compared with other primates and mammals more generally.

There are, of course, real differences between humans and other animals and interesting questions to ask about biological sexes. Yet, when there is less focus on human uniqueness, other compelling explanations can be considered (Dunsworth 2022). While human pregnancy is long, it is not significantly longer than for other apes (30 to 39 weeks). The length of gestation might be more reasonably explained not by brain size and bipedalism, but by the metabolic demands, or energetic needs sustaining both a pregnant individual and a growing and developing fetus. In fact, the energetics of gestation and fetal growth, or EGG, hypothesis applies to not only humans, but also other primates and placental mammals. By centering the bodies of females and pregnant and birthing individuals—instead of presuming they are imperfect variations on male anatomies and biologies—we open the lines of inquiry for a more complete understanding of human evolution.

WHO ASSISTS OR ATTENDS TO BIRTHING PEOPLE: KINSHIP, CARE, AND BIOMEDICALIZATION

Who assists or attends to people during a birth is revealing of the larger model or system of birth in a society or culture. Midwives and doctors represent two contrasting models of birth. The midwifery model is rooted in historical and cross-cultural practices of women caring for other women in birth. Today, it promotes an understanding of birth as a normal physiological process that typically requires minimal intervention. Midwives in the United States today use language such as client or pregnant woman or person, emphasizing their woman-to-woman or person-to-person care. Doctors refer to their patients; the physician-patient relationship is defined and encoded in laws as well as in professional ethics. The biomedical model is oriented toward treating birth as disorderly and risky. Historically, male doctors developed instruments and interventions to assist what they saw as the pathologies of birth. The biomedical model is the globally dominant one today.

The modern English word midwife comes from the Middle English words for with (mid) and woman (wife). The term midwifery has been used to refer to the care provided typically by women to birthing women. Across cultural settings, these women have other names, such as partera, dai, or sage-femme, and tend to the bodily, emotional, and spiritual needs of women during pregnancy, birth, and postpartum (El Kotni 2022). Historically, these birth attendants gained their knowledge and skills under the guidance and supervision of other experienced women. Campaigns to discredit midwifery in the eighteenth and nineteenth centuries were part of active efforts to promote biomedicine, specifically obstetrics. Midwifery followed diverging trajectories in different communities around the world. In Europe, midwifery became professionalized, with schools established to educate young women as midwives. In countries like France, professional midwives became incorporated into the national healthcare system. In the United States, Black and Indigenous midwives and birth attendants were prevented from performing their work and from passing along their knowledge. Concerted efforts were undertaken by physicians to professionalize and increasingly bring birth under biomedical control. Midwifery remained marginalized until the 1960s and 1970s when the women's liberation movement, combined with the struggle for civil rights, inspired an interest in reclaiming women's knowledge and particularly the traditions of midwifery.

In the Global South, the supplanting of traditional midwives is a continuing legacy of the policies and practices enacted by colonial governments. The restrictions on midwifery were presented as beneficial to local communities, but the imposition of colonial medicine was also an effective way of bringing people, literally their bodies, directly under colonial power. Distinctions are now made between "traditional" birth attendants, whose learning occurs outside of formal institutions, and professional midwives, who receive training from formal institutions which grant them credentials and degrees. In areas of the Global South where there are few professional midwives or doctors, traditional birth attendants may become incorporated into the formal healthcare system as community health workers. While they offer important outreach, especially to people living in remote areas, the birth attendants, mostly women, also feel their roles have been diminished and their ability to care for birthing women has been constrained. The marginalization of midwives is both gendered and racialized. Indigenous parteras in Chiapas, Mexico, for instance, have organized to assert their legitimacy as knowledgeable and skilled carers in the face of these restrictions (El Kotni 2022).

The word doctor is derived from the Latin for teacher and the Middle English for learned person. Since the fourteenth century, it has been used in English as a title for academic specialists. Its reference to practitioners of biomedicine is more recent, but this history points to the importance of institutions in defining doctors. Their legitimacy is based on credentials attached to formal learning and their authority is gained in and over the institutional spaces of hospitals to which births were removed from homes. **Obstetrics** is the area of biomedicine focused on pregnancy and birth. Interestingly, the term itself comes from the Latin word for midwife. Its history can be traced to the involvement, in fifteenth-century Europe, of so-called man-midwives in attending births and especially developing instruments to address complications of delivery (Drife 2002). The forceps, invented in the 1600s, became a necessary tool in the late nineteenth century with the use of chloroform and, later, other forms of general anesthesia. The medications, while intended to relieve pain, also incapacitated women so they could not push during birth; obstetricians used forceps to deliver babies instead.

From the nineteenth century onward, obstetricians became established as the authorities over pregnancy and birth and their instruments and interventions became relied upon, not only in complicated and emergency situations, but also in routine practice (Smith-Oka and Spiegel 2024). These practices required the removal of births from homes to hospitals, which also led to the introduction of still more interventions. Robbie Davis-Floyd (2024) applied ritual analysis to question the standard procedures in US hospitals in the 1980s and 1990s. These practices included requiring wheelchairs for pregnant women who are capable of walking and regularly performing episiotomy, a surgical cut in the perineum (between vagina and anus), which may be needed when a doctor is using forceps, but not necessary otherwise. While claimed to be beneficial for birth outcomes, Davis-Floyd argued they were rituals serving the priorities of biomedical doctors. It has been common in doctor-attended births, for example, to recline women on their backs with their legs apart and feet braced on a surface or in stirrups. This position came into common use with man-midwives who could remain standing or sitting during a birth. Yet, historically and cross-culturally, women have delivered their babies while positioned upright, squatting or standing, or on all-fours. Birthing women themselves described being made to feel vulnerable, exposed, and incapable as well as upset and angry about how their perspectives were diminished and not taken seriously. When they attempt to assert themselves, however, they risk being labeled difficult or non-compliant or accused of selfishly putting their experiences ahead of the health and safety of their babies.

In recent years, the sharp lines of contrast between midwifery and biomedicine have become increasingly blurred. Traditional midwives in Mexico and India have claimed the right to administer Pitocin (synthetic oxytocin), an intervention which biomedical doctors use to stimulate contractions. Obstetricians raise questions about the number of Cesarean sections, which are higher than what is estimated to be medically justified; both US and UK rates of Cesarean deliveries are above 30%. Certified nurse midwives provide pregnancy and birth care in hospitals, where they may support people through long courses of labor. By allowing people to walk and move freely during labor, for example, or give birth while positioned upright or on all-fours (instead of supine, or on one's back), births may occur with minimal interventions, including no medications and no need for surgical delivery. This situation is an example of what Davis–Floyd (2024) calls humanistic birth, combining approaches from midwifery and biomedicine (see also Chapter 6).

RACISM, COLONIALISM, AND BIOMEDICINE IN BIRTH

The ascendancy of biomedicine in the United States—similar to Canada, Australia, New Zealand, and other settler colonial states— has a disturbing history as it pertains to women and especially Black and Indigenous women. Gynecology addresses the range of female bodily concerns other than pregnancy and birth, which are the focus of obstetrics. Based on the presumption that male bodies and their functioning represent normal human anatomy and physiology, the predisposition in biomedicine is to treat female bodies as abnormalities. Gynecology and obstetrics are oriented toward approaching even normal and healthy physiological processes, like menstruation or birth, as disorderly or risky.

The establishment of gynecology in the United States is connected directly to the pain and suffering of enslaved Black women.

Infamously, J. Marion Sims became acclaimed as the father of modern gynecology based on the experimental surgeries he performed on the bodies of 12 enslaved women during the 1840s (Cooper Owens 2018). Only the names of three women are known to us today: Anarcha, Betsey, and Lucy. Over the course of five years, they endured the procedures that Sims claimed would fix the women's injuries, which they suffered during birth, and restore their capacities to work and to reproduce (Roberts 1997). The women received no anesthesia because of racist assumptions that Black people feel less pain than white people do. This racist claim has persisted in the twenty-first century. In a 2016 survey of US medical students, about half agreed with statements expressing false beliefs about biological differences between Black and white people, such as the idea that Black skin is thicker than white skin (Hoffman et al. 2016). When biomedical doctors bring these uninformed and unexamined biases into their work, they may fail to provide appropriate care for Black people. Implicit bias is understood to be a factor in the disproportionately higher rate of maternal death among Black women than among other women in the United States today (Saluja and Bryant 2021). This is just one manifestation of the obstetric racism described by Davis (2019) (see also Chapter 6).

In the late nineteenth and early twentieth centuries, obstetricians engaged in active efforts to discredit midwives providing skilled care for other women in their communities, including calls to legally ban their activities which were claimed to be guided by ignorance. By the mid- and late-twentieth century, authoritative knowledge of pregnancy and birth was associated not with female experiences and the perspectives of birthing women and midwives, but with the acquired expertise and credentials of male biomedical doctors. Black and Indigenous birth attendants were particularly targeted due to sexist and racist assumptions about their knowledge and ability, with consequences for the communities they had served.

The experiences of the native people known in the United States as members of the Crow tribe are recounted by Brianna Theobald (2019), a scholar of Native American history, in her book, *Reproduction on the Reservation*. Even after being forced onto reservation lands in Montana during the 1880s, Crow women continued to seek care during pregnancy and birth from other skilled women. By avoiding the white physicians who were assigned to the reservation, Crow women also avoided puerperal fever, also known as childbed fever, which was a major cause of maternal death for white American women at the time. The bacterial infections which cause puerperal fever can be spread by unhygienic practices like the failure of people assisting births to simply wash their hands—a fact that was not understood by scientists until the late nineteenth century. In Europe and North America, midwives were blamed, but the incidences of fever and death were higher among women attended by physicians. The same physicians were reluctant to adopt appropriate hygienic practices (like handwashing) even after one of their peers, the Hungarian physician Ignaz Semmelweis, provided proof of their efficacy. Their initial unwillingness to change their practice produced more maternal deaths.

On the Crow reservation, doctors were initially indifferent to the women's activities. They became more interventionist in their approach to pregnancies and births as the US government became more aggressive in implementing its policies to "assimilate" native people. The US government's focus on the practices of pregnancy and birth is an example of **reproductive governance**, or the exercise of power over people through a range of measures and efforts, including laws, defining and shaping their actions and behaviors of reproduction. Nearly one third of the Crow population is estimated to have died in the 1890s. Awareness of histories like this one is necessary for understanding the imposition of biomedicine as an exercise of colonial power and its continuing legacies today (see Chapter 5 and Chapter 6).

BOX 4.3   CESAREAN SECTION

The global rates of Cesarean section are causes for concern about the care of pregnant and birthing people. Paradoxically, there are both too many and too few surgical deliveries. The World Health Organization sets an "ideal" rate of Cesarean section as 10% to 15% of births representing scientific estimates of the number of medically justified instances. In 2021, the global rate stood at 21.1% with overall trends projecting that 28.5% of births will be surgical deliveries by 2030 (Betran et al. 2021). These high rates of Cesarean section suggest not all of these interventions are medically justified. Within this larger picture, however, attention must be given to the stark disparities between the conditions of birth in high- and low-income countries. The Cesarean section rates in the United States and United Kingdom are higher than 30%. In contrast, across 39 countries in sub-Saharan Africa, only 5% of births are Cesarean sections, indicating unmet needs for pregnant and birthing people, such as access to lifesaving emergency care. These countries also have among the highest numbers of maternal death.

Interestingly, low- and middle-income countries in Latin America and the Caribbean have among the highest numbers of Cesarean rates in the world, averaging about 42.8%. In the Netherlands, one of the wealthiest countries, 14.9% of births are by Cesarean section. These statistics should prompt us to ask about the larger conditions in which people become pregnant and give birth in these varied settings.

Obstetricians have questions about whether their own practices may be creating a necessity for surgical intervention. Electronic fetal monitoring is routinely used in US hospitals to track the rates and patterns of a fetus' heartbeat and a pregnant person's uterine contractions. Since the technology became widely adopted in the 1970s, however, studies show no clear evidence of improved outcomes, such as preventing cerebral palsy (Nelson et al. 2016). Continuous monitoring is evidenced to increase the likelihood of Cesarean section (Paterno et al. 2016). Continuous monitoring (unless newer, wearable monitors are available) requires a birthing person to stay in bed, which makes labor more difficult. A prolonged labor may cause concerns for the birthing person and for the baby. Doctors may suggest surgical delivery to avoid delays and risks for which they might be held responsible. Of biomedical doctors who are sued for medical liability in the United States, a large proportion of claims are made against obstetricians.

The practice of Cesarean section reflects not only the interventionist orientation of biomedicine, but also the circumstances and cultural logics guiding the decisions of birthing people themselves. More than half of births in Brazil are surgical deliveries, including elective procedures which were scheduled in advance. In 2016, in an effort to reduce the high number of Cesarean sections, the country passed a law to prohibit medically unnecessary surgeries before 39 weeks of pregnancy. Pregnant people see their situations quite differently, especially when they may be already caring for other children or have work and other obligations. Rather than confronting the unpredictability of labor and birth—not only when it starts, but how long it lasts—they may see the procedures as necessary to arranging their time. A pregnant person may experience more fear and worry about labor pain than post-surgical recovery. Or they may feel more anxiety and dread about the changes in their bodies resulting from vaginal deliveries than from Cesarean sections. In fact, recovery from the surgeries is associated with pain, prescribed bed rest, and risk of infection (from the incision, or cut into the abdomen). Having a Cesarean section also makes more likely a need for surgical deliveries at subsequent births.

Why there are both too many and too few Cesarean sections is for reasons we ought to understand within the specific contexts of the places and the people in need and want of better care.

WHERE BIRTHS TAKE PLACE: SITES OF SAFETY OR VIOLENCE

The place of birth is important and meaningful. It is striking, for example, that Tarahumara and Ju/'hoansi women seek solitary births in outdoor places, removed from the spaces of home and village (Cheyney and Davis-Floyd 2022). In the Pacific island community of the Ifaluk, women go to a separate birth house where they are attended and cared for by their own mothers and the sisters of their mothers (aunts) and remain in seclusion for ten days after giving birth (Le 2000). Historically, and still to this day in many communities, births have occurred at home, or the space that is shared with kin and family. Sharing a home may be a nuclear family comprised of individuals married to each other and their children or an extended family which includes multiple generations (e.g., parents, their children and partners, and their grandchildren). In patrilocal societies, a custom at marriage is for a woman to leave her family of origin and live with her husband and his parents. At birth, a birthing woman's mother-in-law may be expected to care for her and, afterward, the new baby during a period of postpartum recovery and ritual seclusion for the new mother (see Chapter 5). In other societies, a woman may return to her family of origin to receive attention from her own mother, which has the effect of not only renewing her own ties, but also establishing new ones between her kin and her child. Labor, birth, postpartum recovery, and nurture of the infant at the home can also anchor both mother and baby to the hearth and the house— and to the broader kinship lineage (see Chapter 5). Giving birth at home, then, is a significant practice of family and making kinship.

Ideally, home is a space of familiarity and comfort providing emotional support during birth. It also represents a private and intimate space in which a birthing person feels empowered, in contrast with the public and institutional space of a hospital. Moving births to the hospital was one of the most consequential shifts in the biomedicalization of childbirth and infant care that began earlier in the twentieth century. In turn, seeking safety, support, and empowerment guides the current movements for home birth in the United States, where healthcare is accessed through primarily private medical insurance, which covers hospital births (see also Chapter 6). In the United States and other nations of the Global North, only about 1% or fewer births take place at home. The exception is the Netherlands, where national medical insurance covers home births under the care of professional midwives and 16% of births take place in homes.

At the start of the COVID-19 pandemic in 2020, hospitals in the United States and elsewhere imposed severe limitations on who was allowed to be present at births aside from doctors and nurses, so that a partner or other support person might be restricted from accompanying a birthing person. These restrictions, alongside worries that birthing people suspected of having the virus might be separated from their new babies and fears that going to a hospital by itself posed a risk of getting sick with the virus, have been linked to a bump in the number of home births attended by midwives. The numbers were still quite small, but they increased by 19% from 38,506, or 1% of all US births in 2019 to 45,646 or 1.3% in 2020 (Aragão 2022).

In the European Union, with the exception of the Netherlands, 98% of births occur in hospitals, and in most nations of the Global North, almost all births occur in hospitals, including 97% in Australia and 98% in the United States (Galkova et al. 2022). The situation is starkly different in most nations of the Global South. Namibia, a middle-income country in sub-Saharan Africa, has one of the highest numbers of hospital births (83%), while in neighboring Angola, 35% of births occur in hospitals (Gage et al. 2021). A small number of births also take place in clinics or other institutional settings, but all other births are at home. The location of birth is a concern in the policies and practices of "safe motherhood." The term refers to the aim of reducing the number of pregnancy and birth-related deaths; it is the name given to a global network of programs and series of projects launched in 1987 by organizations like the United Nations and World Bank. One goal of safe motherhood has been to promote hospital births in the Global South where there are high numbers of maternal deaths. Advocates for maternal health and reproductive justice rightly ask, however, whether increasing hospital births addresses the needs of pregnant and birthing people (Strong 2022). They may not have money to cover medical fees and other expenses; for instance, there may be few hospitals and people in rural areas may not have transportation to reach them. Time is essential in emergency care and birthing people and their babies may die due to delays in being referred to the hospital and then taken there. The hospitals, however, may be inadequately resourced and managed. The staff working there may be undertrained and overwhelmed, leading to high rates of maternal mortality.

Obstetric violence is the term used to refer to a range of disrespectful and abusive behaviors directed at birthing people by doctors, nurses, and other professional staff (Oluoch-Aridi et al. 2022). Birthing people may go to a hospital expecting care, but instead may experience mistreatment including verbal or physical abuse and neglect or abandonment of their care. Women who are poor and come from minoritized ethnic communities have been especially subject to obstetric violence, which is clearly connected to inequalities of power and status. Awareness of obstetric violence originates in Latin America as part of the larger movements asserting women's right to live free of violence. In countries of the Global South, activists are organized around the cause of dignified birth. In the United States, Dána-Ain Davis (2019) built on this concept to explore how systemic racism interacts with obstetric violence to produce **obstetric racism** (see Chapter 6).

Structural violence refers to the damage done to people not through physical force, but the actions and inactions of social institutions engaged in their business as usual. These institutions and their activities reflect and reinforce an accumulating range of inequities and injustices, as witnessed in the example of incarcerated women's experiences of pregnancy and birth. The numbers of people of color in prisons or jails have been demonstrated to result from racist disproportionality of policing and convictions with broad and deep impacts on families and communities (Pettit and Gutierrez 2018). Women, many of them mothers, comprise a growing number held in local jails, often while not convicted and waiting to be tried for non-violent property or drug violations (Kajstura and Sawyer 2024). Even while giving birth, incarcerated women have been handcuffed, then been separated from their babies who may be removed to a hospital nursery instead of rooming-in together due to purported concerns for the newborn (Sufrin 2018). This disrupts their bonding and breast-feeding, with profound consequences for maternal and infant health and wellbeing (see Chapter 5). Interventions can and ought to be made to support dignified birth and postpartum care of new mothers and babies—as a larger project to undo the structural violence and obstetric racism reproduced by these conditions. There are ongoing movements and efforts to restore holistic models of care and cultural respect and safety in birth around the world (see Chapter 6).

SUMMARY

- Pregnancy and birth are central experiences of being human that both shape and are shaped by human society, history, culture as well as of human biology and evolution. Anthropologists today seek to analyze and address the inequities that shape the diverse experiences of pregnancy and birth across the world in relation to these biocultural foundations.
- How and why pregnancy and birth came to be understood as conditions requiring biomedical treatment and supervision are connected historically to colonialism and racism. Knowing this history enables us to see the broad and deep roots of reproductive injustices and inequalities that persist and concern us today, and provide insight into systems in place that continue to reproduce these inequities.
- The biomedicalization of birth globally has led to marked shifts in birth attendants, birth place, and birth systems, with the

result of increasingly technological and interventionist treatment of pregnancy and birth. These changes have been accompanied by some improvements but have also been marked by the perpetuation of violence, disempowerment, and pervasive inequities. Control over people's birthing practices has been and still is an exercise of power over people themselves, whether it is men's authority over women or the policies of colonial occupiers implemented on displaced people.

FURTHER EXPLORING

PREGNANCY

See *The Routledge Handbook on Anthropology and Reproduction*, edited by Sallie Han and Cecília Tomori (2022), for chapters by Elise Andaya (2022); Sallie Han (2022); Karen Kramer, Amanda Veile, and Paula Ivey Henry (2022); Richard Powis (2022); Nete Schwennesen and Tine M. Gammeltoft (2022); and Elly Teman and Tsipy Ivry (2022). See the references for more information.

The history of pregnancy testing, especially its ancient history, is a topic of interest for many people, not only researchers. This 2018 article in *Smithsonian* describes some of the scholarship and includes a link to a 1963 article, published in *Medical History*, testing the wheat and barley method of pregnancy diagnosis: www.smithsonianmag.com/smart-news/egyptia n-papyrus-reveals-old-wives-tale-very-very-old-indeed-180970066.

BIRTH

See *The Routledge Handbook on Anthropology and Reproduction*, edited by Sallie Han and Cecília Tomori (2022), for chapters by Melissa Cheyney and Robbie Davis-Floyd (2022); Holly Dunsworth (2022); Mounia El Kotni (2022); Julie Johnson-Searcy and Angela N. Castañeda (2022); April Nowell, Lisa M. Mitchell, and Helen Kurki (2002); Jackline Oluoch-Aridi, Vania Smith-Oka, Jessica Dailey, and Ellyn Milan (2022); Karen R. Rosenberg and Wenda R. Trevathan (2022); and Adrienne Strong (2022). See the references for more information.

Karen Rosenberg discusses her research on birth and human evolution in this short YouTube video by biological anthropologist John

Hawks: "Interview with Karen Rosenberg About the Evolution of the Human Pelvis" (2014) www.youtube.com/watch?v=JY6i8VW7egM.

The exploitation of Black enslaved women in the history of gynecology is the topic of this episode of "Distillations," a podcast produced by the Science History Institute in Philadelphia: www.sciencehistory.org/stories/distillations-pod/the-mothers-of-gynecology.

A statue honoring J. Marion Sims was removed in 2018 from New York City's Central Park where it had been placed in 1959. In 2022, a monument to the women who were subjected unwillingly to Sims' experimental surgeries, called Mothers of Gynecology, was unveiled in Montgomery, Alabama. Learn about it and other creative and community projects honoring these women at this website: www.anarchalucybetsey.org.

REFERENCES

Andaya, Elise. 2022. "Reproductive Governance in Practice: A Comparison of State-Provided Reproductive Healthcare in Cuba and the United States." In *The Routledge Handbook of Anthropology and Reproduction*, edited by Sallie Han and Cecília Tomori, 123–136. Abingdon and New York: Routledge.

Annual Capri Workshop Group. 2020. "Early Pregnancy Loss: The Default Outcome for Fertilized Human Oocytes." *Journal of Assisted Reproduction and Genetics* 37(5): 1057–1063. doi:10.1007/s10815-020-01749-y.

Aragão, Carolina. 2022. "Home Births Rose 19% in 2020 as Pandemic Hit the US." *Pew Research*, July 28. https://pewrsr.ch/3PWTveG.

Betran, Ana Pilar, Jiangfeng Ye, Ann Beth Moller et al. 2021. Trends and Projections of Caesarean Section Rates: Global and Regional Estimates. *BMJ Global Health* 6(6): e005671. doi:10.1136/bmjgh-2021-005671.

Brave Heart, Maria Yellow Horse. 1999. "Gender Differences in the Historical Trauma Response Among the Lakota." *Journal of Health & Social Policy* 10(4): 1–21. doi:10.1300/J045v10n04_01.

Cheyney, Melissa and Robbie Davis-Floyd. 2022. "Rituals and Rites of Childbirth across Cultures." In *The Routledge Handbook of Anthropology and Reproduction*, edited by Sallie Han and Cecília Tomori, 480–493. Abingdon and New York: Routledge.

Cooper Owens, Deirdre. 2018. *Medical Bondage: Race, Gender, and the Origins of American Gynecology*. Athens, GA: The University of Georgia Press.

Craven, Christa. 2019. *Reproductive Losses: Challenges to LGBTQ Family-Making*. Abingdon and New York: Routledge.

Davis, Dána-Ain. 2019. *Reproductive Injustice: Racism, Pregnancy, and Premature Birth.* New York: NYU Press.

Davis-Floyd, Robbie. 2024. *Birth as an American Rite of Passage.* 3rd ed. Berkeley, CA: University of California Press.

Davis-Floyd, Robbie. 2024. "Obstetrics and Midwifery in the United States: The Tensions between the Technocratic and Midwifery Models of Maternity Care." In *A Companion to the Anthropology of Reproductive Medicine and Technology*, edited by Cecilia Coale Van Hollen and Nayantara Sheoran Appleton, 56–69. Hoboken, NJ: John Wiley & Sons.

Drife, J. 2002. "The Start of Life: A History of Obstetrics." *Postgraduate Medical Journal* 8: 311–315. doi:10.1136/pmj.78.919.311.

Dunsworth, Holly. 2022. "There Is No Evolutionary 'Obstetrical Dilemma.'" In *The Routledge Handbook of Anthropology and Reproduction*, edited by Sallie Han and Cecília Tomori, 441–453. Abingdon and New York: Routledge.

El Kotni, Mounia. 2022. "Midwifery in Cross-Cultural Perspectives." In *The Routledge Handbook of Anthropology and Reproduction*, edited by Sallie Han and Cecília Tomori, 454–467. Abingdon and New York: Routledge.

Falu, Nessette. 2022. "Invisible Hands: The Reproductivities of Queer(ing) and Race(ing) Gynecology." In *The Routledge Handbook of Anthropology and Reproduction*, edited by Sallie Han and Cecília Tomori, 305–319. Abingdon and New York: Routledge.

Falu, Nessette and Christa Craven. 2024. "Queer Reproductive Futures." In *A Companion to the Anthropology of Reproductive Medicine and Technology*, edited by Cecilia Coale Van Hollen and Nayantara Sheoran Appleton, 219–233. Hoboken, NJ: John Wiley & Sons.

Ferrara, Mel Lynwood. 2024. "Inconceivable: Cisnormativity and the Management of Trans and Intersex Reproduction." In *A Companion to the Anthropology of Reproductive Medicine and Technology*, edited by Cecilia Coale Van Hollen and Nayantara Sheoran Appleton, 234–249. Hoboken, NJ: John Wiley & Sons.

Gage, Anna D., *et al.*2021. "Hospital Delivery and Neonatal Mortality in 37 Countries in Sub-Saharan Africa and South Asia: An Ecological Study." *PLoS Med* 18(12): e1003843. doi:10.1371/journal.pmed.1003843.

Galkova, Gabriela, *et al.*2022. "Comparison of Frequency of Home Births in the Member States of the EU between 2015 and 2019." *Global Pediatric Health* 9: 1–8. https://journals.sagepub.com/doi/10.1177/2333794X211070916.

Gammeltoft, Tine M. 2015. *Haunting Images: A Cultural Account of Selective Reproduction.* Berkeley, CA: University of California Press.

Ginsburg, Faye and Rayna Rapp. 2024. "Cripping Reproduction: The Intersections of Pregnancy and Disability." In *A Companion to the Anthropology of Reproductive Medicine and Technology*, edited by Cecilia Coale Van Hollen and Nayantara Sheoran Appleton, 282–297. Hoboken, NJ: John Wiley & Sons.

Gray, Peter B., Alex Straftis, and Kermyt G. Anderson. 2022. "Men and Reproduction: Perspectives from Biological Anthropology." In *The Routledge Handbook of Anthropology and Reproduction*, edited by Sallie Han and Cecília Tomori, 52–67. Abingdon and New York: Routledge.

Han, Sallie. 2013. *Pregnancy in Practice: Expectation and Experience in the Contemporary US*. New York and Oxford: Berghahn Books.

Han, Sallie. 2022. "Bringing Language into the Anthropology of Reproduction: The Text and Talk of Pregnancy." In *The Routledge Handbook of Anthropology and Reproduction*, edited by Sallie Han and Cecília Tomori, 396–409. Abingdon and New York: Routledge.

Hodnett, Ellen D., Simon Gates, G. Justus Hofmeyr, and Carol Sakala. 2013. "Continuous Support for Women During Childbirth." *Cochrane Database of Systematic Reviews*, 7: CD003766. doi:10.1002/14651858.CD003766.pub5.

Hoffman, Kelly M., *et al.* 2016. "Racial Bias in Pain Assessment and Treatment Recommendations, and False Beliefs About Biological Differences Between Blacks and Whites." *Proceedings of the National Academy of Sciences* 113(16): 4296–4301. doi:10.1073/pnas.1516047113.

Hrdy, Sarah Blaffer. 2024. *Father Time: A Natural History of Men and Babies*. Princeton, NJ: Princeton University Press.

Ivry, Tsipy. 2010. *Embodying Culture: Pregnancy in Japan and Israel*. New Brunswick, NJ: Rutgers University Press.

Jayashankar, Siva Shantini *et al.* 2023. "Non-Invasive Prenatal Testing (NIPT): Reliability, Challenges, and Future Directions." *Diagnostics* 13(15): 2570. doi:10.3390/diagnostics13152570.

Johnson-Searcy, Julie, and Angela N. Castañeda. 2022. "Doulas: Negotiating Boundaries in Birth." In *The Routledge Handbook of Anthropology and Reproduction*, edited by Sallie Han and Cecília Tomori, 468–479. Abingdon and New York: Routledge.

Jordan, Brigitte. 1993. *Birth in Four Cultures: A Cross-Cultural Investigation of Childbirth in Yucatan, Holland, Sweden, and the United States*. Long Grove, IL: Waveland Press.

Kajstura, Aleks and Wendy Sawyer. 2024. "Women's Mass Incarcerations: The Whole Pie 2024." *Prison Policy*, March 5. www.prisonpolicy.org/reports/pie2024women.html.

Kirczenow MacDonald, Trevor, *et al.* 2020. "Disrupting the Norms: Reproduction, Gender Identity, Gender Dysphoria, and Intersectionality." *International Journal of Transgender Health* 22(1–2): 18–29.

Kramer, Karen L., Amanda Veile, and Paula Ivey Henry. 2022. "Reproduction in Biological Anthropology." In *The Routledge Handbook of Anthropology and Reproduction*, edited by Sallie Han and Cecília Tomori, 19–35. Abingdon and New York: Routledge.

Le, Huynh-Nhu. 2000. "Never Leave Your Little Due Alone: Raising an Ifaluk Child." In *A World of Babies: Imagined Childcare Guides for Seven*

Societies, edited by Judy S. DeLoache and Alma Gottlieb, 199–220. Cambridge: Cambridge University Press.

Moseson, Heidi*et al.*2021. "Abortion Experiences and Preferences of Transgender, Nonbinary, and Gender-Expansive People in the United States." *American Journal of Obstetrics and Gynecology* 224(4): 376.e1–376.e11. doi:10.1016/j.ajog.2020.09.035.

Nelson, Karin B., Thomas Sartwelle, and Dwight Rouse. 2016. "Electronic Fetal Monitoring, Cerebral Palsy, and Caesarean Section: Assumptions Versus Evidence." *BMJ* c355: i6405. doi:10.1136/bmj.i6405.

Nowell, April, Lisa M. Mitchell, and Helen Kurki. 2002. "Conceiving of Reproduction in Archaeology." In *The Routledge Handbook of Anthropology and Reproduction*, edited by Sallie Han and Cecília Tomori, 68–83. Abingdon and New York: Routledge.

Oluoch-Aridi, Jackline, *et al.*2022. "Making Dignified Care the Norm: Examining Obstetric Violence and Reproductive Justice in Kenya." In *The Routledge Handbook of Anthropology and Reproduction*, edited by Sallie Han and Cecília Tomori, 494–509. Abingdon and New York: Routledge.

Paterno, Mary T., Kathleen McElroy, and Mary Regan. 2016. "Electronic Fetal Monitoring and Cesarean Birth: A Scoping Review." *Birth* 43(4): 277–284. doi:10.1111/birt.12247.

Pettit, Becky, and Carmen Gutierrez. 2018. "Mass Incarceration and Racial Inequality." *American Journal of Economics and Sociology*, 77(3–4): 1153–1182. doi:10.1111/ajes.12241.

Powis, Richard. 2022. "From Couvade to 'Men's Involvement': Sociocultural Perspectives of Expectant Fatherhood." In *The Routledge Handbook of Anthropology and Reproduction*, edited by Sallie Han and Cecília Tomori, 410–421. Abingdon and New York: Routledge.

Rapp, Rayna. 1999. *Testing Women, Testing the Fetus: The Social Impact of Amniocentesis in America*. Abingdon and New York: Routledge.

Reed, Richard K. 2005. *Birthing Fathers: The Transformation of Men in American Rites of Birth*. New Brunswick, NJ: Rutgers University Press.

Roberts, Dorothy E. 1997. *Killing the Black Body: Race, Reproduction, and the Meaning of Liberty*. New York: Pantheon Books.

Rosenberg, Karen R. and Wenda R. Trevathan. 2022. "The Obstetrical Dilemma Revisited—Revisited." In *The Routledge Handbook of Anthropology and Reproduction*, edited by Sallie Han and Cecília Tomori, 425–440. Abingdon and New York: Routledge.

Rothman, Barbara Katz. 1986. *The Tentative Pregnancy*. New York: Viking.

Running Bear, Ursula*et al.*2019. "The Impact of Individual and Parental American Indian Boarding School Attendance on Chronic Physical Health of Northern Plains Tribes." *Family & Community Health* 42(1): 1–7. doi:10.1097/FCH.0000000000000205.

Saluja, Bani, and Zenobia Bryant. 2021. "How Implicit Bias Contributes to Racial Disparities in Maternal Morbidity and Mortality in the United States." *Journal of Women's Health* 30(2): 270–273. doi:10.1089/jwh.2020.8874.

Schwennesen, Nete and Tine M. Gammeltoft. 2022. "Prenatal Screening and Diagnosis." In *The Routledge Handbook of Anthropology and Reproduction*, edited by Sallie Han and Cecília Tomori, 351–364. Abingdon and New York: Routledge.

Shostak, Marjorie. 1981. *Nisa: The Life and Words of a !Kung Woman*. Cambridge, MA: Harvard University Press.

Small, Meredith. 2003. "How Many Fathers Are Best?" *Discover*, April 1. www.discovermagazine.com/health/how-many-fathers-are-best.

Smith-Oka, Vania and Simona Spiegel. 2024. "Into Doctors' Hands: Obstetric Praxis in Anthropology." In *A Companion to the Anthropology of Reproductive Medicine and Technology*, edited by Cecilia Coale Van Hollen and Nayantara Sheoran Appleton, 41–55. Hoboken, NJ: John Wiley & Sons.

Strong, Adrienne. 2022. "Maternal Mortality." In *The Routledge Handbook of Anthropology and Reproduction*, edited by Sallie Han and Cecília Tomori, 510–523. Abingdon and New York: Routledge.

Stroumsa, Daphna, Michelle H. Moniz, Halley Crissman, *et al.* 2023. "Pregnancy Outcomes in a US Cohort of Transgender People." *JAMA* 29(21): 1879–1881. doi:10.1001/jama.2023.7688.

Sufrin, Carolyn. 2018. "Making Mothers in Jail: Carceral Reproduction of Normative Motherhood." *Reproductive Biology, Medicine and Society Online* 7, 55–65. doi:10.1016/j.rbms.2018.10.018.

Teman, Elly and Tsipy Ivry. 2022. "Pregnancy and the Anthropology of Reproduction." In *The Routledge Handbook of Anthropology and Reproduction*, edited by Sallie Han and Cecília Tomori, 383–395. Abingdon and New York: Routledge.

Thayer, Zaneta and Theresa Gildner. 2022. "Developmental Origins of Health and Disease: Evidence, Proposed Mechanisms, and Ideas for Future Application." In *The Routledge Handbook of Anthropology and Reproduction*, edited by Sallie Han and Cecília Tomori, 36–51. Abingdon and New York: Routledge.

Theobald, Brianna. 2019. *Reproduction on the Reservation: Pregnancy, Childbirth, and Colonialism in the Long Twentieth Century*. Chapel Hill, NC: University of North Carolina Press.

Twine, France Winddance and Marcin Smietana. 2022. "the Racial Contours of Queer Reproduction." In *The Routledge Handbook of Anthropology and Reproduction*, edited by Sallie Han and Cecília Tomori, 289–304. Abingdon and New York: Routledge.

Wegner, Josef. 2006. "The Magical Birth Brick." *Expedition Magazine* 48(2). www.penn.museum/sites/expedition/the-magical-birth-brick/.

5

POSTPARTUM, INFANT, AND OTHER CARE

In much of the Global North, cultural expectations are that reproduction ends with childbirth. Yet, this is clearly not the case when we look at people's experiences more closely using our anthropological lens. This chapter highlights that reproduction is a process that continues beyond birth and demands collective and cooperative effort. What happens after birth has been often overlooked in narrowly framed conversations about reproduction, yet they are central to understanding reproduction in the first place. The chapter begins with a brief discussion of ideas and practices concerning physical recovery and social reintegration of parents after birth. Next, the chapter turns to the evolutionary importance of closeness and the roots of infant care in human societies, focusing the discussion on breastfeeding and infant sleep. Building on the previous chapter, we highlight how colonial and commercial interests coupled with biomedicalization have transformed care for new parents and babies. These changes—which contrast with evolutionary and cross-cultural models of infant care—led to significant harms in the Global South and perpetuated inequities in the US. The final part of the chapter showcases diverse movements challenging these models and restoring and reclaiming systems of care that have been profoundly disrupted. Our biocultural evolutionary roots and cross-cultural models point the way toward the importance of nurture and collective care. We, too, can support efforts to rebuild these systems and work together toward **reproductive justice** (see Chapter 1).

DOI: 10.4324/9781003379416-5

THE POSTPARTUM PERIOD—CARE, COMMUNITY, AND KINSHIP

Anthropologists have long documented cultural practices postpartum that prescribe a period of rest for the birthing mother where others support her and take over heavy labor, household and other tasks and often assist with infant care as well. This period of rest usually lasts at least 30–40 days. Most cultures recognize this period as a liminal and vulnerable one, which requires special attention and community participation. During this time mothers can focus on healing from birth and caring for the newborn infant, who requires frequent feeding, closeness and intensive care. Usually, more experienced women relatives assist the mother with learning to breastfeed and address any issues that may arise. Other widespread cultural practices include uterine massage, eating special restorative foods while having restrictions on other foods, or staying close to the hearth to warm the body—all aiming to restore health and wellbeing to the mother and to facilitate her ability to feed and care for the newborn.

While in many communities around the world this period of rest is supportive of new mothers' needs, some of the postpartum practices can also be restrictive and impart control over them. Some of the experiences of control have been documented in patrilineal kinship systems, where mothers are recovering at the household of the father's family. In these instances, such as documented in ethnographic work from China, mothers may be isolated from their own natal support systems and experience the postpartum period as more restrictive than helpful. In recent years, well-off expectant couples in South Korea have turned to commercialized postpartum services, shifting the focus from larger kin relations, as when new mothers received care from their own mothers, to conjugal ties as attention is expected from husbands to wives who have given birth (Kang 2014).

Another key element of these postpartum practices includes incorporating the new baby into kinship systems, which may take place over time. Babies may not be considered fully formed persons when they are born. For instance, in some cultures they are considered transient beings or spirits until they are named, which may take place at a later time—usually after the initial dangerous newborn period, when mortality is high, has passed. Among the Beng, in Côte d'Ivoire, for instance, babies are considered to belong to the spirit world initially and they may be called back to that world (Gottlieb 2015). They need to be persuaded to stay using a series of ritual and caregiving practices. Indeed, babies are often not named until a certain number of days have passed when it is more certain that they will survive.

Incorporating the baby into kinship systems is often accomplished gradually, and via various acts of nurture. Breastfeeding is a key process among these. In many settings breastfeeding is directly linked to other bodily substances. For instance, in Malaysia breastmilk is considered to derive from blood, which fed the fetus during pregnancy (Carsten 1997). Blood and milk are also linked to the house and hearth, so breastfeeding a baby simultaneously anchors them to kin networks and to the house. This also means that breastfeeding another's child can also help incorporate them into kinship systems.

Anthropologists have documented **milk kinship**—wherein breastfeeding and breastmilk is recognized to create relatedness—across numerous cultures and across numerous historical traditions dating back many centuries. In these settings breastfeeding is formally recognized as a means of creating lasting kinship ties. This also means that in some contexts there are also prohibitions that would prevent a child who was breastfed by a woman to later marry their milk sibling because that would create an incestuous relationship. This is a common interpretation in Islamic cultures. Because of the potential kinship implications of breastfeeding and even consuming breastmilk from someone other than the biological mother, creating human milk banks to help premature or sick babies has been challenging in some settings. This is because **milk banking** involves pooling milk from multiple people who may be unknown to the recipient, and could lead to the potential for incest in the future. However, there have been efforts to overcome these problems while remaining respectful of local kinship traditions.

Physical proximity is another key element of cross-cultural infant care traditions and plays a role in making kinship, with babies being fed frequently throughout the day and night, and mothers sleeping next to them. As babies grow, they may be carried on the body of the mother, with access to frequent breastfeeding. Others—such as grandmothers, sisters, and siblings—may also carry the baby, and can breastfeed the baby as well when the mother may be away for a period of time. While **cross-nursing**—or breastfeeding another's infant—is common across cultures, it has become less common and even viewed negatively in many settings in the Global North, including in the US, but these practices are returning as breastfeeding becomes more common in these contexts. Notably, someone who has breastfed an infant in the past can re-establish breastfeeding again with stimulation (e.g. grandmothers) even without pregnancy. **Lactation** (the production of milk) can also be induced without prior pregnancy, but this usually requires medication in combination with stimulation. All of these practices play a role in making kinship.

EVOLUTIONARY ROOTS

The common patterns of closeness, carrying, frequent breastfeeding, and proximate sleep across cultures have important evolutionary roots (Trevathan and Rosenberg 2016; Kramer, Veile, and Henry 2022). Anthropologists and biologists have studied other mammals in comparison with humans and have identified some common patterns. Mammals are distinguished by lactation, which is an evolutionary adaptation whose roots date back to the era of dinosaurs. Proto-mammals laid eggs and covered them in a substance that helped to keep the egg hydrated and safe from microbes. This is the evolutionary foundation of secretions that nourished young, and became part of an increasingly sophisticated communication system between parent and child through the adaptation of the nipple and the suckling process that most mammals possess (Power and Schulkin 2016).

Different mammals occupy different environments and have developed different reproductive and lactation strategies. Among them, primates are distinguished by giving birth to few, large-brained young, and caring for them for an extended period of time after birth as they mature. This kind of reproduction requires close proximity to care for relatively immature young, who are carried and cling to their mothers' fur, nursing frequently during day and night, and sleeping in close proximity with one another. Their milk is dilute, reflecting this frequent feeding strategy. This is quite different from other mammals that cache their babies while they forage, such as rabbits, who may be away from their young for extended periods of time and feed them when they return.

Humans also have some special additional characteristics that distinguish us even from other primates (Rosenberg 2021; Trevathan and Rosenberg 2016). Humans are born very vulnerable, with no ability to cling to fur, and adults do not possess fur to cling to. Infant brain functioning is not developed enough to fully regulate body temperature or breathing and many other basic physiological functions, and newborns rely on co-regulation of their mothers derived from closeness and frequent breastfeeding to stay alive. Human babies also have an exceptionally long period of brain maturation after they are born—it takes years for humans to learn to walk, acquire speech, and to eventually be able to care for their basic needs. Humans are a fully biocultural species, and infants experience a tremendous amount of socialization during their infancy, and they also become part of a community during this time.

Closeness is a key element of ensuring survival during the early parts of this very vulnerable time. Closeness via skin-to-skin contact enables physiological co-regulation. Indeed, it is so important for survival that it has been recently recognized by updates of major global guidelines that recommend **kangaroo mother care** that entails continuous skin-to-skin contact for premature, small, and other vulnerable babies as routine care across high-, medium-, and low-resource settings (WHO 2023). This is a major change from previous models that involve separation. Closeness also serves other important evolutionary purposes—it has kept babies safe from other hazards, like cold or bad weather and predation. The mother or another caregiver is there to keep the baby safe and respond in case of illness or natural disasters or threats from other humans as in the case of conflict.

Lactation is a key part of the package of adaptations within this system that is enabled through closeness. Immediate skin-to-skin contact provides the opportunity for babies to initiate breastfeeding right after birth, which plays a key role in setting lactation into motion. These critical early hours and continued opportunities to breastfeed frequently as needed helps to set breastfeeding on a trajectory that helps to ensure that the baby can be successfully fed exclusively for six months, which helps babies grow, stay healthy and develop well. After that, other foods can be gradually introduced alongside breastfeeding, which usually continues for two to three years (see Tomori et al. 2018; Halcrow et al. 2022).

Breastfeeding delivers nutrition, hydration, immunological protection, and a slew of hormones and other bioactive compounds that are continually adapted to the infant's specific needs and environment (Pérez-Escamilla et al. 2023). Lactation responds to both the baby and the environment, changing composition throughout the day and over the course of the babies' development. For instance, in warmer environments, the milk becomes more diluted, ensuring adequate hydration. Hormones in the milk help set the babies' circadian rhythm, helping babies gradually coordinate their wake and sleep cycles in coordination with day- and nighttime. Human milk contains life-saving protection against viruses and bacteria. The babies' saliva helps to send signals to the mother to make tailor-made immune factors that tackle specific microorganisms to which the baby is exposed. Biological anthropologists have studied all these sophisticated mechanisms and even more—like how milk adapts to the challenging environments of high altitude, or how human milk sends signals that help to set the metabolic trajectory of the infant, which has lifelong consequences (Quinn 2021).

Frequent breastfeeding also plays a role in the reproductive trajectories of mothers. Breastfeeding suppresses ovulation, which helps produce birth intervals that provide adequate time for mothers' bodies to recover and to ensure that the infant is able to grow and thrive before the next pregnancy arrives. Breastfeeding is also associated with fewer cases of ovarian and breast cancers, and also helps prevent cardiovascular disease and other metabolic disorders. In these many ways breastfeeding plays a key role in ensuring long-term maternal health, infant and young child survival and in the prevention of infant and young child malnutrition. Important to note is that breastfeeding has always been a biocultural process. This means both that breastfeeding has been intimately intertwined with local cultural beliefs and practices, and that its practice and duration have varied. Bioarchaeological studies with increasingly sophisticated scientific methods provide detailed evidence on breastfeeding patterns and additional foods that were introduced to infants and young children (complementary foods) (see Halcrow et al. 2022). In a case study of a community in Eastern Zhou-dynasty China that lasted over 500 years from 771–221 BCE, Halcrow et al. (2022)

demonstrated breastfeeding lasted from two to four years and complementary foods differed by gender, reflecting broader patterns of the rise of patriarchal social systems. While variation in infant care and feeding patterns always existed, the profound disruptions in these systems in the more recent past are novel.

BOX 5.1   BREASTFEEDING IS A PROCESS—NOT A PRODUCT!

A key anthropological insight is that breastfeeding is a biocultural process entailing the close interaction of mother and child—and sometimes others as well. This process needs to be considered in its fullness, in the entire range of biological and social interactions that it entails, and how these biocultural processes are intertwined. This process cannot be reduced to the product of this interaction—the milk (Van Esterik 1996). While human milk itself is very interesting, and constitutes its own biological system, it originates through the interaction of the lactating person, child, and their environment. This is especially important as human milk is increasingly appreciated by biomedical science for its many complex properties. While this focus on the milk and its components is necessary and overdue, as lactation was largely ignored for many decades and remains understudied, exclusive focus on milk can serve to reduce the complexity of the process of breastfeeding and overlook its significance for human sociality and human development. The narrow focus on milk can also play into other dynamics fueled by an industry that profits from undermining breastfeeding.

WHAT HAPPENED TO THE POSTPARTUM PERIOD AND INFANT CARE?

You might wonder: if rest, closeness, community, and kinship are so important postpartum, then why do some of these practices differ so much across the Global North today? That is the story of a key area of study in anthropology—and directly tied to major social transformations.

The biggest ones entail the major transition to industrial capitalism and colonial expansion by European nations. Migration to urban centers and factory labor set the stage for increasingly challenging labor practices that did not accommodate children and were often accompanied by difficult living conditions, poverty, and disease. At the same time, colonial expansion focused on exploitation of people and extraction of resources in the colonies that rested on made-up racial hierarchies that provided justification for exploitation and pervasive violence. To reflect this intertwining of racial hierarchies with targeted exploitation, scholars have called this process **racial capitalism** (Robinson 2019, see also Chapter 1).

In the colonies, families were violently torn apart, people were transformed into commodities and sold into slavery, and communities experienced displacement, genocide, and repeated atrocities. A key element of colonial rule concerned "civilizing" local populations, and such civilizing efforts were always accompanied by targeting reproduction. Reproduction was, of course, of great interest to colonial powers because it was a key element of controlling populations, and directly influenced the labor power used to fuel resource extraction. For instance, in the Belgian Congo colonizers were quite concerned about breastfeeding that lasted beyond a few months because of its role in suppressing ovulation (Hunt 1998, see also Chapter 2). Colonizers wanted to reduce birth intervals in order to produce more babies, who would grow up to be used as labor for them. Enslavers in the United States and elsewhere were similarly interested in maximizing the productive and reproductive potential of the people they viewed as their property. There are many terrible examples of the tension between maximizing the work that women could carry out while also bearing children who could become profitable for enslavers. Enslaved women were also used to carry out reproductive labor for enslavers, breastfeeding the masters' children while their own may have suffered or died from lack of adequate breastfeeding.

Biomedicalization was closely intertwined with the rise of capitalism and colonialism (see also Chapter 1). In European settings men with medical training increasingly encroached into reproduction, and began marginalizing midwives, who were the traditional caretakers of pregnancy, birth, and postpartum. Once colonial expansion accelerated, medical officers were also an important part of colonial administrations. They played a key role in managing the human populations they controlled, who were treated as commodities and labor power for the extraction of resources. Biomedicalization was also tied up with moral transformation; women's groups often accompanied these medical offers, and targeted communities to adopt a Christian moral framework and relatively novel, "scientific" ways of raising babies that were increasingly common among Euro-Americans.

The intersections of these forces transformed lifeways and the way we understand the world around us. This extends to our understanding of time. Clocks were first synchronized to facilitate the expansion of British railways, which were built to efficiently transport goods derived from resources extracted from the colonies. The coordination of time facilitated the growing focus on efficiency and productivity as measured by the clock. This new, capitalist way of understanding time also made its way into how we understand bodies and fueled new "scientific" ways of measuring and regulating them in biomedical models. For birth, postpartum, and infant care the consequences of this new understanding of time were profound. The clock was wielded as a powerful tool to justify a growing use of medical interventions, and the regimentation of unruly postpartum and infant bodies. In this model there was increasing emphasis on feeding babies by the clock—at set intervals.

With the movement of birth under physician oversight and ultimately into the hospital in Euro-American settings, the postpartum period was fundamentally uprooted. In hospital settings new routines of postpartum and infant care were established that were ostensibly driven by "science." These practices included routine separation of mothers and infants and increasingly medicated births involving numerous interventions where both mother and infant may have needed supportive care. Medicine increasingly fragmented the entire process of childbearing—with obstetricians overseeing birth and pushing midwives—often targeting midwives serving racial and ethnic minority communities—out of practice.

Pediatricians stepped into a space that was previously occupied by midwives who usually cared for women throughout pregnancy and birth, supported them postpartum, and often helped with lactation and other issues. Midwives also often served families across the lifecourse, assisting in times of illness and death. Pediatricians became specialists that oversaw infant care, and while many ostensibly claimed to support breastfeeding, they also expressed contradictory stances that suggested that breastfeeding was inadequate, or even harmful to infants. For instance, the founder of pediatrics in the US, Emmett Holt, expressed these exact contradictory sentiments toward breastfeeding, arguing that breastfeeding was beneficial, while simultaneously arguing that any emotion could damage babies via harming the milk, and also that breastfeeding frequency should be restricted and ultimately quickly eliminated overnight (Tomori 2018b). If babies cried, they were to be allowed to "cry it out"—likely the first documented instance of this ideology that became widespread among elites. In the late nineteenth and early twentieth centuries, pediatricians increasingly argued that babies required separation from their mothers and that their breastfeeding should be restricted. It is no wonder that mothers struggled with breastfeeding, as these practices directly undermined the physiology of breastfeeding.

THE TRANSFORMATION OF BREASTFEEDING TO INFANT FEEDING—AND BACK AGAIN?

Anthropologists have made significant contributions to understanding another intersection of the forces of capitalism, colonialism, and biomedicalization—the development and promotion of infant formula and its role in undermining breastfeeding and perpetuating many inequalities. Physicians and early pediatricians were particularly involved in creating and promoting infant foods that they claimed would help solve what they saw as infant feeding problems or inadequacies of breastfeeding. These problems were usually caused by lack of knowledge about breastfeeding and insufficient skilled support—disruptions of knowledge that were often directly caused by biomedicalization itself. Physicians were making "formulas" derived from cow's milk with modifications to supplement or substitute for breastfeeding. The early pioneer for this was Henry Nestlé, who lacked a medical background altogether, but did possess an entrepreneurial spirit, and who enlisted the support of a high-level Swiss physician to carry out what was in fact a fake study. In that "study" Lébert claimed that breastfeeding was insufficient to meet infants' needs, and they would need Nestlé's product to supplement this deficiency. Nestlé marketed his product to wealthy women, and with medical backing and a series of claims about the health and happiness of infants, these products quickly gained a following, despite any evidence behind them. The products ultimately reached market saturation in Europe, where breastfeeding promotion became more common again in the mid-twentieth century, so infant formula was aggressively promoted in search of new markets to the colonies.

These promotion efforts were buttressed by an entire scientific and biomedical apparatus. Nestlé funded scientific research, conferences and symposia, and other efforts to address malnutrition. Malnutrition, of course, was driven by the colonial exploitation that was concurrently taking place and was impoverishing colonial populations around the world. The scientific apparatus was built to create new markets for Nestlé's products. From the beginning the marketing accompanying the products used biomedical authority to endorse it and lend it credibility. The company—and others that followed suit—established close ties with medical personnel and facilities that would enable them to access maternity wards. They aggressively promoted products both to health professionals and to new mothers themselves. They even employed sales representatives who dressed up like health professionals—so-called Nestlé nurses— who did not actually have any medical credentials. These efforts were highly successful in creating the new markets that formula companies sought. However, instead of addressing malnutrition, they actually caused a devastating crisis of malnutrition, diarrheal disease, and death around the world. The products that were marketed were mixed in settings that lacked sanitation, with unsafe water and equipment that couldn't be easily cleaned, leading to microbial contamination. Formula was also frequently diluted because it was expensive and once the free samples ran out, parents would stretch the formula because they couldn't afford it. Additionally, formula feeding directly undermined breastfeeding, stripping infants from both optimal nutrition and from the immunological protection that it conferred. Together, this caused the sickening of an uncounted number of infants and the deaths of tens of thousands.

The rising number of sick and dying babies prompted communities to raise concerns, and eventually led to the Nestlé Boycott in

1977, which ultimately led to the World Health Assembly (WHA), the decision making body of the World Health Organization (WHO), to adopt an International Code of Marketing of Breast-Milk Substitutes in 1981. The United States voted against it due to its own commercial interests in the companies that profited from this marketing. Despite the adoption of the Code (and even the later proclaimed support for it from the United States), most nations failed to implement the Code as law and enforce it.

At the same time, however, breastfeeding was starting to make a come-back, driven by a wide range of social movements and increasingly supported by medical and public health research that demonstrated its importance for the health of both infants and young children as well as for their mothers. This return of breast-feeding was a conflicted one—since on the one hand mothers were increasingly encouraged to breastfeed, but systems were built for formula feeding and little was done to create the systems that would actually support breastfeeding. Healthcare providers continued to lack training on breastfeeding, and many inadvertently provided advice that was inaccurate or directly contradicted best practices. Hospital practices often directly undermined the physiology of breastfeeding by separation and routine use of commercial milk formula. Formula companies had virtually unfettered access to new parents and marketed their products to them as well as to healthcare providers. It was common to receive "gift" packages of formula with advertisements in bags at the hospital upon discharge—and the use of formula in this early period plays an especially important role in undermining the establishment of breastfeeding and the development of a good milk supply. Early supplementation is associated with lower exclusive breastfeeding and earlier breastfeeding cessation (Pérez-Escamilla et al. 2023). Although breastfeeding has become more accepted in the medical community, training is continuing to be insufficient. Only about a quarter of births take place at a **Baby Friendly Hospital** (BFH) in the United States (Centers for Disease Control and Prevention 2022). To obtain BFH designation, hospitals have to undergo training and implementation of the WHO 10 Steps to Successful Breastfeeding—evidence-based practices that have been shown to improve breastfeeding outcomes—and uphold the International Code of Marketing of Breast-Milk Substitutes.

Even when breastfeeding is initiated after birth at the hospital, where most people give birth, there is serious lack of support when they return home. Skilled lactation support is often lacking, inaccessible, or is poorly coordinated. Additionally, in the United States there is still no federal paid leave, and many parents have to return to work within weeks and even after just a few days. This sets the United States apart from all other high-income nations and nearly all other nations across the world. At work, many employers remain hostile even to milk expression and even fewer provide on-site childcare that would facilitate direct breastfeeding. The PUMP Act, which provides structural support for breastmilk expression at work like breaks and a private space that is not a bathroom, only passed in 2023 and there are still workers whom it does not cover, including those working in the airline industry, which lobbied against the law (US Breastfeeding Committee 2023).

The regulatory landscape also remains challenging. Over 40 years after the adoption of the Code by the WHA, the commercial milk formula sector has grown into a $55 billion industry that has grown and consolidated with a handful of companies—all headquartered in the Global North—controlling the majority of the market. Extensive literature documents that these companies continue to engage in unethical marketing practices that undermine breastfeeding and violate the Code and its subsequent resolutions (Rollins et al. 2023). They manipulate the lack of understanding of baby behaviors and portray them as problematic, in need of solutions that they provide via their products—without evidence to support their claims. They make misleading claims about health, intelligence, and development that are not supported by science. In this effort they create impressions of false equivalence that reduce the process of breastfeeding to human milk, and claim that the components in formula products are the same or even superior to breast milk. These marketing practices target everyone—from caregivers to health professionals, and politicians—in order to capture their audience, change social norms, and ultimately gain profits.

They also systematically target vulnerable communities globally and in wealthier nations. ProPublica, an independent investigative news organization, has recently uncovered documents that showed how the US Trade Representative's Office played a crucial role in changing the language of a WHA resolution to the Code that aimed to stop unethical marketing, ultimately succeeding in watering down the resolution (Waldron and Vogell 2024). They also showed how companies aggressively promote products to poor countries that are entirely unnecessary—such as toddler milks—which contribute to the global obesity crisis (Vogell 2024). In the United States, the industry continues to engage in misleading marketing. Among the many problematic practices, the industry's exclusive contracts with the Women, Infants, and Children (WIC) Supplemental Nutrition program in each state allow companies to build brand loyalty and continue to undermine breastfeeding. Companies also actively promote their products to health professionals with misleading scientific claims delivered via healthcare provider training, conferences, and relationships with professional organizations, including philanthropic efforts that elevate the image of industry. Simultaneously, they lobby politicians to weaken efforts to enhance regulations on marketing and safety.

This situation had profound implications during the 2022 formula crisis. Described in US media as a "shortage," it was in fact caused by the systematic undermining and evasion of regulations to enhance the safety of infant formula manufacturing (Tomori and Palmquist 2022). Contaminated formula sickened and killed some infants, leading to a shut-down of a major plant in Michigan, owned by Abbott, a US-based multinational corporation, which produced a quarter of the nation's formula. Parents whose infants were formula-dependent were sent into crisis. Disproportionately affected were WIC participants who were tied to a specific brand for their formula or who relied on specialty formula products. Moreover, WIC participants are disproportionately racialized minorities—the same populations who have suffered a long history of systemic racism, the destruction of midwifery, and the undermining of breastfeeding in their communities. Unfortunately, although Abbott has since come under investigation by numerous bodies, including the Department of Justice, legislative efforts have not adequately dealt with the root causes of the crisis and have not recognized the link between the industry's highly effective efforts to undermine breastfeeding that leave entire populations vulnerable to the industry's own practices or other system-level shocks. These issues are becoming even more prominent in a time of climate crisis, with communities most affected who have aging infrastructure and have faced systemic neglect—the same communities who have experienced the least support for breastfeeding and face the highest infant mortality. This is just one example of how racial capitalism continues to impact contemporary communities. On the other hand, while a few decades ago only a quarter of mothers had the opportunity to put their babies to breast, today most do so (well over 80%), despite these ongoing inequities and persistent obstacles.

INFANT SLEEP AND BREASTSLEEPING

There are many other consequences of the profound transformation of the postpartum period and infant care that anthropologists have examined in depth (see Ball, Tomori, and McKenna 2019; Rudzik et al. 2022). A key concern has been with infant sleep practices (see Tomori 2018a, 2018b, 2024). Infants routinely slept next to their mothers cross-culturally and historically. Elites, of course, have often relied on others—servants and enslaved persons—to care for their infants, who also usually slept next to them. Over the course of the early twentieth century, the idea of having the baby in a separate room became increasingly fashionable and copied by the middle classes. This was also fueled by the rise of "scientific" parenting that pediatricians advocated, along with regimented feeding practices. Servants were less affordable for the middle classes, and increasingly so even for wealthier individuals. In addition, there were concerns about the quality of these servants, many of whom also breastfed infants. Wealthy people were concerned about "bad" personality characteristics passing on through their milk. These groups were happy to adopt the new practice of scientific infant feeding and formulas promoted by pediatricians, which would remove these undesirable qualities from the equation.

These new practices of separate sleep without another person were not preferred by infants. They protested. Whereas previous literature always noted that infants slept lightly and awoke frequently, this pattern was considered routine and expected, not problematic. As separate sleep took hold as pediatric advice in Europe and in the United States, a new genre of "sleep problems" arose in infant care books. Rather than recognizing that these "problems" were actually caused by the advice itself, experts claimed that the solution was not to respond to infant cries. This advice is exemplified by Holt's approach of letting the baby "cry it out." Although he claimed that this was only to be used if other reasons for crying were ruled out, in fact he discouraged frequent feeding during the night, and claimed it was unnecessary. This is in direct contradiction of the physiology of lactation among primates, and especially humans, who are particularly reliant on frequent feeding. Not responding to the infant does not cause them to sleep "better" as the consolidation of sleep into longer segments is in fact developmental (Ball, Tomori, and McKenna 2019). There are powerful evolutionary reasons for babies to seek proximity—it is a matter of survival for them—and to wake frequently as they require frequent feeding and close contact for co-regulation. When there is no response from caregivers, babies become silent eventually not because they are in peaceful rest but to conserve energy and resources. Separate sleep advice was further reinforced by psychologists who argued for highly regimented interactions with infants that limited contact.

These practices had significant impacts. They established separate sleep for infants as the normative standard for middle class white Americans. They also undermined breastfeeding, since without frequent opportunities for breastfeeding, lactation downregulates and eventually ends. This, too, is an evolutionary mechanism as breastfeeding is an energetically expensive process and without a baby to continually stimulate the breasts, the body does not expend additional resources on it. They also led to the pathologization of shared sleep—particularly notable since shared sleep was, and remains, the cross-cultural standard. Over time, infant deaths that occurred during sleep, that were initially labeled "crib death" and are now more commonly known as sudden infant death syndrome (SIDS), were increasingly blamed on shared sleep.

During this time pediatric advice also shifted to have infants sleep on their bellies. This was aiming to help digestion and discomfort, which was brought about by the rise of formula feeding. However, this advice was lethal. Babies died much more after this advice but reversing this took decades. Current medical advice is to always put babies on their backs—advice that eventually reversed this trend. However, the approach of blaming parents, particularly mothers, for not following medical advice remains even though putting babies on their stomachs is actually rooted in this misguided medical history.

Breastfed babies are rarely put down on their bellies since they cannot breastfeed that way. In fact, anthropologists have shown that when breastfeeding babies sleep next to their mothers, they face the breast, and mothers spontaneously curl up in a C position around them without instruction, likely reflecting an evolutionary adaptation (Rudzik et al. 2022). At the time, however, sleep advice was fragmented from infant feeding advice. Since the baseline norm was now established as separate sleep and formula feeding on a schedule, the connection between breastfeeding and sleep was completely ignored and erased. Parents were told to never bed-share with their infants, and infant deaths in adult beds were blamed on co-sleeping—even when other risks were present. Mode of feeding was simply not considered.

Biological anthropologists were the first to challenge this ideology of separation based on evolutionary anthropology and on video studies that documented the coordination of mother-infant sleep, and later, physiology. These studies have shown that when breastfeeding mothers and babies sleep together, their sleep is coordinated and they wake together, nursing often without fully awakening. Anthropologists called this intertwining of breastfeeding and sleep "breastsleeping"—a term that describes the fundamental interconnectedness of these processes (McKenna and Gettler 2015). Breastsleeping has also been documented in the global ethnographic literature. There are descriptions of mothers unable to respond to questions about the number of times they woke up to nurse their babies. The reason for this is that they were not fully awake for these breastfeeding sessions, and they were not counting them. These descriptions hail from all over the world— from Japan to Côte d'Ivoire, to Guatemala—suggesting a shared evolutionary mechanism that enables the coordination of sleep and breastfeeding (Tomori 2018a). In multiple descriptions they told anthropologists that they did not find these awakenings problematic. This is in sharp contrast with US culture where shared sleep and nighttime awakenings are problematized and considered dangerous or "sleep problems," respectively. Indeed, frequent waking is often considered so problematic that it is frequently recommended to require the intervention of "sleep training," which usually involves some form of "crying it out"—the term first used by Holt. Yet, despite these prohibitions, anthropologists have also documented similar descriptions of breastfeeding and sleep coordination in the United States among breastfeeding parents. This highlights a tension between the physiological coordination rooted in our evolutionary history and the cultural approach to it.

A major issue in the United States is how to deal with this tension as more parents embark on a breastfeeding journey and find themselves falling asleep with their babies—regardless of their intent. Anthropologists have found that middle class, relatively privileged and mostly white parents experience stigmatization of shared sleep driven by breastfeeding, but they are able to hide it and navigate it due to their privilege. In contrast, the racialized minorities have been targeted by public health campaigns that have been particularly stigmatizing and shift blame for sleep-related deaths to mothers and families. These communities have often been the subject of surveillance and could generate scrutiny from child protection services and medical professions for the very same practices.

The medical decision makers were not welcoming of anthropological critique and the sleep experts were not convinced of the role of breastfeeding in reducing SIDS. Over time, as the evidence grew on the importance of breastfeeding, and studies showed that more breastfeeding was associated with decreasing rates of SIDS, they adopted the recommendation to breastfeed. Although contemporary medical advice reversed course on sleep position and now also advocates breastfeeding, the prohibition against shared sleep remains in the United States. Neither evolutionary anthropology nor cultural anthropology are required parts of medical training, so most physicians are not familiar with the deep or more recent history of breastfeeding and shared sleep. In other Global North settings, some nations have reversed course and no longer prohibit co-sleeping, but instead advise on how to make it safer. Additionally, in the United States, the Academy of Breastfeeding Medicine has been informed by anthropological work, and issued protocols for clinicians and parent-directed handouts that similarly help people understand the physiology of nighttime infant care and ways to make shared sleep safer in the context of breastfeeding (Blair et al. 2020; Zimmerman et al. 2023). This is an area where anthropological research has made an important impact even if contradictions between breastfeeding and sleep advice are not fully resolved in the United States.

"TRANSGRESSIVE" BREASTFEEDING AND MILK SHARING

Although breastfeeding is now embraced as the recommended form of infant feeding, its practice often continues to be stigmatized—such as outside the home, or under a variety of circumstances that are not endorsed by the medical establishment (e.g. in the context of shared sleep as above). Those who are not heterosexual or who occupy gender diverse identities have experienced pervasive stigmatization of their breastfeeding, **chestfeeding**, or **bodyfeeding** practices (Walks 2018). These may be preferred terms among transgender and gender expansive individuals who do not identify as women. The lack of inclusive skilled lactation support from healthcare providers is a major barrier for these parents and is an area of necessary work identified by both anthropologists and public health professionals.

One of the areas that has been particularly well studied by anthropologists is the rise of the practice of **milk sharing**, which can involve either cross-nursing mentioned above or providing human milk for another's child (see Reyes-Foster, Carter, and Hinojosa 2015; Palmquist and Doehler 2016). While nursing others' children was common practice in the past and remains so in many cultures, shared breastfeeding went out of fashion due to the rise of commercial milk formula and later concerns about HIV transmission via breastfeeding. With the return of breastfeeding in the Global North, milk sharing has also made a come-back. Milk banks have been established that primarily focus on helping premature and fragile infants who are at particularly high risk of illness and death. These milk banks screen milk donors and treat milk to kill pathogenic organisms. However, many infants who would greatly benefit from human milk continue to be unable to access it because their parents lack skilled lactation support and paid leave to be able to spend time with their infants. Donor milk may also be unavailable or unaffordable and not covered by insurance.

Other parents are aware of the importance of breastfeeding for their babies but struggle with lactation or perhaps are adoptive parents who are not able to breastfeed. Some parents have infants who have not responded well to commercial milk formulas. Some of these parents engage in informal milk sharing—where parents identify others who are willing to donate milk to their infants, usually via social media. Despite some medical portrayals of milk sharing as inherently unsafe, anthropologists have documented these practices and the careful planning and screening that people use to ensure that the milk is safe for their babies. This practice relies on generosity and networks of care, which often binds donors and recipients together (see Palmquist 2020; Tomori, Quinn, and Palmquist 2022; Quinn, Palmquist, and Tomori 2023). These relations can build similar kinds of relationships that anthropologists have documented in instances of milk kinship. This is a very different process from selling milk, which may have different motivations and different levels of care going into the process. Informal milk sharing can address many different challenges in this cultural setting where breastfeeding is recommended but where structural support is often lacking for it. Milk sharing expands the community of those who nurture the infants and resists the individualized, biomedical approach to breastfeeding.

Other kinds of shared breastfeeding have also been increasingly documented in these settings that once again demonstrate the widespread cultural significance of breastfeeding and bodily closeness for building kinship ties. For instance, anthropologists have documented how foster and adoptive parents have induced lactation and breastfed their infants and slept next to them, helping to establish the closeness they desired (Wilson 2018). This can be risky as foster parents are not allowed to engage in these practices according to the US legal system and can be accused of sexual misconduct and risk losing the children they are caring for. However, these parents see such acts of nurture as critical to their child's development and healing from the often-traumatic separations they have already experienced prior to entering their care.

BREASTFEEDING AND INFECTIOUS DISEASE

A wealth of anthropological literature addresses breastfeeding and infant feeding in the context of the HIV epidemic. At the beginning of the epidemic, public health guidance was issued to avoid breastfeeding when infected with HIV because of the concern about transmission to infants which would ultimately result in death. When this guidance was issued, however, the consequences of the advice were not adequately considered; the risk of death from not breastfeeding may be higher in many settings than the risk of transmission of the virus. It also produced the unintended effect of stigmatizing women who were feeding their babies with formula in predominantly breastfeeding settings because it identified them as infected with HIV—a highly stigmatized condition—whether or not they were. With the development of antiretroviral treatment, the global guidance was reversed in 2010 and breastfeeding is now recommended for women with HIV. This began to undo some of the damage from earlier advice, although the implementation of updated guidance was also confusing. Additionally, in many high-income settings the guidance remained prohibitive against breastfeeding with HIV despite the global guideline shift. This has been increasingly challenged in the past decade, including by anthropological research and interdisciplinary collaborative teams. As a result, some of these settings have adopted more relaxed policies that enable breastfeeding with HIV. In the United States, it is still not recommended, but shared decision-making is encouraged and breastfeeding with HIV with appropriate treatment has been allowed since 2023 (US Department of Health and Human Services, 2023). In an important shift, mothers who decide to breastfeed are no longer referred to Child Protection Services which could lead to the removal of their children. The American Academy of Pediatrics has followed suit and updated its recommendations in April 2024 (Abuogi, Noble, and Christiana Smith 2024). This is particularly significant, since racialized and marginalized communities are at elevated risk for HIV transmission. These communities also face higher maternal and infant mortality, and breastfeeding plays a key role in reducing these inequities. These guideline changes are a welcome update that begins to address some of these issues. More anthropological attention is anticipated in this crucial area of work in light of these updates.

Breastfeeding has also been the subject of anthropological attention in the context of other infectious diseases. Most important among them is breastfeeding during the COVID pandemic. The global response to the pandemic was variable and fragmented. In some settings, mothers and infants were separated and were prohibited from breastfeeding, while others followed the WHO recommendations and kept mothers and infants together while practicing other precautions, such as wearing a well-fitting mask. In the United States, mothers and infants were separated during the early phase of the pandemic. Anthropologists played a role in critiquing these guidelines, which were ultimately reversed (Tomori et al. 2022). The response of the US medical community to the pandemic with automatic separation was unsurprising based on the history of US biomedicalization, in which mother-infant separation was a hallmark, and which remains a pervasive challenge in maternity and postpartum care. Both pregnancy and lactation were also overlooked in the initial phase of the COVID vaccine rollout, leaving many in limbo and having to interpret evidence without adequate medical support. This left room for misinformation to take root and resulted in further inequities for birthing and postpartum populations and their infants. It remains to be seen whether lessons have been learned from this experience and whether they are implemented in policy responses for future pandemics, whose threat is rising with climate change.

BREASTFEEDING AND EMERGENCIES

Breastfeeding in the context of emergencies is another area to which anthropologists have contributed. The historical lack of understanding and appreciation of the importance of breastfeeding that was described in the earlier part of this chapter has meant that breastfeeding has often been overlooked by global health as well as in public health efforts within high-income countries. This has left a major gap in preparedness and response—which can lead to poor outcomes as well as inappropriate donations of formula from companies who aim to enhance their reputation but may instead cause considerable harm. Formula-fed infants are much more vulnerable in emergencies, and parents may not be able to access safe water, electricity, and clean supplies with which to prepare formula, or even a reliable source of formula over time. These infants can end up in the same situation as was documented earlier in the century with the aggressive promotion of formula—dehydrated, suffering from diarrheal disease, and even dead. Ensuring preparedness includes provision of skilled lactation support and safe infant and young child feeding instructions and supplies. Anthropologists have played an important role in building this into policies across the globe (see Quinn, Palmquist, and Tomori 2023).

With the rise of armed conflicts and the climate crisis at the same time around the world, these policies play a particularly important role (see Chapter 6). Breastfeeding is a matter of basic food and water security. Its erasure from many conversations around these issues is a perfect reflection of the historical transformations that have undermined it and erased it from many settings until recently. Understanding the central importance of breastfeeding and its role in ensuring survival is essential to mitigating these crises, and addressing current gaps requires an anthropological lens.

COLLECTIVE MODELS OF CARE

The ethnographic literature is rich with collective models of infant care. Indeed, they represent the cross-cultural norm while the nuclear family, coupled with biomedicalized and fragmented models of care, stands out as quite unusual. Evolutionary biologists have argued that community care has played a critical role in the success of the human species. Care provided from mothers and others is so widespread, that these other carers have been termed **alloparents** and biological anthropologists have argued that **cooperative breeding** is built into our evolution—meaning in evolutionary terms that reproductive success is achieved by sharing reproductive labor among kin (Hrdy 2005; Palmquist 2020; see also Herlosky and Crittenden 2022; Kramer, Veile, and Henry 2022). Most of this care is delivered by mothers' own sisters and mothers (grandmothers) and children's older siblings. Fathers also play an important role in care, although their role varies widely across cultures and settings. Evolutionary anthropologists have argued that hunter-gatherer communities have more of this shared model of care across genders while agriculture facilitated women moving to their husband's household and created more patriarchal gender norms. Still, we have evidence that fatherhood, and specifically proximity and caring for infants, also has biological effects on men (Gray, Straftis, and Anderson 2022). This has been elegantly demonstrated in studies of shared sleep with infants (e.g. Gettler 2014), as well as in other care practices.

Grandmothers deserve special mention in these networks of collective care as they often take on responsibilities of teaching new mothers and supporting them in the postpartum period, helping them learn breastfeeding and infant care and sharing the load (Block 2022). Recent evolutionary work also indicates that there is a link between extended period of maternal care and longer lifespan, which provides further opportunities for grand-mothering (Zipple et al. 2024). In ethnographic work we have seen grandmothers taking over the full array of infant care responsibilities when mothers leave for extended periods of time for work or when they become ill or die. This was particularly prominent at the height of the HIV/AIDS crisis before anti-retroviral treatment became more available globally. In these cases, grandmothers cared for infants and breastfed them as well—a spe-cial feature of lactation described above, as it can be stimulated again once a woman has given birth previously.

There are of course many other models of networks of infant and child care that are worth attention in the global ethnographic literature. **Adoption, fostering**, and **child circulation** are parti-cularly important practices (see Leinaweaver and Marré 2022). All three can mean forms of kinship relationships, but they can take different forms. Adoption refers to the permanent assignment of kinship between the adoptive family and the adoptee, while fos-tering generally refers to a more temporary model of care that may have legal or informal status, and child circulation means caring for children (usually of a relative) that may also be temporary but likely not accompanied by legal recognition (see Leinaweaver 2008). In some cases, these practices serve to incorporate infants and young children into households when their parents are not available—due to a wide range of circumstances. Some of these practices are mostly used by kin who take on these care responsi-bilities sometimes only for a short period of time. However, there are also elements of inequities that can structure these relations. This can mean that parents circulate their children temporarily to other kin because they do not have the resources to care for them, and the kin who takes in the child may exploit the child's labor for their own purposes. On the global stage, Western adoption prac-tices have often been directly linked to systemic inequities driven by colonialism and postcolonial economic systems that have left the Global South impoverished. Wealthy Western, primarily white parents have adopted from other countries that are more permis-sive with adoption practices. In some of these cases, as in Peru, children who were temporarily fostered by other families were made available to these parents, permanently cutting them off from their kin. The systemic inequities in global adoption practices have given rise to wide-ranging anthropological study.

REPRODUCTIVE JUSTICE AND THE RETURN TO COMMUNITY POSTPARTUM AND INFANT CARE

In the last few decades, there have been growing challenges to bio-medicalized models of birth and postpartum care. These efforts have diverse roots across multiple different social change movements dating to the 1960s and 1970s, such as natural parenting, hippy (peace), and civil rights activism. These movements, coupled with developments in research in public health and allied medical disciplines, have fueled a rising interest in midwifery models of care that (re)unite prenatal, birth, and postpartum care. One example is the growth of birth and postpartum **doulas**, who provide support during birth and the postpartum period, respectively (see Chapter 4). With more research and momentum in biomedicine to back breastfeeding, there has been a shift from ad hoc and peer-to-peer lactation support to increased reliance on professional lactation consultants who may provide support within birth settings (including in hospitals) and in the homes of new parents after they return from the birth. Anthropologists have examined how the emerging profession of lactation consultants is shaped by tensions between the pressure to adopt biomedicalized approaches to care and gain professional licensure required to be recognized as legitimate members of the healthcare team and to receive appropriate pay—and the desire to provide community-based lactation support grounded in models of care and kinship that challenge these biomedicalized models in the first place. Ideally, knowledge about lactation, like other aspects of childbearing, has been transmitted across the generations, but when it has not been, community-based support that reflects the make-up of the community and responds to its needs are effective in restoring lactation knowledge and skills. Although specialists may also be required, they are far less commonly necessary if breastfeeding is appropriately supported across the prenatal to the postnatal period.

A central concern is the continued lack of adequate and accessible lactation support in many communities, disproportionately affecting communities with racialized minorities. This is tied to the crisis of maternal mortality in the United States fueled by racism and reflected by the growing absence of maternity services that some have called maternity care deserts. The treatment of Black, Indigenous, Latine, and other women of color is marked by discrimination, lack of adequate listening and appropriate care, and ultimately the disproportionately high maternal mortality and morbidity among these populations within the United States. Indeed, these rates and inequities set the United States apart from all other similar high-income nations. This is particularly relevant because of the troubled history of structural racism and the dismantling of midwifery and undermining of breastfeeding in these communities (see Chapter 4). Since the 1990s, the reproductive justice movement in the United States has been at the forefront of re-establishing community-based support systems around every aspect of reproduction and childbearing and has had a profound impact in addressing these injustices. This movement (see Chapter 1) has centered racialized and marginalized communities and has also been buoyed by intersections with public health researchers who are informed by this framework and have demonstrated that postpartum care and breastfeeding support are fundamental health equity and health justice issues. A key element of this movement is peer-to-peer support involving people who are from the communities being served. The restoring and uplifting of community traditions actively counters the medical racism that is pervasive across the reproductive spectrum and has a significant positive impact in Black, Indigenous, Latine, and other communities of color (see also Chapter 6).

Similar movements have also grown in First Nations communities in Canada, Aboriginal communities in Australia, and Maori communities in New Zealand, among others. There are many opportunities for those interested in the anthropology of reproduction to learn from these movements. Among these lessons is to better appreciate the importance of the postpartum period in a broader context, including holistic models of care that do not fragment childbirth, postpartum, and the multiple, intertwined dimensions of infant care. In these holistic models, we see the emphasis on kinship, community, and nurture. Initiatives that aim to design more effective and respectful maternity care can learn a great deal both from our evolutionary roots and from these movements and communities, and improve health equity and work toward reproductive justice.

SUMMARY

- Cultures around the world emphasize that rest and care after childbirth are essential to enable recovery and infant care, however this period is not always adequately supported by policies in many settings.
- This period is also an essential part of making kinship through a variety of embodied nurture and care for infants, including close physical contact and breastfeeding, which are also foundational to infant survival.
- Colonialism, racial capitalism and medicalization have dramatically transformed models of infant care, and resulted in cultural norms of limited physical contact, formula feeding, and separate sleep. These models had harmful consequences and perpetuated global inequities whose legacies are still manifest today, but are actively challenged and have been renegotiated with some notable successes that shift the standard toward more nurturing models of care with greater social support.
- Diverse forms of collective care are also reflected in adoption, fostering, and child circulation, although each of these may be fraught and shaped by broader patterns of inequities.
- Our evolutionary history and cross-cultural practices offer alternatives to dominant individualistic models of care, and a path towards restoring and reclaiming nurturing and collective care practices. Much work remains to fully support these models and move toward reproductive justice.

FURTHER EXPLORING

In *The Routledge Handbook on Anthropology and Reproduction* (2022), see chapters on breastfeeding and infant sleep by Cecília Tomori, E.A. Quinn, and Aunchalee Palmquist (2022); on alloparents by Kristen Herlosky and Alyssa Crittenden (2022); grandmothers by Ellen Block (2022); fatherhood by Peter Gray, Alex Straftis, and Kermyt Anderson (2022); and reproduction in biological anthropology by Karen Kramer, Amanda Veile, and Paula Ivey Henry (2022). See the references for more information.

BREASTFEEDING AND LACTATION

For more readings on breastfeeding, see the review article on biocultural lactation by Quinn, Palmquist, and Tomori (2023) and *Breastfeeding: New Anthropological Approaches*, edited by Tomori, Palmquist, and Quinn (2018). The authors also created a podcast series, *Anthrolactology*, which can be streamed from this website: https://anthrolactology.com/anthrolactology-podcast.

The topic of this presentation, given by Cecília Tomori as part of The 2023 Lancet Breastfeeding series, is "Ensuring Breastfeeding Success in a Market-Driven World": https://youtu.be/1HwF2n10CKo?si=kMczSqjItqlNZw00.

Aanoodizewin is a podcast series examining the commercial determinants of Indigenous health for people in Canada and worldwide. This episode is focused on infant formula: www.youtube.com/watch?v=y7v0WW2O4UM.

This lecture by Siân Halcrow provides an overview of bioarchaeological insights into life histories, infant feeding, and care in the past: https://youtu.be/WICpIU0IF1s?si=aUNh0RbLax2yFUgg.

INFANT SLEEP

Anthropologist Helen Ball is one of the foremost experts on the topic of infant sleep. She created this website, the Baby Sleep Information Source (BASIS), to present information to parents and researchers on what is biologically normal sleep: www.basisonline.org.uk.

Ball provides an overview in this 2020 lecture, "What Is Normal Infant Sleep: The View from Anthropology": www.youtube.com/watch?v=g5fOogsUpIk.

She is also featured in this 2023 presentation, "Mother-Baby Sleep Contact: Biology, Behavior and Culture": www.youtube.com/watch?v=5KFnn1gRHwI.

ALLOPARENTS

Sarah Hrdy's work on parenting and human evolution has been influential outside of anthropology as well as within the discipline. She is featured on the podcast *UnSILOed* in this episode,

"Alloparenting and Allomothering: Learning How to Parent": www.youtube.com/watch?v=2cjzcCcWJy0.

The grandmother hypothesis is the topic of this episode of *Origin Stories*, a podcast produced by the Leakey Foundation: www.youtube.com/watch?v=Z_VBUJ0s4Qo.

In this 2021 piece, published in *Nature Human Biology*, Robin Nelson argues for the necessity of communal care, demonstrating the relevance of insights from biological anthropology for social policy. A PDF of the article can be downloaded from here: www.nature.com/articles/s41562-020-01037-w.

REFERENCES

Abuogi, Lisa, Lawrence Noble, and Christiana Smith. 2024. "Infant Feeding for Persons Living With and at Risk for HIV in the United States: Clinical Report." *Pediatrics* 2024: e2024066843.

Ball, Helen L., Cecilia Tomori, and James J. McKenna. 2019. "Toward an Integrated Anthropology of Infant Sleep." *American Anthropologist* 121(3): 595–612.

Blair, Peter S., Helen L. Ball, James J. McKenna, Lori Feldman-Winter, Kathleen A. Marinelli, Melissa C. Bartick, and Academy of Breastfeeding Medicine. 2020. "Bedsharing and Breastfeeding: The Academy of Breastfeeding Medicine Protocol# 6, Revision 2019." *Breastfeeding Medicine* 15(1): 5–16.

Block, Ellen. 2022. "the Shifting Role of Grandmothers in Global Reproduction Strategies." In *The Routledge Handbook of Anthropology and Reproduction*, edited by Sallie Han and Cecília Tomori, 590–603. Abingdon and New York: Routledge.

Carsten, Janet. 1997. *The Heat of the Hearth: The Process of Kinship in a Malay Fishing Community*. Oxford: Oxford University Press.

Centers for Disease Control and Prevention. 2022. *Breastfeeding Report Card, United States 2022*. Centers for Disease Control and Prevention. www.cdc.gov/breastfeeding/data/reportcard.htm#:~:text=In%202021%2C%20over%201%20in,that%20more%20work%20is%20needed.

Gettler, Lee T. 2014. "Applying Socioendocrinology to Evolutionary Models: Fatherhood and Physiology." *Evolutionary Anthropology: Issues, News, and Reviews* 23(4): 146–160.

Gottlieb, Alma. 2015. *The Afterlife Is Where We Come From*. 2nd ed. Chicago, IL: University of Chicago Press.

Gray, Peter B., Alex Straftis, and Kermyt G.Anderson. 2022. "Men and Reproduction: Perspectives from Biological Anthropology." In *The Routledge Handbook of Anthropology and Reproduction*, edited by Sallie Han and Cecília Tomori, 52–67. Abingdon and New York: Routledge.

Halcrow, Siân E., Melanie J. Miller, Kate Pechenkina, Yu Dong, and Wen-quan Fan. 2022. "The Bioarchaeology of Infant Feeding." In *The Routledge Handbook of Anthropology and Reproduction*, edited by Sallie Han and Cecília Tomori, 541–558. Abingdon and New York: Routledge.

Herlosky, Kristen N., and Alyssa N. Crittenden. 2022. "Alloparenting: Evolutionary Origins and Contemporary Significance of Cooperative Child-rearing as a Key Feature of Human Reproduction." In *The Routledge Handbook of Anthropology and Reproduction*, edited by Sallie Han and Cecília Tomori, 604–617. Abingdon and New York: Routledge.

Hrdy, Sarah B. 2005. "Evolutionary Context of Human Development: The Cooperative Breeding Model." In *Family Relationships: An Evolutionary Perspective*, edited by C.A. Salmon & T.K. Shackelford, 39–68. Oxford: Oxford University Press. doi:10.1093/acprof:oso/9780195320510.003.0003.

Hunt, Nancy Rose. 1998. "'Le Bebe en Brousse': European Women, African Birth Spacing and Colonial Intervention in Breast Feeding in the Belgian Congo." *The International Journal of African Historical Studies* 21(3): 401–432.

Kang, Yoonjung. 2014. "Love and Money: Commercial Postpartum Care and the Reinscription of Patriarchy in Contemporary South Korea." *Journal of Korean Studies* 19(2): 379–397.

Kramer, Karen L., Amanda Veile, and Paula Ivey Henry. 2022. "Conceiving Reproduction in Biological Anthropology." In *The Routledge Handbook of Anthropology and Reproduction*, edited by Sallie Han and Cecília Tomori, 19–35. Abingdon and New York: Routledge.

Leinaweaver, Jessaca B. 2008. *The Circulation of Children: Kinship, Adoption, and Morality in Andean Peru*. Durham, NC: Duke University Press.

Leinaweaver, Jessaca, and Diana Marré. 2022. "Adoption and Fostering." In *The Routledge Handbook of Anthropology and Reproduction*, edited by Sallie Han and Cecília Tomori, 618–630. Abingdon and New York: Routledge.

McKenna, James J., and Lee T. Gettler. 2015. "There Is No Such Thing as Infant Sleep, There Is No Such Thing as Breastfeeding, There Is Only Breastsleeping." *Acta Paediatrica* 105(1): 17–21.

Palmquist, Aunchalee. 2020. "Cooperative Lactation and the Mother-Infant Nexus." In *The Mother-Infant Nexus in Anthropology: Small Beginnings, Significant Outcomes*, edited by Rebecca Gowland and Siân Halcrow, 125–142. Berlin: Springer International Publishing.

Palmquist, Aunchalee E.L., and Kirsten Doehler. 2016. "Human Milk Sharing Practices in the US." *Maternal & Child Nutrition* 12(2): 278–290.

Pérez-Escamilla, Rafael, Cecília Tomori, Sonia Hernández-Cordero, Phillip Baker, Aluisio J.D. Barros, France Bégin, Donna J. Chapman et al.2023. "Breastfeeding: Crucially Important, but Increasingly Challenged in a Market-Driven World." *The Lancet* 401(10375): 472–485.

Power, Michael L., and Jay Schulkin. 2016. *Milk: The Biology of Lactation.* Baltimore, MD: JHU Press.

Quinn, Elizabeth A. 2021. "Centering Human Milk Composition as Normal Human Biological Variation." *American Journal of Human Biology* 33(1): e23564.

Quinn, Elizabeth A., Aunchalee E.L. Palmquist, and Cecília Tomori. 2023. "Biocultural Lactation: Integrated Approaches to Studying Lactation Within and Beyond Anthropology." *Annual Review of Anthropology* 52: 473–490.

Reyes-Foster, Beatriz M., Shannon K. Carter, Melanie S. Hinojosa. 2015. Milk Sharing in Practice: A Descriptive Analysis of Peer Breastmilk Sharing. *Breastfeeding Medicine* 10(5): 263–269.

Robinson, Cedric J. 2019. *On Racial Capitalism, Black Internationalism, and Cultures of Resistance.* London: Pluto Press.

Rollins, Nigel, Ellen Piwoz, Phillip Baker, Gillian Kingston, Kopano Matlwa Mabaso, David McCoy, Paulo Augusto Ribeiro Neves*et al.*2023. "Marketing of Commercial Milk Formula: A System to Capture Parents, Communities, Science, and Policy." *The Lancet* 401(10375): 486–502.

Rosenberg, Karen R. 2021. "The Evolution of Human Infancy: Why It Helps to Be Helpless." *Annual Review of Anthropology* 50: 423–440.

Rudzik, Alanna E.F., Cecília Tomori, James J. McKenna, and Helen L. Ball. 2022. "Biocultural Perspectives on Infant Sleep." In *The Routledge Handbook of Anthropology and Reproduction*, edited by Sallie Han and Cecília Tomori, 559–572. Abingdon and New York: Routledge.

Tomori, Cecília. 2018a. "Breastsleeping in Four Cultures 1: Comparative Analysis of a Biocultural Body Technique." In *Breastfeeding: New Anthropological Approaches*, edited by Cecília Tomori, Aunchalee E.L. Palmquist, and E.A. Quinn, 55–68. Abingdon and New York: Routledge.

Tomori, Cecilia. 2018b. "Changing Cultures of Night-Time Breastfeeding and Sleep in the US." In *Social Experiences of Breastfeeding*, edited by Sally Dowling, David Pontin, and Kate Boyer, 115–130. Bristol: Policy Press.

Tomori, Cecília. 2024. *Nighttime Breastfeeding: An American Cultural Dilemma.* 2nd ed. New York and Oxford: Berghahn Books.

Tomori, Cecília, Karleen Gribble, Aunchalee E.L. Palmquist, Mija-Tesse Ververs, and Marielle S. Gross. 2020. "When Separation Is Not the Answer: Breastfeeding Mothers and Infants Affected by COVID-19." *Maternal & Child Nutrition* 16(4): e13033.

Tomori, Cecília, and Aunchalee E.L. Palmquist. 2022. "Racial Capitalism and the US Formula Shortage: A Policy Analysis of the Formula Industry as a Neocolonial System." *Frontiers in Sociology* 7: 961200.

Tomori, Cecília, Aunchalee E.L. Palmquist, and Elizabeth A. Quinn, eds. 2018. *Breastfeeding: New Anthropological Approaches.* Abingdon and New York: Routledge.

Tomori, Cecília, Elizabeth A. Quinn, and Aunchalee E.L. Palmquist. 2022. "Making Space for Lactation in the Anthropology of Reproduction." In *The Routledge Handbook of Anthropology and Reproduction*, edited by Sallie Han and Cecília Tomori, 527–540. Abingdon and New York: Routledge.

Trevathan, Wenda R., and Karen R. Rosenberg, eds. 2016. *Costly and Cute: Helpless Infants and Human Evolution*. Santa Fe, NM: School for Advanced Research Press.

US Breastfeeding Committee. 2024. *The PUMP Act Explained*. www.usbreastfeeding.org/the-pump-act-explained.html.

US Department of Health and Human Services. 2023. *Panel on Treatment of HIV During Pregnancy and Prevention of Perinatal Transmission. Recommendations for the Use of Antiretroviral Drugs During Pregnancy and Interventions to Reduce Perinatal HIV Transmission in the United States*. https://clinicalinfo.hiv.gov/en/guidelines/perinatal.

Van Esterik, Penny. 1996. "The Cultural Context of Breastfeeding and Breastfeeding Policy." *Food and Nutrition Bulletin* 17(4): 1–6.

Vogell, Heather. 2024. "The US Government Defended the Overseas Business Interests of Baby Formula Makers. Kids Paid the Price." *ProPublica*. www.propublica.org/article/how-america-waged-global-campaign-against-baby-formula-regulation-thailand.

Waldron, Lucas, and Heather, Vogell. 2024. "Documents Show Internal Clash Before US Officials Pushed to Weaken Toddler Formula Rules." *ProPublica*. https://projects.propublica.org/toddler-formula-documents/.

Walks, Michelle. 2018. "Chestfeeding as Gender Fluid Practice." In *Breastfeeding: New Anthropological Approaches*, edited by Cecília Tomori, Aunchalee E.L. Palmquist, and E.A. Quinn, 127–139. Abingdon and New York: Routledge.

Wilson, K.J., 2018. *Others' Milk: The Potential of Exceptional Breastfeeding*. New Brunswick, NJ: Rutgers University Press.

World Health Organization. 2023. *Kangaroo Mother Care—Implementation Strategy for Scale-Up Adaptable to Different Country Contexts*. www.who.int/publications/i/item/9789240071636.

Zimmerman, Deena, Melissa Bartick, Lori Feldman-Winter, Helen L. Ball, and Academy of Breastfeeding Medicine. 2023. "ABM Clinical Protocol# 37: Physiological Infant Care—Managing Nighttime Breastfeeding in Young Infants." *Breastfeeding Medicine* 18(3): 159–168.

Zipple, Matthew N., H. Kern Reeve, and Orca Jimmy Peniston. 2024. "Maternal Care Leads to the Evolution of Long, Slow Lives." *Proceedings of the National Academy of Sciences* 121(25): e2403491121.

6

STRUGGLES AND MOVEMENTS TOWARD REPRODUCTIVE JUSTICE

Whether or not to have children, when to have them, how many of them, and how to ensure that they are born and raised in health and safety—these questions represent both longstanding human concerns and deeply significant exercises of our individual agency. Recognizing and actively enabling and supporting our rights, as humans, to make these decisions—and to raise our children so that they, too, can survive and thrive—are the aims of **reproductive justice**, which merges activist and scholarly efforts in the movements for reproductive rights and social justice (Ross and Solinger 2017). Additionally, it demands sexual autonomy and gender freedom. The framework of reproductive justice brings into perspective that while we have rights as individuals, we also make our decisions as selves who are encumbered within relationships with various other people, such as partners and kin and family, and as members of our societies and cultures. Our decisions are influenced by the economic, social, and political conditions in which we live, how we understand our ability to care for and raise up our children, including what prospects we see for them.

As we have discussed throughout this book, the anthropological study of reproduction requires us to think and talk not only about differences of custom and habit which may exist across cultures, but also, even more importantly, about the exercises of power and the inequalities and inequities shaping every dimension of reproductive experience. What follows in this chapter are discussions of present and past struggles and movements for reproductive justice. First, we address fertility crises and how they are shaped by state interests that assert control, or exercise **reproductive governance**,

DOI: 10.4324/9781003379416-6

over individual, family, and community reproductive desires using pronatalist and anti-natalist policies. Next, we look at examples of the most extreme forms of reproductive governance—exercised by states that wish to undermine, limit, or eliminate the reproductive capacity of communities or entire people through armed conflict, war, and genocide. These crises make clear that the roots of reproductive justice lie in **human rights**—which also address the basic rights to ensure the safety, survival, and reproduction of individuals and communities. The third section turns to ongoing core struggles for reproductive rights, freedom, and justice in relation to the colonial legacies of gendered oppression, attacks on diverse sexualities, and the ability to birth and care for children in racist systems. The final section broadens the lens to examine our collective reproductive future in light of the intersecting global threats of the climate crisis, the era of pandemics, and the concept of planetary health and environmental justice.

The aim here is to examine not only the inequities that constrain people's abilities to make decisions about their reproductive lives, but even more importantly to take heed of how people resist, challenge, overcome, and reinvent their possibilities and opportunities. The discussion also demonstrates the insights we gather when we think about reproduction using the critical perspectives of anthropology. In this chapter, as in the other chapters of this book, our use of language is purposeful, so that when we refer to women and mothers, we do not assume biologically determined status, but understand them as meaningful identities within historical, social, and cultural contexts. Drawing on the diverse social movements and struggles that have shaped the histories of the reproductive justice movement, we argue for a future filled with radical hope for reproductive justice and freedom even, and especially, in the face of the threats we describe above.

POPULATION AND FERTILITY CRISES IN CONTEXT

Population matters for a range of reasons. Among them, it represents the size of both the needs and wants of a group or country and the capacity to meet these demands. This is a reason why nations are concerned with the numbers of people who are very young and very old in proportion to the numbers of people who can provide the labor required to sustain all of us. Political and economic stability are understood to be linked to each other and to increases or decreases in a population that occur with births, deaths, and migrations of people in and out of a country. States seek to control or at least manage their numbers through population policies that are implemented through laws, practices, and institutions like public hospitals (Browner and Sargent 2022). One aim of population policies is to influence and shape the behaviors contributing directly and indirectly to reproduction, specifically births. Because population policies are directed at regulating births, not surprisingly, their effects are felt most especially among women and people who can become pregnant and give birth. Laws and practices create the conditions in which people make decisions and take actions to prevent pregnancies with birth control, end one with an abortion, seek fertility treatment, and receive healthcare during pregnancy, birth, and postpartum. Other laws and practices impose requirements and restrictions on people, such as mandatory sterilization of women and men.

Pronatalist policies are oriented toward the growth of populations and encourage pregnancies and births. **Anti-natalist** policies attempt to limit growth and discourage births. The orientation of a state can shift over time. Today, we can observe countries pursuing pronatalism or anti-natalism—or both at the same time. While we typically think about population as the total number of people in a country, we can also talk about populations as the numbers of people grouped by categories like age, gender, or race and ethnicity. Populations may not be equally valued. Are there too many or too few babies being born today? The answer depends not only on who you are asking, but also whom you are asking about.

FROM ANTI-NATALISM TO PRONATALISM IN SOUTH KOREA

A country's **fertility rate** refers to an estimated average of how many children a woman will have in her lifetime. A fertility rate of 2.1 is considered replacement level, meaning the numbers of people will neither increase nor decrease, aside from changes due to immigration. In 2022, Niger, a low-income country in West Africa, had a fertility rate of 6.7, one of the world's highest. In the same year, South Korea, a high-income country in East Asia, had a fertility rate of 0.78, one of the world's lowest.

Within South Korea, also known as the Republic of Korea, women are blamed for the low number of births in popular media and conservative political discourses. They accuse feminists of luring young women away from their roles and responsibilities as wives and mothers. Outside of Korea, observers frequently cite culture as the reason for a feminist rejection. In their telling, cultural ideas and practices are even more problematically patriarchal in Korea than elsewhere. What both attempts at explanation have in common is their reductiveness, or biased oversimplification. To understand how and why the fertility rate is so low in South Korea today requires attention to economic, political, historical, social, and indeed cultural processes and patterns, which need to be taken together, not singly or independently of each other.

Japan's occupation of Korea began in 1910 and ended in 1945 with the division of the Korean peninsula. The Korean War began in 1950 when the China-backed Communist forces of North Korea moved to "reunify" the peninsula by force, which was resisted by the UN and US-backed forces of South Korea. The conflict ended with an armistice agreement in 1953 establishing a demilitarized zone that is now the border between the Democratic People's Republic of Korea (North) and the Republic of Korea (South). In the aftermath of the war, Korea was one of the world's poorest countries. Between 1960 and 1980, the Republic of Korea aggressively pursued economic development goals to bring the country from least developed to developed status, earning it the moniker of the "miracle on the Han River."

South Korea's nationalist development agenda included anti-natalist policies that transformed it from a high-fertility country to one with one of the lowest rates in the world (Kang 2021). In 1960, the country had a rate of 6.0, which declined to 4.53 in 1970. By 1983, Korea reached the replacement fertility rate of 2.1. During the 1980s, Korea's fertility rate continued to decline, falling below replacement, and by 1996, the country had largely abandoned its anti-natalist policies. Efforts to increase births initially lost momentum, however, with the 1997 Asian financial crisis. Under austerity measures imposed by the International Monetary Fund, male breadwinners lost their jobs and women felt pressure to earn an income while maintaining the hierarchical privilege of husbands over wives (Kim and Finch 2002).

During these years, more than 200,000 children from Korea were adopted overseas, primarily in the United States and countries in Europe (see Chapter 3). Many were so-called GI babies born to Korean women and US soldiers stationed in Korea during and after the war. As historian Arissa Oh (2015) notes, these mixed-race children, particularly those born of Black fathers, represented violations of the "purity" of the Korean people—an idea employed in the nationalist rhetoric of Park Chung Hee, who aggressively oversaw his country's development agenda during his 18 years in power. Cultural ideas about bloodlines also discouraged the adoption of "fully" Korean children by families who did not share biogenetic kinship. "Saving" these children by adopting them became a cause for Christians in the United States, whose efforts laid the groundwork for a system of international adoption. In South Korea, the discourse on adoption has shifted since the 1980s, when the number of "child exports" became a source of global controversy during the 1988 Olympics hosted in Seoul. Overseas, there were increasing sensitivities about transracial adoption; additionally, questions were raised about whether children had been voluntarily relinquished.

By 2023, the fertility rate had decreased to 0.72. Popular and political discourses accuse feminists of creating this demographic crisis. Drawing special ire these days is the 4B movement, the online-based activism of Korean feminists primarily in their 20s. The English letter B is a homophone for the Korean prefix (bi) meaning not or no, and 4B stands for the Korean words for no marriage (bihon), no birth (bichulsan), no romance (biyeonae), and no sexual relationships (bisekseu). 4B feminists offer a critique of what they see as the root causes of women's unequal status in Korean society. In addition, as anthropologists Jieun Lee and Euisol Jeong (2021) explain, they articulate a concrete vision for women to plan for lives independent of men. Social media posts offer pragmatic advice, for example on establishing and maintaining financial self-sufficiency.

Like other movements which require understanding of the specific contexts where they emerge, 4B feminism needs to be understood as a response of Korean women to their own society, culture, and recent history. South Korea has one of the world's largest economies. Yet, compared with other countries in the Organization for Economic Co-operation and Development (OECD), an intergovernmental trade agency, it also has one of the largest gender gaps in employment and pay. The 20% difference in women's and men's employment appears to be a care gap, with women leaving the workforce to shoulder the burdens of child (and elder) care while the 20% difference between women's and men's pay is a gender gap, observed among younger unmarried women and men then compounding over time and life courses (Stansbury et al. 2023).

Political scientist and Korea scholar Katharine H.S. Moon (2022) notes that Korea ranks low across global measures of gender equality, including high rates of reported harassment and sexual violence. The situation, then, points not to a problem with women, but with misogyny. Young men themselves have become involved in alt-right groups whose homophobic rhetoric accuses feminists of being man-hating lesbians and blames women for their own dimmed economic prospects and the broader political and social uncertainties affecting everyone in Korea. Not only has the number of births fallen, but so has the rate of marriages (No 2024).

Over the years, Korean feminists have been pushing back against not only the narratives accusing young women of selfishly avoiding marriage and motherhood, but also the cultural expectations and social structures that define what women are and are not allowed to do and be. "We are not birth-machines" became a rallying cry (Lee and Jeong 2021). In recent years, the state has made efforts like offering childcare subsidies to encourage motherhood, but they do not address women's fundamental concerns. As of 2023, Korea was one of only two OECD nations with no anti-discrimination laws, including those prohibiting discrimination on the basis of gender or of sexual orientation (Cho and Richards 2023). The fertility rate is projected to fall from 0.72 in 2023 to 0.68 in 2024.

The efforts of South Korea to raise the number of births are being watched in other countries also concerned with their low and still declining fertility rates. There is no evidence of success from pronatalist policies that address mothers, but not women; childcare, but not work; and, indeed, women, but not men.

ANTI-NATALISM, ANTI-IMMIGRATION, AND PRO-NATIONALISM

In 2023, India became the world's most populous country, surpassing China. Both countries count more than one billion people each, but their fertility rates have been declining since the 1960s. In 2022, India's fertility rate was 2.0; China's was 1.2. China implemented its anti-natalist "one-child policy" in 1979 to curb population growth and to meet gender equality goals. While the policy improved girls' and women's ability to pursue education and employment, it also created an imbalance in the number of males and females, as Chinese parents acted upon cultural preferences for sons over daughters (Browner and Sargent 2022). The efforts made to bring down the number of births included coercive measures, like mandatory abortion and sterilization, as well as positive incentives for better work opportunities and pay. Amid concerns also about a shrinking workforce and aging population, China shifted to a pronatalist two-child policy in 2015. It includes revised measures that remain coercive, like restricting divorce and abortion, and new incentives, like coverage for fertility treatments (see Chapter 3). There is talk among Chinese authorities about allowing unmarried women to access services like in vitro fertilization (IVF) and egg freezing (Master 2023). By the time China officially ended its one-child policy, it already had been pursuing both anti-natalist and pronatalist policies for years, encouraging more births in the majority Han ethnic population and discouraging them among minority communities such as the Uyghurs, a predominantly Muslim ethnic group in northwestern China.

The numbers of births and the numbers of people migrating into a country contribute to the increases and decreases in a population, and population policies are targeted at controlling or managing reproduction and immigration. These concerns appear to be particularly intertwined for the United States, which grants unrestricted birthright citizenship to individuals born in the country or its territories, whether or not an individual's parents are also US citizens. In recent years, anti-immigration rhetoric includes derogatory phrases like "anchor baby" or "birth tourism" to claim—with no substantial evidence—that foreign nationals were purposefully entering the United States to give birth and gain legal protections. There are currently about 10.5 million undocumented immigrants, or people who entered the country without a valid visa or overstayed legal permission to live here. Many work and pay taxes. As of 2022, there are also 580,000 active recipients of temporary legal residency through the Deferred Action for Childhood Arrivals

(DACA) program for undocumented immigrants who were brought into the country when they were age 16 or younger. DACA was announced by then-president Barack Obama in 2012 and rescinded under then-president Donald Trump in 2017.

The US-Mexico border is not only a geographical location, but also a powerful symbol of immigration and particularly of "illegal immigration." In 2018, the Trump administration enforced a "zero-tolerance" policy targeting families seeking asylum at the border. An estimated 5,000 children, including infants, were separated from their parents and guardians and held in juvenile facilities (French 2024). The adults were detained elsewhere then deported without their children. John Kelly, then the White House Chief of Staff, acknowledged it was intended to be a "tough deterrent" for migrants and force Congress to act. It was, in short, a political weaponization of migrant children. Because there was no system to track and link children and their parents, up to 2,000 children were still separated from their families in 2024. The children remaining in the United States may be living now with other relatives or family friends, placed in foster care, or have been adopted (Bennett 2023).

The involuntary sterilization of migrant women was brought to light by a whistleblower complaint from a nurse, Dawn Wooten, who had worked at the Irwin County Detention Center in Georgia. The women had been detained by Immigration and Customs Enforcement and later discovered they were unable to conceive. They had not been informed or given consent to the procedures that left them infertile. Shocking as this situation might seem, Leith Mullings notes this instance of sterilization abuse along with the weaponization of migrant children represent the latest chapter in a long history of what she calls the necropolitics of reproduction: "Not only policies that value some lives more than others, but the use of political power to determine who will live and who will die" (Mullings 2022, 107).

REPRODUCTION IN TIMES AND PLACES OF ARMED CONFLICT AND WAR

No fiber in the fabric of a society is left untouched by armed conflicts, especially the experiences of reproduction. Since the early 2000s, anthropologists have documented and critically examined the consequences of the wars in Afghanistan and Iraq, waged by the United States and its allies, in addition to civil wars (between organized groups in the same country), which continue to be felt in their long aftermaths in places such as Sierra Leone, Uganda, and Guatemala (Mazzarino, Inhorn, and Lutz 2019). All told, tens of millions of people around the globe have been forced to flee their homes and communities, as internally displaced people within their countries or as refugees outside their borders, taking shelter in camps which are overcrowded and unsafe. The costs of war are high and manifold. They include not only the killing and injuring of combatants (soldiers, militia, and contractors) and civilians, both directly and indirectly by military operations, but also the long-reaching and lasting impacts on the physical, psychological, and social health of individuals and communities (Mazzarino 2024). Studies of embodiment, or the biological impacts of people's prolonged experiences of adverse social conditions like poverty or war, and of the developmental origins of health and disease demonstrate that the effects on health may be felt across generations (Clarkin 2019). Bayla Ostrach and Merrill Singer (2012) use the term "syndemics of war" to describe the overlapping and compounding impacts of physical and emotional trauma; food insecurity and hunger; spread of infectious disease; and destruction of social infrastructure. From healthcare systems to kin and family life to both formal schooling and informal learning and teaching from older to younger generations, every aspect of a society—and every dimension of human reproduction—is disrupted, as witnessed in Gaza and Ukraine.

PREGNANCY, BIRTH, AND BREASTFEEDING IN GAZA, 2023–2024

Pregnant and birthing women and children, whether intentionally targeted or not, have borne terrible impacts in Israel's war on Hamas. Between October 2023 and May 2024, more than half of the estimated 35,000 people killed in Gaza were women and children; in fact, about half of the population is age 18 or younger. In October 2023, Israel declared war on Hamas, the military organization governing Gaza, which launched surprise attacks, killing around 1,200 people and abducting about 250 others. The current war in Gaza, a Palestinian territory in southern Israel, is part of a longer history of violently disputed claims for Israeli and Palestinian sovereignty. As of August 2024, the United Nations estimates at least 1.9 million people across Gaza, or 90% of the population, have been displaced from their communities and homes, including those who have been displaced up to ten times (UNRWA 2024). In addition, 80% of educational facilities, including universities, in Gaza, have been damaged or destroyed with the result that children there have no access to schooling, a situation that the United Nations (2024) calls scholasticide.

The UN Human Rights Office expressed concerns in February 2024 about "a pattern of attacks by Israeli forces striking essential life-saving civilian infrastructure in Gaza, especially hospitals" (Shamdasani 2024). Claiming that Hamas is embedded inside the facilities, Israel has carried out ground and air strikes on hospitals—an action that is prohibited by international humanitarian laws. Some attacks have targeted facilities sheltering birthing women and infants, including premature infants who may require supportive care that is impossible without electricity. In addition, Gaza's health ministry estimates that at least 490 healthcare workers were killed between October 2023 and February 2024 (Fick et al. 2024). The near total collapse of Gaza's healthcare system, which was stretched thin even before the current war, has particularly awful consequences for pregnant and birthing women. The fertility rate here is high (3.38 births per woman) and about 180 women give birth on any given day (Stancati and Ayyoub 2024). Now, without medical care during pregnancy, even a commonly occurring and easily treated condition like anemia (iron deficiency) is left unaddressed. Also not diagnosed is preeclampsia, a serious condition of hypertension, or high blood pressure, that can be life-threatening for a pregnant woman and her baby. Even one month after ground and air strikes on Gaza, shortages of medical supplies forced doctors to perform surgical deliveries on women without anesthesia (BBC 2023). With women forced to give birth in temporary shelters or tents at refugee camps, with little or no medical attention, a group called Safe Birth in Palestine Project created and posted short videos offering instructions, in Arabic, on emergency unassisted birth (Walker 2024).

The hazards for women and their children in Gaza do not end with birth. Concerns about postpartum recovery require keeping a watchful eye for hemorrhage (excessive blood loss) as well as infection, particularly after surgical delivery. Feeding mothers and babies is the most urgent need. Before the war, only half of mothers in Gaza were breastfeeding beyond six weeks (Hegarty 2024) and they may lack skilled lactation support to help them. Now, infant formula is scarcely available and there is no safe water to mix it. Formula-fed infants are especially vulnerable in these emergencies and are at the earliest risk of malnutrition, illness, and death—which is a reason why structural support for breastfeeding is a critical matter of food security (Tomori 2023). Cross-nursing (breastfeeding someone else's child, can be occasional) and relactation (restarting breastfeeding after a previous period of weaning) can help, but they rely on having knowledge and skilled support, the latter of which is particularly lacking because humanitarian aid is severely restricted. Although breastfed infants are more likely to survive, without adequate additional foods after six months, they, too, are at high risk of malnutrition. Additionally, mothers themselves face starvation and dehydration. As of May 2024, the UN World Food Program described a state of "full-blown famine" in northern Gaza and the International Criminal Court announced bringing charges against Israel's prime minister and defense minister for starvation as a method of warfare, which is defined as a war crime in international law. More than 40% of food in Gaza had been locally produced; however, since the start of the war, around 45% of agricultural land has been damaged (Tabrizy Piper, and Berger 2024). More than half of water and sanitation sites have been damaged or destroyed, so there is limited availability of clean water (Devlin et al. 2024). The physical growth of children is a clear marker of the impacts of war and the stunting of Palestinian children younger than five years old had been documented after the Second Intifada in 2000 (Clarkin 2019). These children are today's adults and parents. The disproportionate and known impacts of war on mothers and children reaffirm the social significance of reproduction as a site of struggle for survival and reproductive justice.

FEMALE COMBATANTS, SEXUAL VIOLENCE, AND THE REMOVAL OF CHILDREN IN UKRAINE, 2022–2024

In Ukraine, there is a mandatory draft for men. Yet about 65,000 women voluntarily serve in the military, including 4,000 in combat positions (Tung 2024). While women are frequently perceived as non-combatants in war, Jan Brunson (2022) considers the experiences of Nepalese women fighting in the People's Liberation Army (PLA) against government forces. During the ten-year span of the Maoist People's War, from 1996 to 2006, women combatants became pregnant and gave birth to children, whom they left in the care of other family members. With the signing of a peace agreement, former combatants entered formal processes of reintegration into society. Women, however, described tensions between the ideals of gender equity that had motivated their participation in the PLA and the post-war realities of cultural expectations for wives and mothers.

Targeting women is waging war on every dimension of reproduction. Similar to Gaza, there are documented targeted attacks on maternity and children's hospitals, most famously in Mariupol, which Russia claimed were military targets. Additionally, women suffer sexual violence resulting in physical injuries and reproductive problems, psychological trauma, and social stigma (Mazzarino, Inhorn, and Lutz 2019). Rape is used as a deliberate and planned military strategy. Forced pregnancy resulting from rape or other coerced sexual relationships is recognized as an act of genocide, as witnessed in Bosnia, Rwanda, and elsewhere during the 1990s. Across these settings, abortion and infanticide are documented responses to unwanted pregnancies. What happens to the children born of war rape is seldom discussed among survivors and scholars, but Kimberly Theidon (2015) uncovers how the names given by women who were raped to their children are revealing of their histories. "These children's names can be a form of narrating the past, of attesting to the legacies of violence in the present, and of denouncing the harm done, for which no redress has yet been found" (Theidon 2015, S195).

In Ukraine, men, too, were the victims of sexual violence. In a May 2024 interview with CNN, Oleksii Sivak, a 39-year-old civil volunteer in Kherson, described having been detained, beaten, and tortured by Russian officers. "They said, 'we're going to sterilize you now' and things like that, while they were electrocuting my genitals" (Kottasová and Voitovych 2024). This kind of taunting feeds larger fears of a genocidal campaign to destroy Ukraine as a country, people, and culture. Ukraine has accused Russia of carrying out the forcible transfer of 19,000 children from Ukraine to

Russia for this purpose (Bubola 2022). Of these children, only 400 were returned to their families in the first year of the war. They were sent to what Ukrainian officials describe as indoctrination camps where lessons were taught on Russian language and history. Roman Tarasov, 16, was told: "Forget your Ukrainian if you want to continue studying" (Gall et al. 2023). This theft of children, under the guise of supposed benevolence from the Russian state, is a direct attack on the reproduction of a people.

CONTINUING FIGHTS FOR REPRODUCTIVE RIGHTS, FREEDOM, AND JUSTICE

The fight for safety, shelter, food, medicine, and water are critical human rights issues that shape the ability to survive and reproduce. In addition to these most acute threats, other ongoing struggles continue over fundamental tenets of human rights that are deeply anchored in reproduction, as we have discussed throughout this book. They are highlighted here because they are fundamentally interconnected as touchstones of reproductive justice.

FIGHTING FOR ACCESS TO BIRTH CONTROL AND ABORTION

Despite decades of social movements expanding access to birth control, the ability not to have children remains a key area of struggle across the world. Without contraception, women can be coerced into having babies regardless of their wishes. Women in Japan, for instance, fought for decades to gain access to the birth control pill, which only became legalized in 1999—after approval had been given to Viagra to treat men's erectile dysfunction. Emergency contraception is still only available via a physician.

Across large portions of the Global North, right wing movements have challenged efforts to expand and defend rights and access to birth control and abortion. These attacks are linked to pronatalist and ethnonationalist movements that emphasize racial and ethnic purity and naturalize women as primarily childbearers and mothers, challenging their equal legal status. Poland, for instance, imposed dramatic restrictions on abortion during the 1990s (Mishtal and de Zordo 2022). Here and elsewhere, however, the majority of people have voted to oppose these restrictions (see

Chapter 2). Counter-movements have fought back and even overturned longstanding restrictions, such as in Ireland, Argentina, Mexico, and Colombia (Zissis et al. 2023).

In Brazil, efforts to decriminalize abortion continue, leaving women to seek unsafe abortion or travel abroad, if they have the means to do so. While the law provides exceptions for rape, survivors often face obstacles, like requesting police reports, that make getting a timely abortion nearly impossible and leading to further complications from an unwanted pregnancy or unsafe abortion (Henderson 2024). Brazilians with African and Indigenous ancestry are disproportionately affected by rape and unsafe abortion, clearly making safe abortion access a racial justice and equity issue (Diniz et al. 2023; Barzallo 2024; Henderson 2024).

In the United States, abortion access has been dramatically restricted since the Supreme Court's 2022 ruling in the Dobbs v. Jackson case, which overturned its 1973 decision in Roe v. Wade. Post-Dobbs, the right for people to have an abortion is no longer federally protected and a series of anti-abortion laws have been rolled out in US states controlled by Republican legislatures, banning abortion in 14 states, and dramatically restricting access in an additional 11 states (KFF 2024). Notably, the majority of women in these states support legal abortion and the passage of laws that protect abortion (Kearney et al. 2024). Anti-abortion efforts have been based on far-reaching claims on the status of personhood for fetuses and, more recently, for embryos (see Chapter 3). Frozen embryos, produced in IVF procedures, were legally recognized as children by the state of Alabama's highest court in 2024.

Around the world and in the United States, medication abortion (involving the use of prescribed drugs during early pregnancy; see Chapter 2) has been increasingly relied upon in reproductive healthcare. Providers have been using telehealth as a way to support those seeking medication abortion (Ungar 2024). Professional societies have spoken against bans and restrictions on both medication abortions and the use of telehealth. Providers are being driven out of training and practice in the US states where these restrictions are in place (Ogrera and Grover 2024), leading to further provider healthcare shortages piling on top of already existing ones (Sonenberg and Mason 2023). Community support groups have been facilitating access to abortion services, including medication abortion, for people living in US states with restrictions, and state and national organizations are working to overturn these laws as well as to expand abortion-supportive policies (Ungar and Mulvihill 2024). Although access to mifepristone, one of the drugs used in medication abortion, remains legal after a June 13, 2024 Supreme Court ruling, this access can end with future challenges (Ahmed 2024) or if a national ban is enacted. Powerful right-wing groups are pouring resources, including money, into lobbying and influencing the three branches of the US government. Donald Trump's 2024 re-election sets the stage for the passage of a national ban on abortion modeled on the nineteenth century Comstock Act (Siegel and Ziegler forthcoming). The Republican-majority House of Representatives endorsed a ban in March 2024.

THE STRUGGLE FOR LGBTQ+ RECOGNITION

LGBTQ+ people have long struggled for basic human rights, among which the first is the legal recognition and protection of their sex and gender identities and their sexualities. There remain places in the world where, by law, people may face imprisonment, torture, and even death for being gay or transgender. Globally, however, movements have been gaining successes in changing this landscape (see Williamson 2023). For instance, in 2022, the South Korean Supreme Court affirmed the right of adults to change their sex, even when they had underage children—a right that was previously denied—in a ruling that has broader implications beyond the single parents with children to whom it directly applies (Kuhn 2022).

The implications for reproduction are multiple. The basic legal status of LGBTQ+ individuals is required for the recognition of their partnerships, including marriages, and their children and families. As of 2024, same-sex marriage is legal in more than 36 countries (Human Rights Council n.d.), but remains unrecognized or banned elsewhere. The right to have a child and make a family continues to be another key site of struggle. It may be especially meaningful for queer individuals themselves who were rejected and disowned by their own parents and kin. Although the right to adoption and access to infertility treatment and assisted reproductive technologies has expanded in recent years, it remains limited globally (see Chapter 3). Reproductive tourism is an important pathway for LGBTQ+ couples to have children, but it is accessible only to people with the resources to travel and seek care elsewhere. Ironically, while reproductive tourism may offer an escape from anti-LGBTQ+ discrimination, it can reinforce still other existing inequities as wealthy queer couples from the Global North rely on the bodies of poor, racialized women from the Global South to build their families (Twine and Smietana 2022).

LGBTQ+ people find themselves at the crossroads of multiple lines of attacks on reproductive justice, experiencing fallout from the Dobbs decision and the continuing, even escalating, resistance to recognition of their basic rights and those of their children (Mackenzie 2022). In the United States, right-wing attacks have moved toward targeting children and youth, prompting the parents of LGBTQ+ individuals to become advocates in the struggle for reproductive justice, asserting their right to raise children in safety. Under the guise of protecting children against abuse and harm, access to gender-affirming care has been banned or restricted in US states led by Republican legislatures and governors. Their impacts are profound for trans children and youth, who suffer from further marginalization, poor mental health, and disproportionately high rates of suicide (see, for instance, Green et al. 2022). Families have been forced to flee to other states (Londoño et al. 2023) or make plans to live outside the United States (Mackenzie 2022). This kind of mobility is not equally available to all. Reproductive justice encompasses queer reproductive justice and racial justice (Twine and Smietana 2022).

STRUGGLES AGAINST RACISM IN SEXUALITY, BIRTH, AND INFANT CARE

Racism is a critical axis of reproductive struggles. Historically, the constructs of race and racial hierarchies were created in the cultural imaginaries of Western European elites and used to justify colonial expansion that was enacted with horrific violence, genocide, enslavement, and the displacement and profound exploitation of people and resources. The concept of **racial capitalism** (Robinson 2019, see also Chapter 1) explains the fundamental interrelationships between the exploitation of labor (referring to the human effort or work of reproduction and production) and the accumulation of capital (wealth) within the framework of racial hierarchies. Asserting control over reproduction was at the center of colonialism. In turn, struggles against these colonial structures have always been part of people's histories. They continue into the current postcolonial era that is built upon the inequities brought about by colonialism.

The colonial past is still present and global conditions are experienced locally, as anthropologists remind us. Around the world, struggles for reproductive justice are organized around common causes like abortion access and LGBTQ+ rights, but in each setting, the movement reflects the local configurations of how racial hierarchies were imposed and embedded into legal systems and other structures of everyday life. For instance, in India, legal measures imposed by British colonial rule criminalized homosexuality and deemed unacceptable local manifestations of gender and sexuality embodied in hijras, or third-gender individuals who have been recognized in Hindu religious traditions for centuries. After many years of activism, the colonial era Section 377 law was finally overturned in 2018 (Beyrer 2019), but the law's social impacts and the colonial framing of sexuality have been far-reaching and long-lasting. The movements to fight discrimination on the basis of gender and sexuality are locally complex. Hijras, for example, do not necessarily identify or entirely align themselves with contemporary LGBTQ+ identities or political advocacy. In October 2023, the country's Supreme Court declined to legalize same-sex marriage (Pathi 2023). The LGBTQ+ struggle in India continues.

Religion is another dimension of colonial legacy with continuing consequences in people's reproductive experiences. In India, colonial governance sought to curtail specific local religious practices, like those concerning hijras, which the British regarded culturally as offensive. In South America, too, religious prohibitions have been introduced by colonial missionization and by more recent proselytizing. White Christian evangelical movements have aimed to constrain and reframe reproduction in their own terms (Barzallo 2024). In settings such as Brazil, activists call out the religious prohibitions on reproductive freedoms as colonial legacies and call for reproductive justice as postcolonial resistance.

The roots of present-day inequities in the United States run deep and are intertwined in colonialism and racism. Historically, the United States was established as a settler colonial nation, with the unlawful taking of territory by the brutal displacement and violent elimination of the people already inhabiting it. The nation's wealth was generated with labor extracted from enslaved Africans. Historians, legal scholars, and social scientists have explored the centrality of reproductive control and coercion to this entire enterprise (see Morgan 2004, 2021; Roberts 2014 [1997]). Native American survivors of dispossession and genocide were further suppressed through practices like separating children from their families and sending them to boarding schools to become "civilized." Regarding enslaved Africans, the concern was maintaining a labor pool that not only produced commodities, but was itself a commodity that reproduced itself. Enslaved women were forced to bear children who could later be sold as property; exploited for reproductive labor such as wet-nursing and caring for white women and children, often to the detriment of their own children; and coerced into being available for white men's sexual desires (Jones-Rogers 2019; Morgan 2021). Enslaved women suffered experimental surgeries, without anesthesia, which established modern gynecology (Washington 2006). In their struggles against these violations of themselves as humans, enslaved people staged uprisings and engaged in various forms of resistance that also included daily practices to take control of their reproductive capacities, for example sharing knowledge of plant-based abortifacients and using breastfeeding to space births.

Although enslavement in the United States was abolished in 1865, its legacies continue to be felt as an institution contributing to the country's founding. Structural racism remains in force and racism pervades the entire reproductive spectrum. In the past decade, there has been growing attention to the startlingly high US maternal mortality rates—two or three times as high as in other similar high-income nations—and the profound inequities evidenced in them (Gunja et al. 2024). Black women face extremely high rates of mortality (49.5 / 100,000 versus 22.3 / 100,000 overall). Biomedical research led primarily by white scientists has largely focused on race as a "risk factor" for these poor outcomes. Yet, there are problems with this use of race as a variable. Race is a socially used label that does not, in fact, correspond to any biogenetic differences between groups of people that could meaningfully explain differential outcomes in health and disease. It is the effects of racism, not race, that put Black people at risk during pregnancy and birth. This is a critical point made by Black feminists leading the reproductive justice movement.

In her book, *Reproductive Injustice*, Dána-Ain Davis (2019), describes how racism structures every aspect of the experiences of Black families with infants in neonatal intensive care units. These babies are there because Black women are put at higher risk for premature births—a situation that Davis (2019) describes as medical racism. It is not only that Black people may receive less attention and experience poor support or violence from individual care providers with racist biases, but also that racism pervades larger social structures and medical institutions creating these risks and harms. Black birth workers themselves are challenging this system of obstetric racism—a concept that combines medical racism and obstetric violence (see Chapter 4)—in which Black pregnant and birthing people are continually undermined, dismissed, discredited, and mistreated. These practices put the lives and health of Black pregnant and birthing people and their infants at risk. Obstetric racism offers an analytical lens for understanding how unequal perinatal outcomes are produced (see also Davis 2018 and Scott and Davis 2021). By reclaiming the practices of midwifery and holistic care, birth workers point to alternative paths. These traditions had been disrupted by the systematic destruction of midwifery in the early part of the twentieth century (Fraser 1995) and by enslavement and its long aftermath of historical traumas. Black birth workers support families in hospitals as both midwives and doulas, or non-medical carers who can provide continuous emotional support (see Chapter 4). Black midwives offer support for home births and have been working to establish free-standing birth centers grounded in the concepts of respectful and culturally congruent care. One example is the Roots Community Birth Center in Minnesota, where 284 families were served over four years, with no preterm births (Proujansky 2019).

In the context of obstetric racism, challenging the biomedical models of pregnancy, birth, and infant care is part of the struggle for reproductive justice. Worth noting is the much higher reliance on obstetricians and gynecologists in the United States than on midwives, who provide most pregnancy and birth care in other countries with lower rates of maternal and infant mortality. The World Health Assembly in May 2024 introduced a draft position paper on globally transitioning to midwifery models of care. The call affirms the demands for respectful care among Black and Indigenous people around the world often experiencing what might be collectively described as the "violence of care" (Mulla et al. 2021). Indigenous communities around the world have endured colonization and racialized mistreatment and discrimination and continue facing stark inequities in maternal and infant health outcomes. The reproductive struggles of Aboriginal and Torres Straits Islanders have been well documented for decades. The Birthing on Country initiative, a First Nations-led project, acknowledges the long arc of injustices and asserts the importance of culturally safe environments for birth based on an understanding of the connection of land, people, and community (Davis 2022; Hickey, Ireland, and Roe 2022; Woods 2024). This work has already demonstrated an increase in prenatal visits, reduction in preterm births, and growing support for exclusive breastfeeding (Kildea et al. 2021). These successes are prompting calls to improve funding for "Indigenous-led solutions to perinatal health inequities for Indigenous families in well-resourced settler-colonial countries" (Hickey et al. 2021, 303).

Black, Latine, and Indigenous models of midwifery emphasize the importance of breastfeeding practices that have been systematically undermined by colonialism and racial capitalism. Today, breastfeeding is the focus of not only movements specifically focused on restoring and reclaiming practices, but also of other efforts more broadly promoting cultural continuity and first-food sovereignty. The reintegration of birth and breastfeeding as unified concerns is itself a significant assertion made by Indigenous activists. One reason why movements for midwifery and breastfeeding around the world have been separate, not unified, is the biomedical fragmentation of birth, postpartum, and infant care into discrete parts. This fragmentation is replicated even in new initiatives to transform models of care. In Canada and the United States, First Nations and Indigenous midwives and lactation supporters have been leading the way to restore and reintegrate traditions of birth, breastfeeding, and food sovereignty (see Tomori and Palmquist 2022). For instance, in Washington State, Hummingbird Indigenous Family Services, led by Cammie Goldhammer, offers wrap-around support to Indigenous families for pregnancy, birth, and lactation that reaffirms traditional knowledge (www.hummingbird-ifs.org). Here, reproduction is imagined as both a central and holistic experience of transformative potential for families and communities.

Any effort to successfully struggle against racism in reproductive care must address the root causes of racism and colonialism head on. It requires a fundamental reorientation toward models of reproductive care that are grounded in the desires of communities globally for reproductive justice and freedom and led by their members who are enabled to restore and support the autonomy, safety, nurture, and continuity of families and communities.

CONCEIVING OUR FUTURE

The struggles for reproductive justice are, ultimately, struggles for continuing existence as individuals and communities. At this moment, we are keenly aware of the existential threats of environmental and climate crisis resulting from human activity—a situation summarized by the term Anthropocene. In the continuing aftermath of the COVID-19 pandemic, we are forced also to acknowledge the risks of continuously evolving diseases that have and still can spread across species and become rapidly communicated across human populations through our interconnected global networks.

Environmental justice movements around the world have articulated clearly the connections between reproduction and environment and climate. First, these movements offer a critique of colonial and neocolonial concerns about "overpopulation," drawing attention to how these discourses are used to justify the interventions by rich and powerful nations of the Global North to regulate and limit the fertility of people in the Global South. Yet, it is the populations of the Global North who consume far more of the planet's resources than those of the Global South. Second, environmental justice movements also emphasize that the most significant causes of global warming were and still are the activities of Global North countries that gained their wealth through the extraction and exploitation of natural resources taken and controlled by colonial conquest. Those who gained the least will likely suffer the most as the impacts of the climate crisis are experienced most profoundly in the Global South and in communities marginalized by race and class in the Global North. For environmental justice movements, the problems of environment and climate lie with the practices of the Global North, not the populations of the Global South.

The transdisciplinary approach and social movements of **planetary health** offer a framework for "analyzing and addressing the impacts of human disruptions to Earth's natural systems on human health and all life on Earth" (Planetary Health Alliance 2024). Planetary health prompts us to consider the direct and immediate impacts of environment and climate on human reproduction as well as on the long-term consequences for future human reproductive capacity and survival, especially in communities who are most threatened by these impacts. The key reproductive impacts of the climate crisis include the detrimental effects of heat, air pollution, and lack of available safe water for pregnant women and people, infants, and young children; and the increased frequency and severity of catastrophic weather events that undermine basic safety as well as water and food security (WHO 2024). These threats result in greater risk of poor outcomes for pregnant and birthing people and for infants, especially when born prematurely and at low birth weight. Industrial pollution poses reproductive risks. The release of what are called forever chemicals into soil, air, and water can damage male and female fertility, cause preterm births or harmful abnormalities in children, and create other effects on the health of individuals later in life and over the course of generations as in utero exposures may have accumulating and compounding impacts (Lappé et al. 2019; Thayer and Gildner 2022; see also Chapter 4).

Scholarly approaches, including in anthropology, offer ways of talking and thinking about the interconnectedness of politics, economics, society, history, and culture in shaping both environment and reproduction, which themselves are interrelated. Lappé and colleagues (2019) describe an "environmental politics of reproduction" that addresses these intersections from multiple angles. They highlight how environmental and reproductive politics unite in an emerging area of intersectional environmental reproductive justice framework. This approach is grounded in histories of activism around both reproduction and the environment as well as the growing body of research in environmental health sciences that examines the intersection of planetary health and human reproduction. The growing understanding of impacts on reproduction across the lifecourse provides another dimension to this. Recent anthropological work has also engaged with the lived experiences of reproduction in what Lappé et al. (2019) term "dystopian times" wherein people are reckoning with these existential threats to our collective future. Recent scholarship also highlights the potential of anthropology across the subfields to contribute to interventions in environmental reproductive justice, calling for more work in the anthropology of reproduction that is focused on the continued efforts of communities themselves (see Bond 2021; Vaughn, Guarasci, and Moore 2021; McMullen and Dow 2022; Bharadwaj 2024).

Threats to planetary health are directly linked to the rise of infectious diseases. Habitat destruction and global warming create new environments for certain pathogens; industrial practices facilitate human-animal contacts in ways that accelerate transmission. This is a key reason why some scientists are calling the current era the **pandemicene**, or marked by the rise of pandemics. Readers of this book have just survived the major global pandemic of COVID-19, witnessing the disproportionate impacts on marginalized communities in the United States and other countries in the Global North. Much of the Global South had very limited access to vaccines; indeed, the struggle for vaccine equity continues. The COVID-19 pandemic also had specific effects on people's reproductive experiences. In the early days of lockdown in 2020, pregnant and birthing people could not fully access healthcare; hospitals restricted who could accompany birthing people for needed emotional support; and newborn infants could be separated from parents suspected of having the virus, interfering with breastfeeding. People seeking fertility treatment were unable to receive it during this time (Whittaker and Manderson 2024). All told, the impacts of the virus at these physiologically complex moments, together with the practices of lockdown, isolation, and separation, further compounded already existing inequities that disadvantage communities and led to a sharp increase in maternal mortality in the United States (Tomori et al. 2020; Tomori et al. 2022; Gunja et al. 2024).

Pushing back, people have organized efforts to demand vaccine equity globally and locally. Networks of community-based organizations and public health professionals have come together to ensure that people embarking on their reproductive journeys receive support and accurate information. This last point is significant because campaigns of misinformation actively discouraged people in the United States from receiving COVID-19 vaccines, with false claims that they caused infertility in men and women. Although the vaccines were recommended as safe for even young children, circulating among parents were parental rights and anti-vax discourses, which had previously emerged around hesitancy and resistance to vaccinations that were mandatory for children's school enrollment.

More pandemics are anticipated. Currently, we are facing the possibility of H5N1 and other similar viruses spilling over to humans. By June 2024, a large number of cattle herds had been infected and there were several reports of farmworkers who had become ill (Madad et al. 2024; STAT 2024). The pattern of transmission follows an expected one that echoes the structural inequities we witnessed during the COVID pandemic: dairy farm workers are disproportionately poor Latine migrants who may lack information about risks of transmission or prevention, are not supplied with personal protective equipment to do their work, and are not provided testing for sickness or financial support if they are ill. Under these circumstances, potential cases are likely under-reported. We do not yet know what risks may arise from transmission from sexual contact or during pregnancy, but as always the additional vulnerabilities during reproduction must be considered for pandemic preparedness. Unfortunately, we may expect to see disproportionate harms to immigrant communities of color. Whether this virus evolves in new ways remains to be seen, but the likelihood of other future pandemics is certain—and so are their unequal impacts.

Reproductive justice for all can and ought to be both an aim and a means of planetary health and continued human existence. The diverse social movements addressing the health of the planet and the local environment, those who serve communities during emergencies like pandemics and other disasters that are accelerated by climate change, and the movements that aim to forge peace and fight against colonial and postcolonial racist, gendered, and sexually oppressive injustices will ultimately need to unite to ensure reproductive justice for all in the coming decades. This requires imagining a different future, and a commitment to recognize and uplift a multitude of voices in the greater struggle for reproductive justice and freedom across diverse communities.

Reproduction—and these struggles and movements—are ultimately acts of radical hope to enact a better, just, and free future where all people can create and nurture their families and communities in safety.

SUMMARY

- Reproduction has always been fraught with struggle. Movements for reproductive justice and freedom have challenged dominant models of reproduction and coercive control over it asserted by powerful interests and states (both one's own and others) as well as global and local patterns of inequities.
- Fertility is a key site of struggle with states implementing both pronatalist and anti-natalist policies that shape and conflict with the reproductive desires of local people.
- Reproduction plays a central role in armed conflict and war, which threatens basic safety and survival, and ultimately the continuity of communities. Targeted attacks on reproduction reflect the recognition of the importance of reproductive justice as the assertion of the right to exist as a people.
- The struggle for contraception and abortion, for LGBTQ+ recognition and inclusion, and resistance against racism in the context of birth and infant care represent movements for reproductive justice and freedom that challenge deep histories of oppression wrought by racist and gendered colonial and neocolonial policies.
- Our collective reproductive futures as the human species depend on our ability to traverse different axes of oppression and unite to protect the health of the planet, create peace, and work toward reproductive justice across diverse communities.

FURTHER EXPLORING

"Geographies of Kinship" (2020) examines the history of international adoption from Korea and its complicated legacies as told through the stories of four adults, two raised in the United States, one in Sweden, and one in Switzerland. Director Deann Borshay Liem is also noted for two other films, "First Person Plural" (2000) and "In the Matter of Cha Jung Hee" (2010), recounting her own experiences as an adoptee. "Geographies of Kinship" is available to be streamed at https://worldchannel.org/episode/america-reframed-geographies-of-kinship.

"'No anaesthesia, painkillers': Giving birth in Gaza" is a short video clip from November 2023 featuring two new mothers and one doctor describing their recent experiences and the conditions of birthing in Gaza hospitals: www.bbc.com/news/av/world-middle-east-67365679.

The title of the film, "Victoria," refers to the daughter born to Alex, a man who was born female. Set in Jalisco, Mexico, this 2023 short documentary film, directed by Eloisa Diez, follows Alex's journey, which includes gender affirming care and fertility treatment. It can be viewed at *The New York Times* website: www.nytimes.com/video/opinion/100000008463528/victoria.html?action=click&module=video-series-bar&region=header&pgtype=Article&playlistId=video/op-docs.

Native American activists for reproductive justice are featured in "Fighting for Reproductive Sovereignty," a 2022 episode of the KFF Health News podcast, *American Diagnosis*, that can be streamed here: https://kffhealthnews.org/news/article/podcast-american-diagnosis-rezilience-season-4-episode-7-reproductive-sovereignty.

The importance and necessity of anthropological perspective, centered on people and the inequities structuring their reproductive experiences, is the topic of this November 2022 talk by Sallie Han, given as part of the University of Nevada Las Vegas Anthropology Speaker Series: www.youtube.com/watch?v=djCb7IRfuLU.

REFERENCES

Ahmed, Aziza. 2024. The Supreme Court Sides with the FDA on the Abortion Pill—for Now. *The Nation*, June 13. www.thenation.com/article/society/supreme-court-fda-mifepristone-abortion/.

Barzallo, Gabriella. 2024. In Brazil, an Abortion Debate Pits Feminists Against the Church. *Al Jazeera*, April 12. www.aljazeera.com/news/2024/4/12/in-brazil-an-abortion-debate-pits-feminists-against-the-church.

BBC. 2023. "'No Anaesthesia, Painkillers': Giving Birth in Gaza." *BBC*, November 9. www.bbc.com/news/av/world-middle-east-67365679.

Bennett, Geoff. 2023. "Hundreds of Migrant Children Remain Separated from Families Despite Push to Reunite Them." *PBS News Hour*, Feb. 6. www.pbs.org/newshour/show/hundreds-of-migrant-children-remain-sepa rated-from-families-despite-push-to-reunite-them.

Beyrer, Chris. 2019. "Section 377: Why Sodomy Statutes Matter." *African Journal of Reproduction and Gynaecological Endoscopy* 22(5): e25285. doi:10.1002/jia2.25285.

Bharadwaj, Aditya. 2024. "Afterword: Reproducing on an Impaired Planet." In *A Companion to the Anthropology of Reproductive Medicine and Technology*, edited by Cecilia Coale Van Hollen and Nayantara Sheoran Appleton, 502–506. Hoboken, NJ: John Wiley & Sons.

Bond, D., 2021. "Contamination in Theory and Protest." *American Ethnologist*, 48(4): 386–403.

Browner, Carole and Carolyn Sargent. 2022. "Reproduction and the State." In *The Routledge Handbook of Anthropology and Reproduction*, edited by Sallie Han and Cecília Tomori, 87–105. Abingdon and New York: Routledge.

Brunson, Jan. 2022. "Reproduction Through Revolution: Maoist Women's Struggle for Equity in Post-Development Nepal." In *The Routledge Handbook of Anthropology and Reproduction*, edited by Sallie Han and Cecília Tomori, 137–149. Abingdon and New York: Routledge.

Bubola, Emma. 2022. "Using Adoptions, Russia Turns Ukrainian Children Into Spoils of War." *The New York Times*, October 22. www.nytimes.com/ 2022/10/22/world/europe/ukraine-children-russia-adoptions.html.

Cho, Hyein Ellen and Eva Rose Richards. 2023. "Why South Korea Can't Pass Anti-Discrimination Laws." *Asialink*, October 20. https://asialink.unim elb.edu.au/insights/why-south-korea-cant-pass-anti-discrimination-laws.

Clarkin, Patrick F. 2019. "The Embodiment of War: Growth, Development, and Armed Conflict." *Annual Review of Anthropology* 48(1): 423–442.

Conectas Human Rights. 2024. "The Offensive Against Reproductive Justice and the Debate Surrounding Abortion in Brazil." *Conectas Human Rights*, March 8. www.conectas.org/en/noticias/the-offensive-against-reproducti ve-justice-and-the-debate-surrounding-abortion-in-brazil/.

Davis, Alexus. 2022. "Writing and Birthing on Country: Examining Indigenous Australian Birth Stories from a Reproductive Justice Lens." In *The Palgrave Handbook of Reproductive Justice and Literature*, edited by Beth Widmaier Capo and Laura Lazzari, 333–355. Cham: Springer International Publishing.

Davis, Dána-Ain 2018. "Obstetric Racism: The Racial Politics of Pregnancy, Labor, and Birthing." *Medical Anthropology* 38(7): 560–573. doi:10.1080/ 01459740.2018.1549389.

Davis, Dána-Ain. 2019. *Reproductive Injustice: Racism, Pregnancy, and Premature Birth*. New York: NYU Press.

Davis, Dána-Ain and Kelley Akhiemokhali. 2023. "How Eugenics Shaped the US Prenatal Care System." *Sapiens*, August 29. www.sapiens.org/culture/black-maternal-health-prenatal-care/.

Devlin, Kayleen, Maryam Ahmed, and Daniele Palumbo. 2024. "Half of Gaza Water Sites Damaged or Destroyed, BBC Satellite Data Reveals." *BBC*, May 9. www.bbc.com/news/world-middle-east-68969239.

Diniz, Debora, Marcelo Medeiros, Pedro H.G. Souza, and Emanuelle Goés. 2023. "Abortion and Race in Brazil, National Abortion Surveys 2016 to 2021." *Ciência & Saúde Coletiva* 28: 3085–3092.

Fick, Maggie, Ahmed Aboulenein, and Saleh Salem. 2024. "Gaza's Doctors Were Building a Health System: Then came war." *Reuters*, June 4. www.reuters.com/investigates/special-report/israel-palestinians-gaza-health/.

Fraser, Gertrude. 1995. "Modern Bodies, Modern Minds: Midwifery and Reproductive Change in an African American Community." In *Conceiving the New World Order: The Global Politics of Reproduction*, edited by Faye D. Ginsburg and Rayna Rapp, 42–57. Berkeley, CA: University of California Press.

French, Piper. 2024. "Left Apart." *New York Magazine*, Feb. 27. https://nymag.com/intelligencer/article/separated-families-border-trump-zero-tolerance-immigration.html.

Gall, Carlotta, Oleksandr Chubko, and Cora Engelbrecht. 2023. "Ukraine's Stolen Children." *The New York Times*, December 26. www.nytimes.com/interactive/2023/12/26/world/europe/ukraine-war-children-russia.html.

Green, Amy E., Jonah P. DeChants, Myeshia N. Price, and Carrie K. Davis. 2022. "Association of Gender-Affirming Hormone Therapy with Depression, Thoughts of Suicide, and Attempted Suicide Among Transgender and Nonbinary Youth." *Journal of Adolescent Health* 70(4): 643–649.

Gunja, Munira Z., Evan D. Gumas, Relebohile Masitha, and Laurie C. Zephryn. 2024. "Insights into the US Maternal Mortality Crisis: An International Comparison." *The Commonwealth Fund*, June 4. www.commonwealthfund.org/publications/issue-briefs/2024/jun/insights-us-maternal-mortality-crisis-international-comparison.

Hegarty, Stephanie. 2024. "Born on 7 October: Gaza Mum's Fight to Feed Her Baby." *BBC*, March 15. www.bbc.com/news/world-middle-east-68542331.

Henderson, Garnet. 2024. "Under Brazil's Abortion Ban, 'Lack of Information Kills.'" *Rewire*, May 9. https://rewirenewsgroup.com/2024/05/09/under-brazils-abortion-ban-lack-of-information-kills/. Hickey, Sophie, Sarah Ireland, and Yvette Roe. 2022. "Birthing on Country Services Centre First Nations Cultures and Empower Women in Pregnancy and Childbirth." *The Conversation*. https://theconversation.com/birthing-on-country-services-centre-first-nations-cultures-and-empower-

women-in-pregnancy-and-childbirth-170641#:~:text=And%20if%20they
%20don%27t,land%20and%20unique%20birthing%20practices.

Hickey, Sophie, Yvette Roe, Sarah Ireland, Sue Kildea, Penny Haora, Yu
Gao, Elaine Läwurrpa Maypilama*et al*.2021. "A Call for Action That
Cannot Go to Voicemail: Research Activism to Urgently Improve Indi-
genous Perinatal Health and Wellbeing." *Women and Birth* 34(4): 303–305.

Human Rights Council. n.d. *Marriage Equality Around the World*. www.hrc.
org/resources/marriage-equality-around-the-world.

Jones-Rogers, Stephanie E. 2019. *They Were Her Property: White Women as
Slave Owners in the American South*. New Haven, CT: Yale University Press.

Kang, Yoonjung. 2021. *A Plurality of Care: The Politics of Postpartum Care
Practices in Contemporary South Korea*. Doctoral dissertation, University of
Illinois at Urbana-Champaign. https://hdl.handle.net/2142/110828.

Kearney, Audrey, Ashley Kirzinger, Liz Hamel, and Alina Salganicoff. 2024.
"Women's Views of Abortion Access and Policies in the Dobbs Era:
Insights from the KFF Health Tracking Poll." *KFF*, April 5. www.kff.org/
womens-health-policy/poll-finding/womens-views-of-abortion-access-a
nd-policies-in-the-dobbs-era-insights-from-the-kff-health-tracking-poll/.

KFF. 2024. *Abortion in the United States Dashboard*. www.kff.org/womens-hea
lth-policy/dashboard/abortion-in-the-u-s-dashboard/.

Kildea, Sue, Yu Gao, Sophie Hickey, Carmel Nelson, Sue Kruske, Adrian
Carson, Jody Currie*et al*.2021. "Effect of a Birthing on Country Service
Redesign on Maternal and Neonatal Health Outcomes for First Nations
Australians: A Prospective, Non-Randomised, Interventional Trial." *The
Lancet Global Health* 9(5): E651–E659.

Kottasová, Ivana and Olga Voitovych. 2024. "Survivors Say Russia Is Waging
a War of Sexual Violence in Occupied Areas of Ukraine. Men Are Often
the Victims." *CNN*, May 30. www.cnn.com/2024/05/30/europe/russia
-sexual-violence-occupied-ukraine-intl-cmd/index.html.

Kuhn, Anthony. 2022. "South Korea's Supreme Court Rules on Legal
Transgender Recognition." *NPR*, November 25. www.npr.org/2022/11/
25/1139190242/south-koreas-supreme-court-rules-on-legal-tra
nsgender-recognition.

Lappé, Martine, Robbin Jeffries Hein, and Hannah Landecker. 2019. "Environmental Politics of Reproduction." *Annual Review of Anthropology* 48: 133–150.

Lee, Jieun, and Euisol Jeong. 2021. "The 4B Movement: Envisioning a
Feminist Future with/in a Non-Reproductive Future in Korea." *Journal of
Gender Studies* 30(5): 633–644. doi:10.1080/09589236.2021.1929097.

Londoño, Ernesto, Azeen Ghorayshi, and Jamie Kelter Davis. 2023. "Fight or
Flight: Transgender Care Bans Leave Families and Doctors Scrambling."
The New York Times, July 1. www.nytimes.com/2023/07/06/us/transgen
der-health-care-bans.html.

Mackenzie, Sonja. 2022. "Stratifications of Queer Families after Roe." *Society for Cultural Anthropology Forum*, October 3. https://culanth.org/fieldsights/stratifications-of-queer-families-after-roe.

Madad, Syra, Carlos del Rio, Scott J. Becker, and Ewa King. 2024. "With the Threat of H5N1 Bird Flu, Hospitals Must Stay Prepared." *Stat News*, June 18. www.statnews.com/2024/06/18/h5n1-bird-flu-hospitals-should-prepare-now-experts-say/.

Master, Farah. 2023. "Beijing to Cover IVF, Other Fertility Treatments for Couples from July." *Reuters*, June 15. www.reuters.com/world/china/beijing-cover-ivf-other-fertility-treatments-couples-july-2023-06-15/.

Mazzarino, Andrea. 2024. "Reproduction in the Time of War: A Review of Ethnographic Studies from the United States' War on Terror and Beyond." In *A Companion to the Anthropology of Reproductive Medicine and Technology*, edited by Cecilia Coale Van Hollen and Nayantara Sheoran Appleton, 185–200. Hoboken, NJ: John Wiley & Sons.

Mazzarino, Andrea, Marcia C. Inhorn, and Catherine Lutz. 2019. "Introduction: The Health Consequences of War." In *War and Health: The Medical Consequences of the Wars in Iraq and Afghanistan*, edited by Catherine Lutz and Andrea Mazzarino, 1–37. New York: NYU Press.

McMullen, Heather, and Katharine Dow. 2022. "Ringing the Existential Alarm: Exploring BirthStrike for Climate." *Medical Anthropology* 41(6–7): 659–673.

Méheut, Constant. 2023. "New Evidence Found of Rape and Torture by Russian Forces in Ukraine." *The New York Times*, October 21. www.nytimes.com/2023/10/21/world/europe/russia-war-crimes-ukraine.html.

Mishtal, Joanna and Silvia De Zordo. 2022. "Policy, Governance, Practice: Global Perspectives on Abortion." In *The Routledge Handbook of Anthropology and Reproduction*, edited by Sallie Han and Cecília Tomori, 150–164. Abingdon and New York: Routledge.

Mohammad, Linah. 2023. "Children Make Up Nearly Half of Gaza's Population. Here's What It Means for the War." *NPR*, October 19. www.npr.org/2023/10/19/1206479861/israel-gaza-hamas-children-population-war-palestinians.

Moon, Katharine H.S. 2022. "South Korea's Misogyny Problem." *East Asia Forum*, December 9. https://eastasiaforum.org/2022/12/09/south-koreas-misogyny-problem/.

Morgan, Jennifer. 2004. *Laboring Women: Reproduction and Gender in New World Slavery*. Philadelphia, PA: University of Pennsylvania Press.

Morgan, Jennifer L. 2021. *Reckoning with Slavery: Gender, Kinship, and Capitalism in the Early Black Atlantic*. Durham, NC: Duke University Press.

Mulla, Sameena, Rayna Rapp, James Doucet-Battle, Annie Menzel and Dána-Ain Davis. 2021. "Book Forum: Reflections on Dána-Ain Davis's Reproductive Injustice: Racism, Pregnancy, and Premature Birth."

Somatosphere. https://somatosphere.com/2021/book-forum-davis-reproductive-injustice-introduction.html/.

Mullings, Leith. 2022. "The Necropolitics of Reproduction: Racism, Resistance, and the Sojourner Syndrome in the Age of the Movement for Black Lives." In *The Routledge Handbook of Anthropology and Reproduction*, edited by Sallie Han and Cecília Tomori, 106–122. Abingdon and New York: Routledge.

No, Kyung-min. 2024. "Marriages in Korea Fall by 40% Within a Decade." *The Korea Herald*, March 3. www.koreaherald.com/view.php?ud=20240303050103.

Oh, Arissa H. 2015. *To Save the Children of Korea: The Cold War Origins of International Adoption.* Palo Alto, CA: Stanford University Press.

Orgera, Kendal and Atul Grover. 2024. "States with Abortion Bans See Continued Decrease in US MD Senior Residency Applicants." *AAMC Research Institute*, May 9. www.aamcresearchinstitute.org/our-work/data-snapshot/post-dobbs-2024.

Ostrach, Bayla and Merrill Singer. 2012. "Syndemics of War: Malnutrition-Infectious Disease Interactions and the Unintended Health Consequences of Intentional War Policies." *Annals of Anthropological Practice* 36: 257–273. doi:10.1111/napa.12003.

Pathi, Krutika. 2023. "India's Supreme Court Declines to Legalize Same-Sex Marriage, Saying It's Up to Parliament." *PBS News*, October 17. www.pbs.org/newshour/world/indias-supreme-court-declines-to-legalize-same-sex-marriage-saying-its-up-to-parliament.

Planetary Health Alliance. 2024. "What is Planetary Health?" www.planetaryhealthalliance.org/planetary-health.

Proujansky, Alice. 2019. "The Black Midwives Changing Care for Women of Color—Photo Essay." *The Guardian*, July 24. www.theguardian.com/society/2019/jul/24/black-midwives-photo-essay.

Roberts, Dorothy. 2014 [1997]. *Killing the Black Body: Race, Reproduction, and the Meaning of Liberty.* New York: Vintage.

Robinson, Cedric J. 2019. *On Racial Capitalism, Black Internationalism, and Cultures of Resistance.* London: Pluto Press.

Ross, Loretta J. and Rickie Solinger. 2017. *Reproductive Justice: An Introduction.* Berkeley, CA: University of California Press.

Scott, Karen A., and Dána-Ain Davis. 2021. "Obstetric Racism: Naming and Identifying a Way Out of Black Women's Adverse Medical Experiences." *American Anthropologist* 123(3): 681–684.

Shamdasani, Ravina. 2024. "UN Human Rights Concerned by Pattern of Israeli Raids on Gaza Medical Facilities." Speech, Geneva, Feb. 15.

Siegel, Reva, and Mary Ziegler. forthcoming. "Comstockery: How Government Censorship Gave Birth to the Law of Sexual and Reproductive Freedom, and May Again Threaten It." *Yale Law Journal.*

Sonenberg, Andrea, and Diana J. Mason. 2023. "Maternity Care Deserts in the US." *JAMA Health Forum* 4(1): e225541–e225541.

Stancati, Margherita and Abeer Ayyoub. 2024. "Women in Gaza Give Birth in Tents and Public Bathrooms." *The Wall Street Journal*, Feb. 6. www.wsj.com/world/middle-east/women-in-gaza-give-birth-in-tents-and-public-bathrooms-be0a0c71.

Stansbury, Anna, Jacob Funk Kirkegaard, and Karen Dynan. 2023. "Gender Gaps in South Korea's Labour Market: Children Explain Most of the Gender Employment Gap, but Little of the Gender Wage Gap." *Applied Economics Letters*, May, 1–6. doi:10.1080/13504851.2023.2206103.

STAT. 2024. "H5N1 Bird Flu." *STAT News*. www.statnews.com/topic/h5n1-bird-flu/.

Stavig, Lucía Isabel. 2022. "To Birth on Their Own Terms." *Anthropology News*, Dec. 6. www.anthropology-news.org/articles/to-birth-on-their-own-terms/.

Tabrizy, Nilo, Imogen Piper, and Miriam Berger. 2024. "Israel's Offensive Is Destroying Gaza's Ability to Grow Its Own Food." *The Washington Post*, May 3. www.washingtonpost.com/investigations/interactive/2024/gaza-israel-agriculture-food-fisheries.

Thayer, Zaneta and Theresa Gildner. 2022. "Developmental Origins of Health and Disease: Evidence, Proposed Mechanisms, and Ideas for Future Application." In *The Routledge Handbook of Anthropology and Reproduction*, edited by Sallie Han and Cecília Tomori, 36–51. Abingdon and New York: Routledge.

Theidon, Kimberly. 2015. "Hidden in Plain Sight: Children Born of Wartime Sexual Violence." *Current Anthropology* 56: S12,S191–S200.

Tomori, Cecília. 2023. "Global Lessons for Strengthening Breastfeeding as a Key Pillar of Food Security." *Frontiers in Public Health* 11: 1256390.

Tomori, Cecília, and Aunchalee E.L. Palmquist. 2022. "Racial Capitalism and the US Formula Shortage: A Policy Analysis of the Formula Industry as a Neocolonial System." *Frontiers in Sociology*, 7: 961200.

Tomori, Cecília, Bhavana Penta, and Rebecca Richman. 2022. "Centering the Right to Health of Childbearing People in the US During the COVID-19 Pandemic." *Frontiers in Public Health* 10: 862454.

Tomori, Cecília, Karleen Gribble, Aunchalee E.L. Palmquist, Mija-Tesse Ververs, and Marielle S. Gross. 2020. "When Separation Is Not the Answer: Breastfeeding Mothers and Infants Affected by COVID-19." *Maternal & Child Nutrition* 16(4): e13033.

Tung, Nicole. 2024. "'It's a Way of Life': Women Make Their Mark in the Ukrainian Army." *The New York Times*, March 24. www.nytimes.com/2024/03/10/world/europe/ukraine-women-soldiers-army.html.

Twine, France Winddance and Marcin Smietana. 2022. "The Racial Contours of Queer Reproduction." In *The Routledge Handbook of Anthropology and Reproduction*, edited by Sallie Han and Cecília Tomori, 298–304. Abingdon and New York: Routledge.

Ungar, Laura. 2024. "After Roe, the Network of People Who Help Others Get Abortions See Themselves as 'the Underground.'" *AP News*, May 4. https://apnews.com/article/abortion-help-navigators-pill s-roe-v-wade-f760b2817126d56e6cfa5144c9f7e547.

Ungar, Laura and Geoff Mulvihill. 2024. "8,000 Women a Month Got Abortion Pills Despite Their States' Bans or Restrictions, Survey Finds." *PBS News*, May 14. www.pbs.org/newshour/health/8000-women-a-month-got-abor tion-pills-despite-their-states-bans-or-restrictions-survey-finds.

United Nations. 2024. "Gaza: UN Experts Decry 'Systemic Obliteration' of Education System." *UN News*, April 11. https://news.un.org/en/story/ 2024/04/1148716.

UNRWA. 2024. *UNRWA Situation Report #132 on the Situation in the Gaza Strip and the West Bank, Including East Jerusalem.* August 30. www.unrwa.org/ resources/reports/unrwa-situation-report-132-situation-gaza-strip-and-west-bank-including-east-Jerusalem.

Vaughn, Sarah E., Bridget Guarasci, and Amelia Moore. 2021. "Intersectional Ecologies: Reimagining Anthropology and Environment." *Annual Review of Anthropology* 50: 275–290.

Walker, Adria. 2024. "'This Is a War on Birth': How One US Organization Helps Pregnant Palestinians from Afar." *The Guardian*, Feb. 7. www.thegua rdian.com/world/2024/feb/07/gaza-pregnant-women-safe-birth-in-palesti ne-project.

Washington, Harriet A. 2006. *Medical Apartheid: The Dark History of Medical Experimentation on Black Americans from Colonial Times to the Present.* New York: Doubleday Books.

The White House. 2024. *White House Fact Sheet: House Republicans Endorse a National Abortion Ban with Zero Exceptions in Latest Budget.* March 22. www. whitehouse.gov/briefing-room/statements-releases/2024/03/22/fact-shee t-house-republicans-endorse-a-national-abortion-ban-with-zero-exception s-in-latest-budget/.

Whittaker, Andrea, and Lenore Manderson. 2024. "Coronavirus Disease and Assisted Reproduction in South Africa: A Qualitative Study." *Global Reproductive Health* 9(2): e0081.

Williamson, Myles. 2023. "A Global Analysis of Transgender Rights: Introdu cing the Trans Rights Indicator Project (TRIP)." *Perspectives on Politics.* doi:10.1017/S1537592723002827.

Woods, Cat. 2024. "Indigenous Mothers Are Being 'Failed' in Australia—So They Are Taking Measures into Their Own Hands." *BBC News*, April 29. www.bbc.com/future/article/20240429-indigenous-mothers-are-being-fa iled-in-australia-so-they-are-taking-measures-into-their-own-hands.

World Health Assembly. 2024. *Implementing Midwifery Models of Care to Improve Maternal and Newborn Outcomes: A Country Roundtable Discussion*. https://pmnch.who.int/news-and-events/events/item/2024/05/28/default-calendar/implementing-midwifery-models-of-care-to-improve-maternal-and-newborn-outcomes-a-country-roundtable-discussion.

World Health Organization. 2024. *Experts Warn of Serious Health Impacts from Climate Change for Pregnant Women, Children, and Older People*. www.who.int/news/item/05-06-2024-experts-warn-of-serious-health-impacts-from-climate-change-for-pregnant-women–children–and-older-people#:~:text=Ambient%20air%20pollution%20increases%20the,foetal%20brain%20and%20lung%20development.

Yoon, Lina. 2023. "South Korea Court Recognizes Equal Benefits for Same-Sex Couple." *Human Rights Watch*, February 22. www.hrw.org/news/2023/02/22/south-korea-court-recognizes-equal-benefits-same-sex-couple.

Zissis, Carin, Chase Harrison, Jon Orbach and Jennifer Vilcarino. 2023. "Explainer: Abortion Rights in Latin America." *AS/COA*, November 21. www.as-coa.org/articles/explainer-abortion-rights-latin-america#:~:text=That%20changed%20in%20December%20of,America%20have%20now%20done%20so.

GLOSSARY

Abortifacient	Can induce an abortion, or end of a pregnancy.
Adoption	The permanent assignment of kinship between an adoptive family and an adoptee.
Alloparents	Individuals other than biogenetic parents who care for offspring.
Amenorrhea	The absence of periods.
Anthropology	The discipline known as the study of humanity, organized into the four fields of archaeology, biological anthropology, cultural anthropology, and linguistic anthropology.
Anti-natalism	The orientation of practices and ideas to discourage births.
Archaeology	One of the four fields of anthropology, focused on the recovery and interpretation of material remains from the human past.
Assisted reproductive technologies (ARTs)	Techniques, like in vitro fertilization (IVF) and intracytoplasmic sperm injection (ICSI), that enable human conception and others like surrogacy that enable human gestation.
Authoritative knowledge	The knowledge that is socially recognized to matter most.
Baby Friendly Hospital (BFH)	A designation given to US hospitals following international guidelines and evidence-based practices that have been shown to improve breastfeeding outcomes.

DOI: 10.4324/9781003379416-7

Biocultural	Describes the integration of biological and cultural in perspectives or processes.
Biological anthropology	One of the four fields of anthropology, focused on human evolution and human biological variation.
Biomedicalization (also, *medicalization*)	The historical shift from seeing experiences like reproduction in the broader context of people's lives to more narrowly reducing them to biological events, processes, and functions that may require interventions from biomedicine.
Biomedicine	The medical system that is grounded in biological sciences and technologies and accessed through institutions like hospitals. It is now the globally dominant form.
Cesarean section	A surgery to deliver a baby through an incision into the birthing person's abdomen and uterus.
Chestfeeding (also, *bodyfeeding*)	A term that may be preferred by gender diverse people to refer to feeding an infant milk from a lactating person's chest.
Colonialism	The historical projects of territorial expansion and resource extraction undertaken by wealthy nations located in Europe, North America, and Australia.
Child circulation	Caring for children (usually of a relative) in arrangements that are often temporary and generally have no legal recognition.
Cooperative breeding	The sharing of reproductive labor by kin.
Couvade	The ritual involvements of men in pregnancy and birth.
Cross-nursing	Breastfeeding another individual's infant.
Cultural, or *sociocultural*, *anthropology*	One of the four fields of anthropology, focused on human cultures and societies.
Cultural relativism	The principle that any given practice or idea cannot be fully understood, let alone appreciated or evaluated, in isolation from its larger cultural context.

Culture	The totality of learned and taught habits of acting, talking, thinking, and feeling that includes humans as members of a group. It can also explain differences between people.
Doulas	Non-medical carers who offer support before, during, and after birth.
Emmenagogues	Remedies to stimulate menstruation.
Ethnocentrism	The tendency of people to assume that the practices and ideas they learned and were taught in their own culture are or ought to be the normal or correct and even superior ones.
Ethnography	A research process and strategy based on immersion into a group of people for the purpose of documenting and understanding their experiences.
Feminism (also, *feminist*)	A framework of social action and thought that is critical of the unequal status of women and people based on their genders.
Fertility rate	An estimated average of how many children a woman will have in her lifetime.
Fostering	A temporary arrangement of care that may have legal status.
Gender affirming care	Various forms of healthcare, including hormone-based therapies, that allow people to align their bodies and gender identities.
Global North	A term referring to countries that historically gained their wealth and power from colonialism and continue to dominate global economics and politics.
Global South	A term referring to countries with less power and wealth that were subjugated under colonialism and continue to be dominated in global economics and politics.
Grandmother hypothesis	The proposed understanding that the survival of offspring depends upon the efforts of not only mothers and parents, but also of grandmothers or older females.

Holism	An integrated perspective that in anthropology means being human is never reduced to a single dimension like genetic heritage. Humans are always simultaneously biological, social and cultural, and linguistic beings.
Human rights	The basic rights to ensure the safety, survival, and reproduction of human individuals and communities.
Hysterectomy	The surgical removal of the uterus.
Intersectionality	An analysis of inequality recognizing that people's experiences may be compounded and amplified by overlapping systems of discrimination, like racism combined with sexism.
Kangaroo mother care	Continuous skin-to-skin contact for premature, small, and other vulnerable babies.
Kinship	In anthropology, a concept describing and explaining how relatedness and families are made in and through social and cultural practices, not simply given as "natural" biological facts.
Lactation	The production of milk.
Liminality	A state of transition.
Linguistic anthropology	One of the four fields of anthropology, focused on human language.
Milk banking	The pooling of breastmilk from multiple people who may be unknown to the recipient.
Milk kinship	Relatedness that is created by *milk sharing*.
Milk sharing	Arrangements involving either *cross-nursing* or providing human milk for another's child.
Obstetrics	The area of biomedicine focused on pregnancy and birth.
Paleoanthropology	The area of biological anthropology that examines fossil evidence of human evolution.
Pandemicene	A term referring to the current historical time period as marked by pandemics.

Planetary health

A framework of social action and thought to address the impacts of human activities on Earth's interconnected systems supporting the health and lives of all species, including humans.

Primatology

The area of biological anthropology that compares modern humans and other living primates like chimpanzees.

Pronatalism

The orientation of practices and ideas to encourage births.

Race

A social label associated with skin color and other observed features of physical appearance. Historical claims about race as a marker of real differences in human biology have been discredited, but their legacies are still felt in the continuing impacts of *racism*.

Racial capitalism

The systematic exploitation of colonial populations and the accumulation of wealth and capital based on historical claims about race.

Racism

The system of economic, political, and social discrimination, or unequal treatment, based on historical claims about race.

Reproductive governance

The ways that state and non-state actors influence people's experiences of reproduction.

Reproductive justice

The principles and the movements for change organized around the integrated causes of reproductive rights and social justice originating in the efforts of Black feminists in the United States.

Rites of passage

Rituals specifically marking the transformation of individuals from one status to another, like childhood to adulthood.

Rituals

Activities that are performed to express or symbolically demonstrate a community's beliefs and values.

Scientific racism	The efforts of scientists, including anthropologists, to find evidence to support claims that Black, Indigenous, and other non-white people have distinctive biologies different from white people.
Settler colonialism	Colonialism that established permanent occupation of the territory by forcibly displacing or removing people already living on the lands.
Society	The organization of individuals as members of a large group that also includes arrangements of smaller groups like households and families.
Solitary birth	A birth without the presence or assistance of other individuals.
Sterilization	Surgical procedures for permanent birth control. See *hysterectomy, tubal ligation,* and *vasectomy.*
Stratified reproduction	A concept describing people's unequal access to the resources, power, and opportunities enabling them to have and raise children based on their race, ethnicity, gender, sexuality, class, or other social categories of discrimination.
Taboos	Ritual prohibitions.
Tubal ligation	Used as a form of *sterilization,* the blocking of the fallopian tubes by surgically cutting or "tying" them to prevent eggs from reaching the uterus.
Vasectomy	Used as a form of *sterilization,* the surgical blocking of the vas deferens to prevent sperm from reaching the semen.

INDEX

For Product Safety Concerns and Information please contact our EU
representative GPSR@taylorandfrancis.com
Taylor & Francis Verlag GmbH, Kaufingerstraße 24, 80331 München, Germany

www.ingramcontent.com/pod-product-compliance
Lightning Source LLC
Chambersburg PA
CBHW071740270326
41928CB00013B/2742